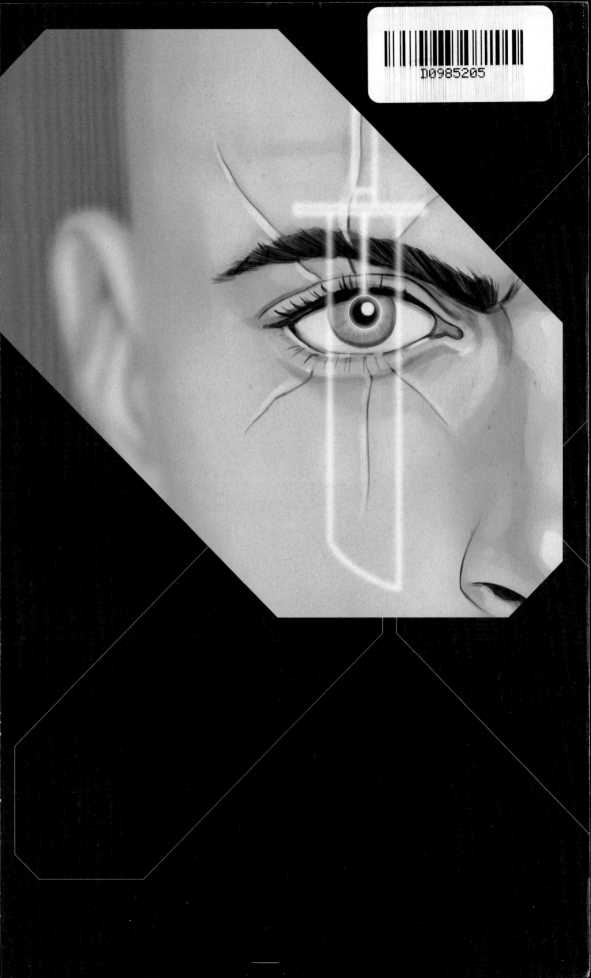

REIGN OF X VOL. 11. Contains material originally published in magazine form as WAY OF X (2021) #2, CABLE (2020) #11-12 and CHILDREN OF THE ATOM (2021) #4-5. First printing 2022. ISBN 978-1-302-93406-4. Published by MARVEL WORLDWIDE, INC., a subsidiary of MARVEL ENTERTAINMENT, LLC. OFFICE OF PUBLICATION: 1290 Avenue of the Americas, New York, NY 10104. © 2022 MARVEL No similarity between any of the names, characters, persons, and/or institutions in this book with those of any living or dead person or institution is intended, and any such similarity which may exist is purely coincidental. **Printed in the Canada.** KEVIN FEIGE, Chief Creative Officer; DAN BUCKLEY, President, Marvel Entertainment; JOE QUESADA, EVP & Creative Director; DAVID BOGART, Associate Publisher & SVP of Talent Affairs; TOM BREVOORT, VP, Executive Editor; NICK LOWE, Executive Editor, VP of Content, Digital Publishing; DAVID GABRIEL, VP of Print & Digital Publishing; MARK ANNUNZIATO, VP of Planning & Forecasting; JEFF YOUNGQUIST, VP of Production & Special Projects; ALEX MORALES, Director of Publishing Operations; DAN EDINGTON, Director of Editorial Operations; RICKEY PURDIN, Director of Talent Relations; JENNIFER GRÜNWALD, Director of Production & Special Projects; SUSAN CRESPI, Production Manager; STAN LEE, Chairman Emeritus. For information regarding advertising in Marvel Comics or on Marvel.com, please contact Vit DeBellis, Custom Solutions & Integrated Advertising Manager, at vdebellis@marvel.com. For Marvel subscription inquiries, please call 888-511-5480. **Manufactured between 2/4/2022 and 3/8/2022 by SOLISCO PRINTERS, SCOTT, QC, CANADA.**

10 9 8 7 6 5 4 3 2 1

REIGN OF X

Volume
11

X-Men created by Stan Lee & Jack Kirby

Writers:	Si Spurrier, Gerry Duggan & Vita Ayala
Artists:	Bob Quinn, Phil Noto & Paco Medina
Color Artists:	Java Tartaglia, Phil Noto & David Curiel
Letterers:	VC's Clayton Cowles, Joe Sabino & Travis Lanham
Cover Art:	Giuseppe Camuncoli & Marte Gracia; Phil Noto; R.B. Silva & Jesus Aburtov; and R.B. Silva & Erick Arciniega
Head of X:	Jonathan Hickman
Design:	Tom Muller
Assistant Editor:	Shannon Andrews Ballesteros
Associate Editor:	Annalise Bissa
Editors:	Jake Thomas & Jordan D. White
Collection Cover Art:	Phil Noto
Collection Editor:	Jennifer Grünwald
Assistant Editor:	Daniel Kirchhoffer
Assistant Managing Editor:	Maia Loy
Associate Manager, Talent Reltaions:	Lisa Montalbano
VP Production & Special Projects:	Jeff Youngquist
SVP Print, Sales & Marketing:	David Gabriel
Editor in Chief:	C.B. Cebulski

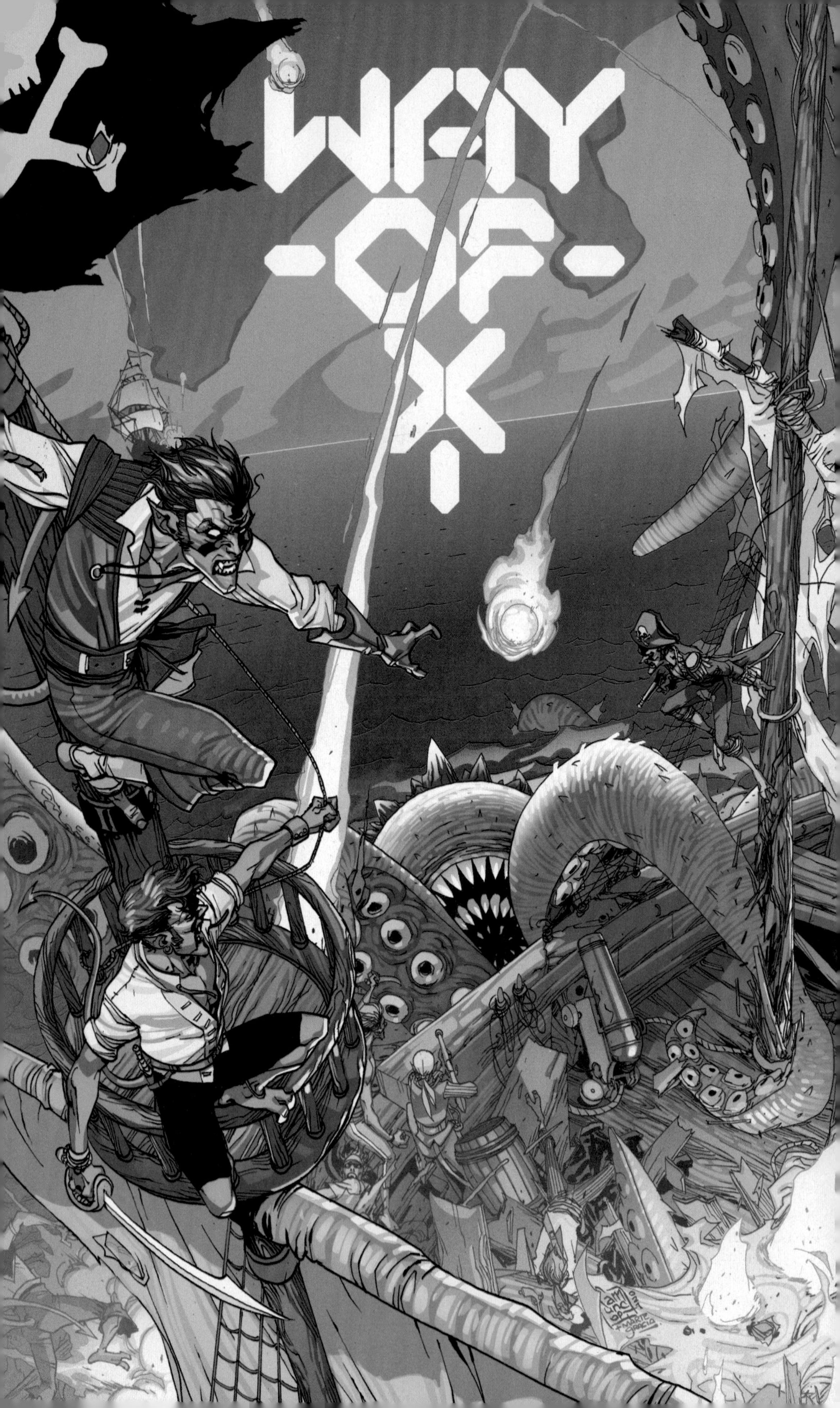
WAY
-OF-
X
1

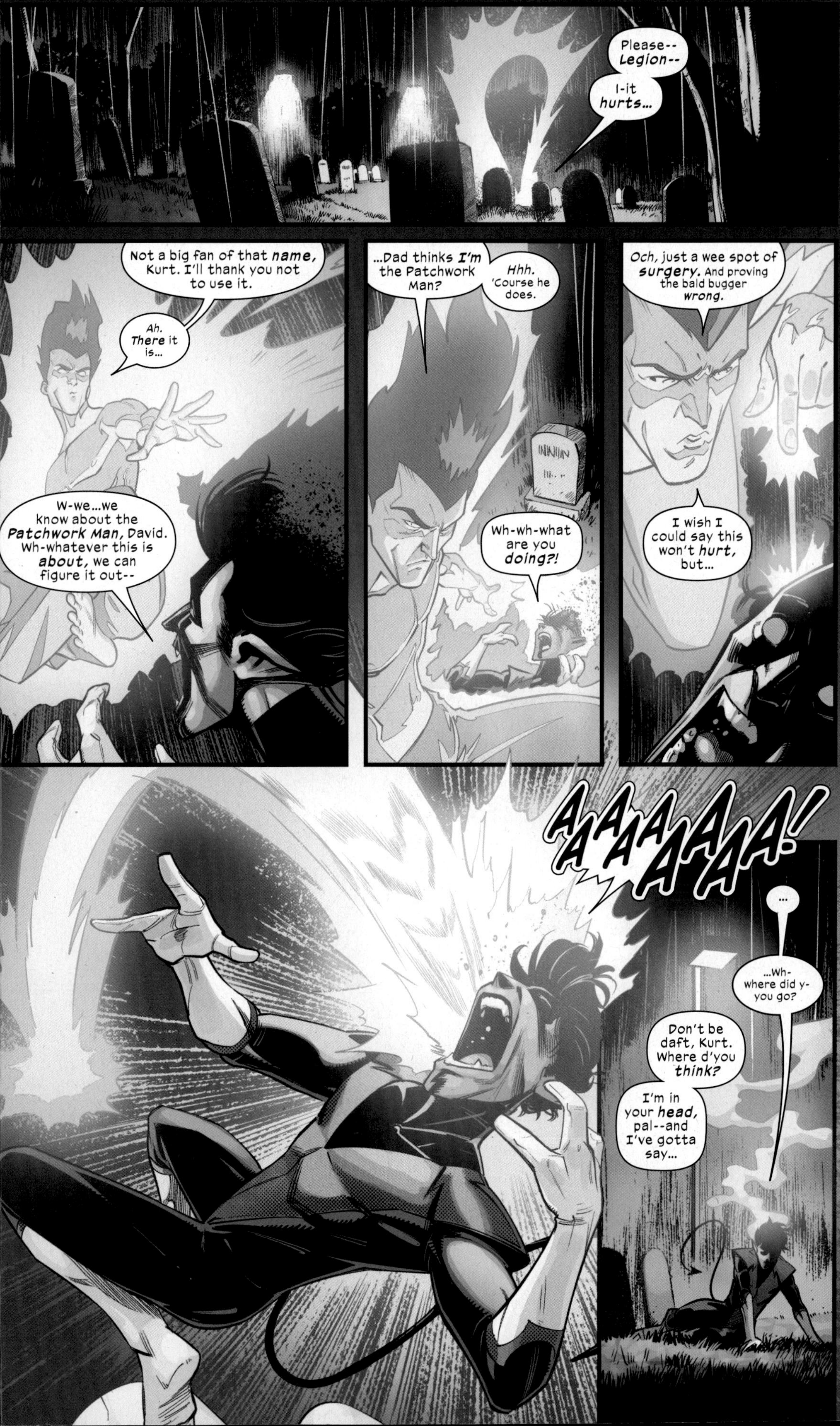
Please--
Legion--
I-it hurts...
Not a big fan of that name, Kurt. I'll thank you not to use it.
Ah. There it is...
W-we...we know about the Patchwork Man, David. Wh-whatever this is about, we can figure it out--
...Dad thinks I'm the Patchwork Man?
Hhh. 'Course he does.
Wh-wh-what are you doing?!
Och, just a wee spot of surgery. And proving the bald bugger wrong.
I wish I could say this won't hurt, but...
AAAAAAAAA!
...
...Wh-where did y-you go?
Don't be daft, Kurt. Where d'you think?
I'm in your head, pal--and I've gotta say...

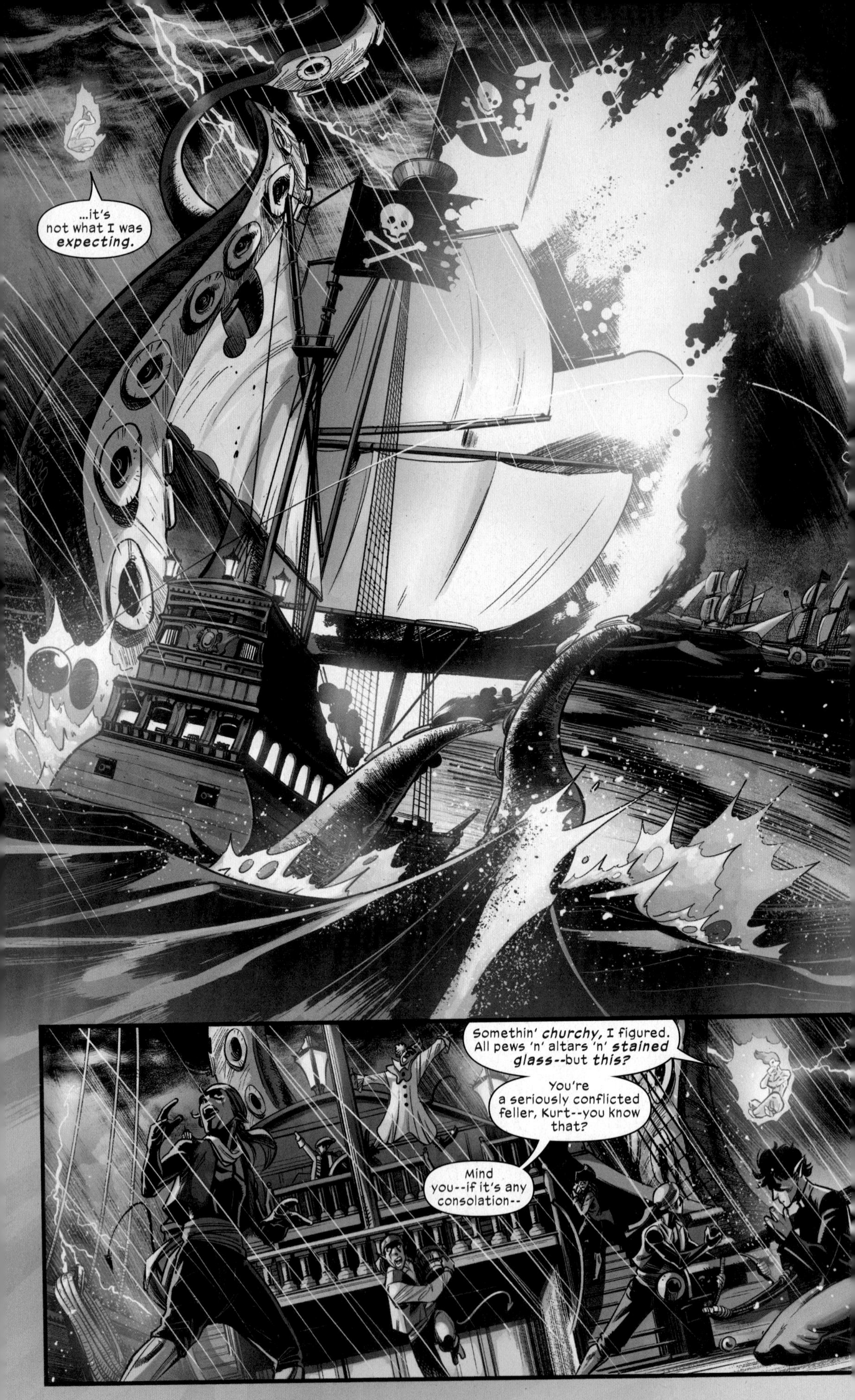

...it's not what I was *expecting.*
Somethin' *churchy,* I figured. All pews 'n' altars 'n' *stained glass*--but *this?*
You're a seriously conflicted feller, Kurt--you know that?
Mind you--if it's any consolation--

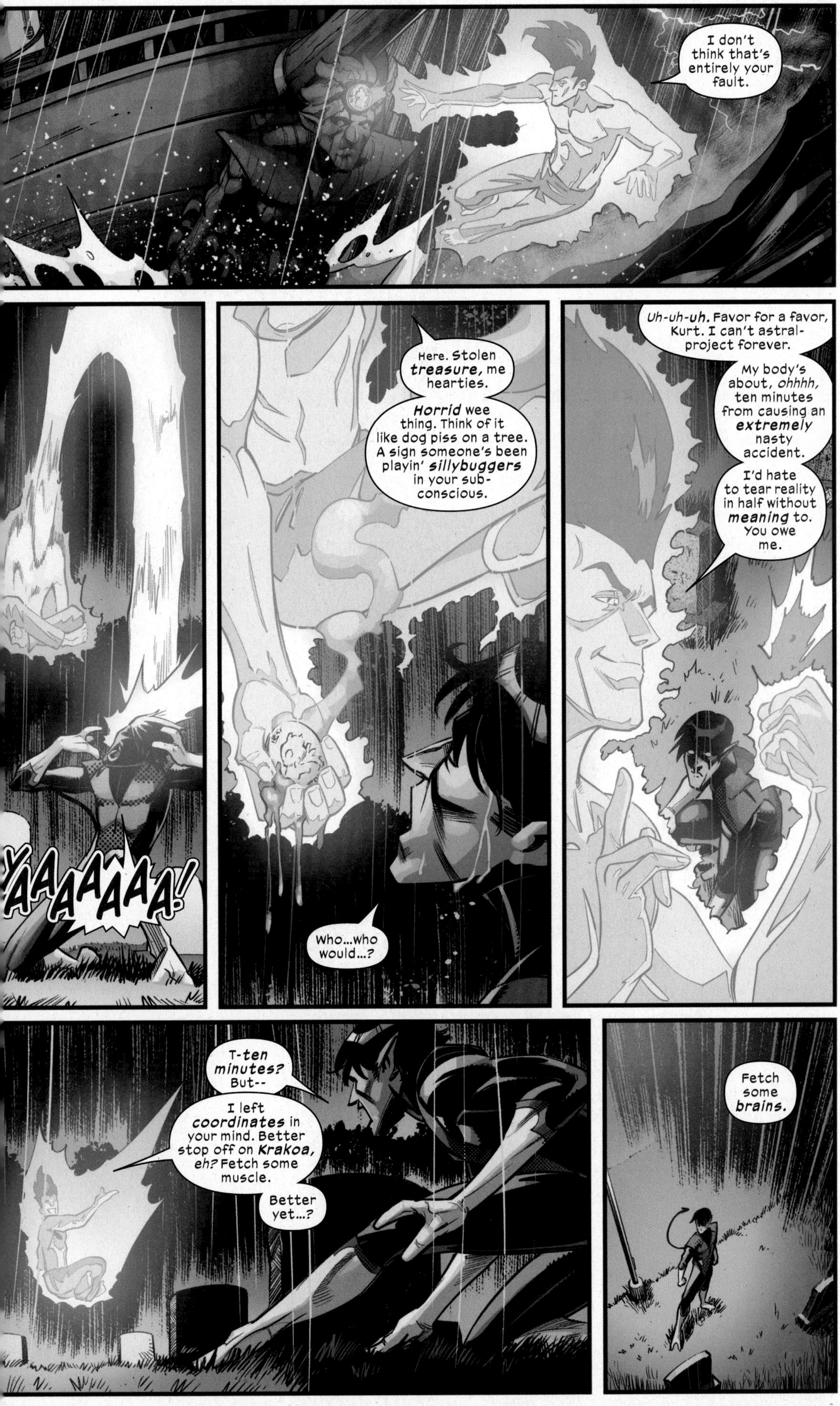

I don't think that's entirely your fault.
YAAAAAAA!
Here. Stolen treasure, me hearties.
Horrid wee thing. Think of it like dog piss on a tree. A sign someone's been playin' sillybuggers in your sub-conscious.
Who...who would...?
Uh-uh-uh. Favor for a favor, Kurt. I can't astral-project forever.
My body's about, ohhhh, ten minutes from causing an extremely nasty accident.
I'd hate to tear reality in half without meaning to. You owe me.
T-ten minutes? But--
I left coordinates in your mind. Better stop off on Krakoa, eh? Fetch some muscle.
Better yet...?
Fetch some brains.

CHANGE MY MIND

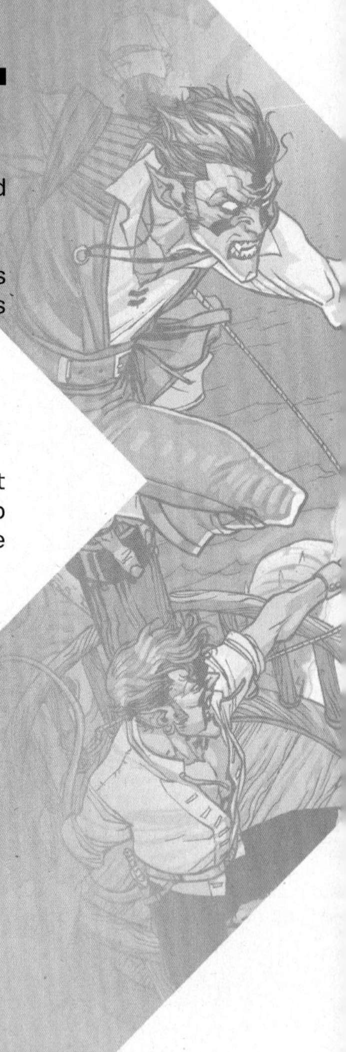

Mutantkind has a new home.

Krakoa! An island of wonders where sins are absolved and the future is bright.

...Or so it seems. In truth, something is rotten in the hearts and minds of mutants, leading to self-destructive behaviors and savage cultural movements.

Kurt Wagner -- Nightcrawler -- is determined to fix it. Unfortunately, he has no idea where to begin.

So when Charles Xavier detects an Omega-level mutant preying on the nightmares of Krakoans and assumes it to be his own wayward son, Legion, Nightcrawler jumps at the chance to investigate.

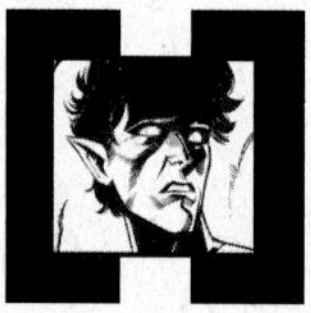

Nightcrawler

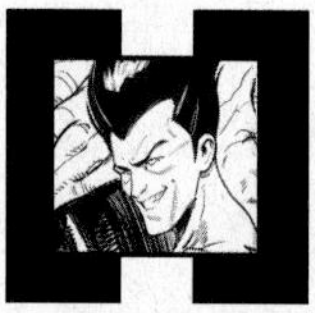

Legion

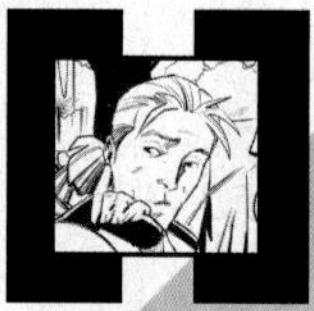

Fabian Cortez

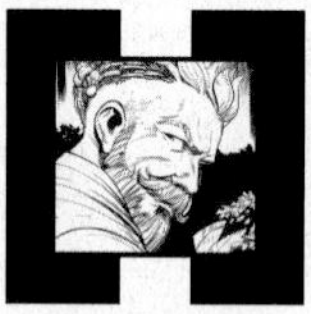

Doctor Nemesis

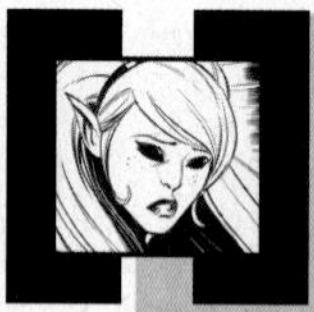

Pixie

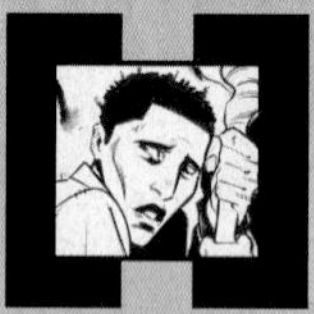

Lost

[00_WAY_]
[00_OF_X]

WAY OF X
[X_02]

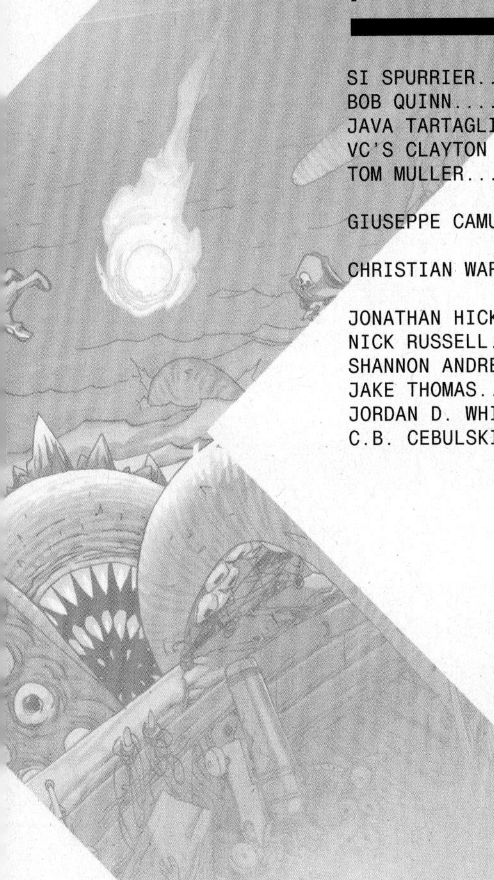

[ISSUE TWO]........................LET US PREY

SI SPURRIER..[WRITER]
BOB QUINN..[ARTIST]
JAVA TARTAGLIA...............................[COLOR ARTIST]
VC'S CLAYTON COWLES.............................[LETTERER]
TOM MULLER...[DESIGN]

GIUSEPPE CAMUNCOLI & MARTE GRACIA...........[COVER ARTISTS]

CHRISTIAN WARD......................[VARIANT COVER ARTIST]

JONATHAN HICKMAN................................[HEAD OF X]
NICK RUSSELL....................................[PRODUCTION]
SHANNON ANDREWS BALLESTEROS.............[ASSISTANT EDITOR]
JAKE THOMAS..[EDITOR]
JORDAN D. WHITE..............................[SENIOR EDITOR]
C.B. CEBULSKI...............................[EDITOR IN CHIEF]

[00_way__]
[00_of___]

[00_00...0.]
[00_00...2.]

[00______]
[00____X_]

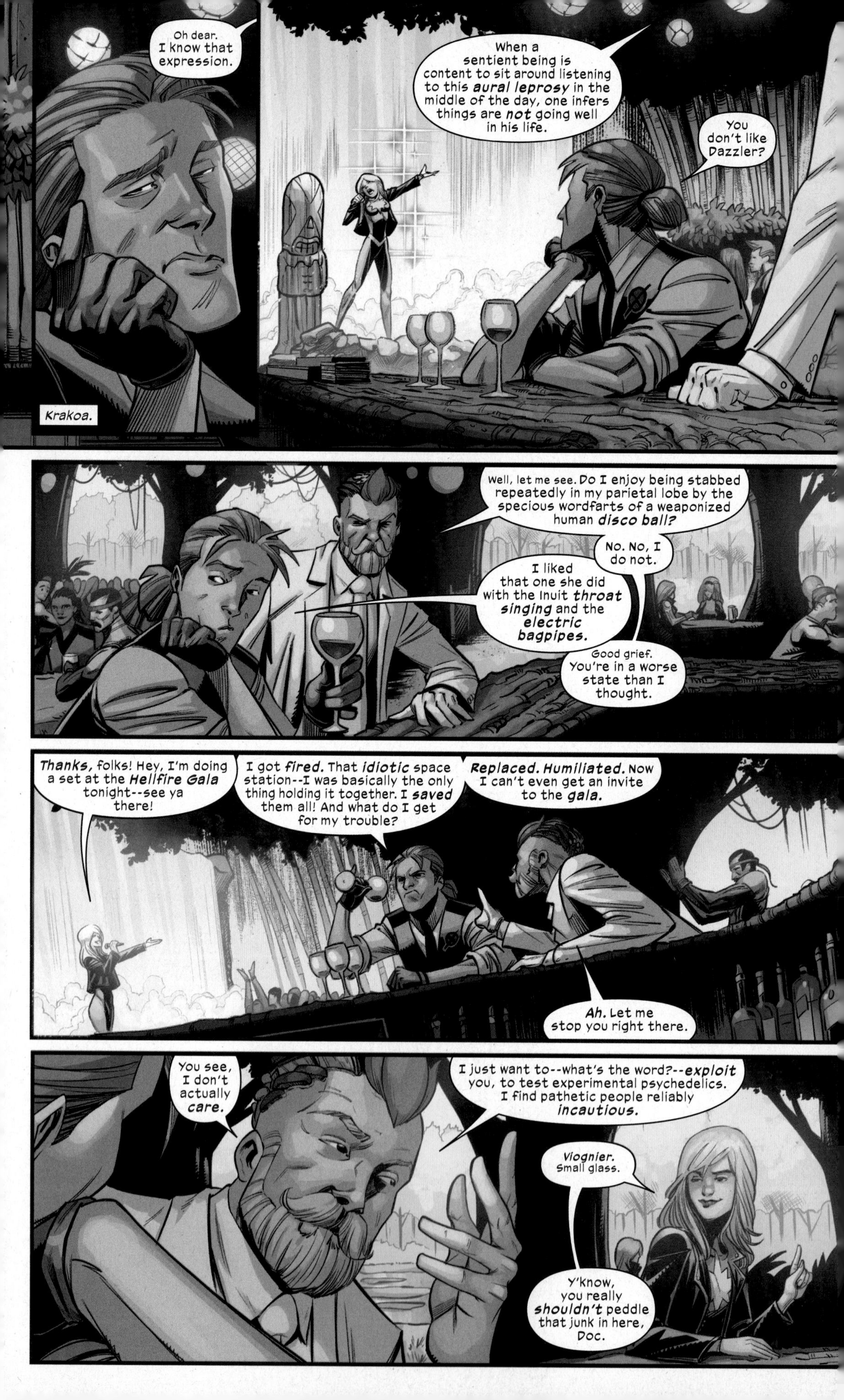
Krakoa.
Oh dear. I know that expression.
When a sentient being is content to sit around listening to this aural leprosy in the middle of the day, one infers things are not going well in his life.
You don't like Dazzler?
Well, let me see. Do I enjoy being stabbed repeatedly in my parietal lobe by the specious wordfarts of a weaponized human disco ball?
No. No, I do not.
I liked that one she did with the Inuit throat singing and the electric bagpipes.
Good grief. You're in a worse state than I thought.
Thanks, folks! Hey, I'm doing a set at the Hellfire Gala tonight--see ya there!
I got fired. That idiotic space station--I was basically the only thing holding it together. I saved them all! And what do I get for my trouble?
Replaced. Humiliated. Now I can't even get an invite to the gala.
Ah. Let me stop you right there.
You see, I don't actually care.
I just want to--what's the word?--exploit you, to test experimental psychedelics. I find pathetic people reliably incautious.
Viognier. Small glass.
Y'know, you really shouldn't peddle that junk in here, Doc.

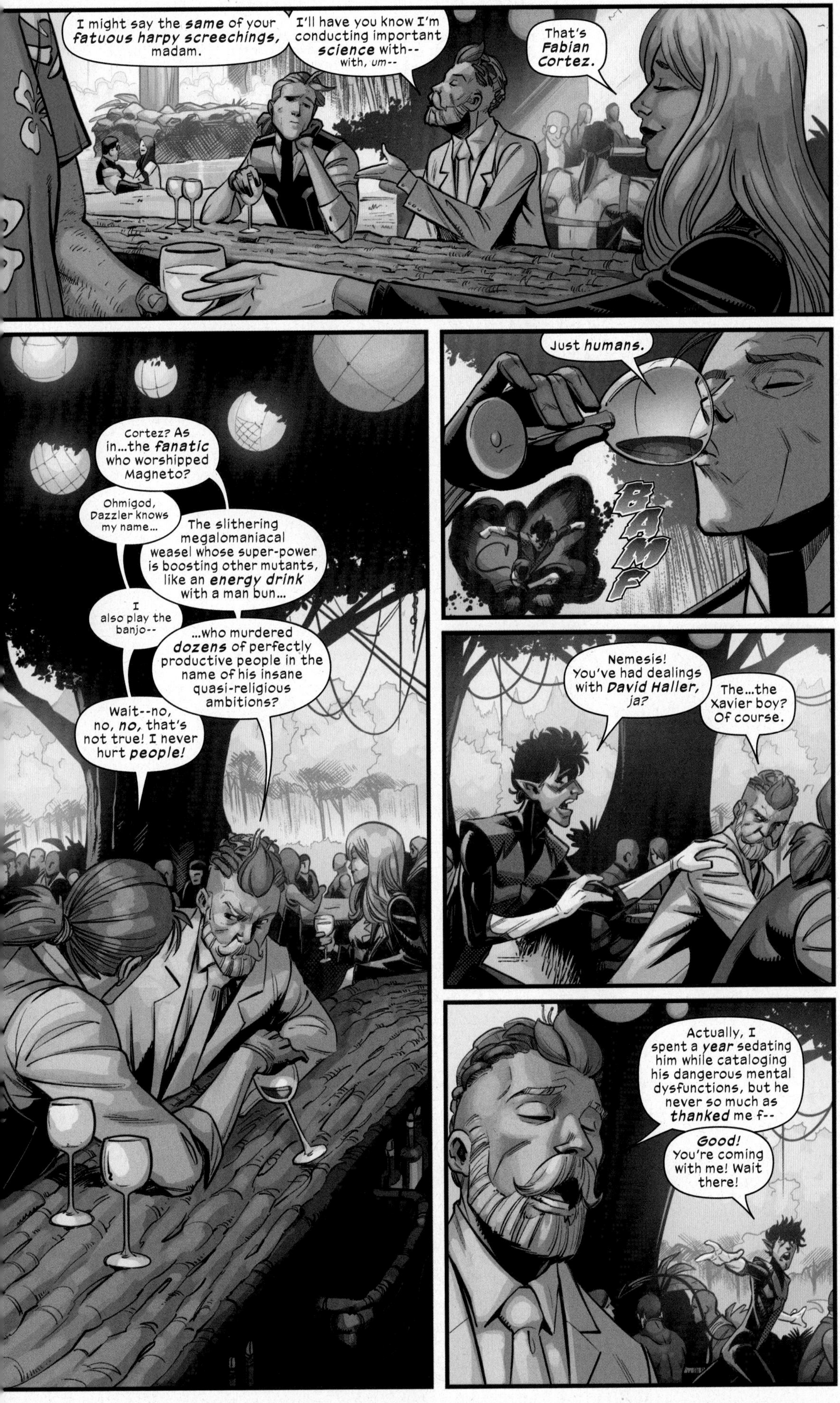
I might say the *same* of your *fatuous harpy screechings,* madam.
I'll have you know I'm conducting important *science* with-- with, *um*--
That's *Fabian Cortez.*
Cortez? As in...the *fanatic* who worshipped Magneto?
Ohmigod, Dazzler knows my name...
The slithering megalomaniacal weasel whose super-power is boosting other mutants, like an *energy drink* with a man bun...
I also play the banjo--
...who murdered *dozens* of perfectly productive people in the name of his insane quasi-religious ambitions?
Wait--no, no, *no,* that's not true! I never hurt *people!*
Just *humans.*
BAMF
Nemesis! You've had dealings with *David Haller, ja?*
The...the Xavier boy? Of course.
Actually, I spent a *year* sedating him while cataloging his dangerous mental dysfunctions, but he never so much as *thanked* me f--
Good! You're coming with me! Wait there!

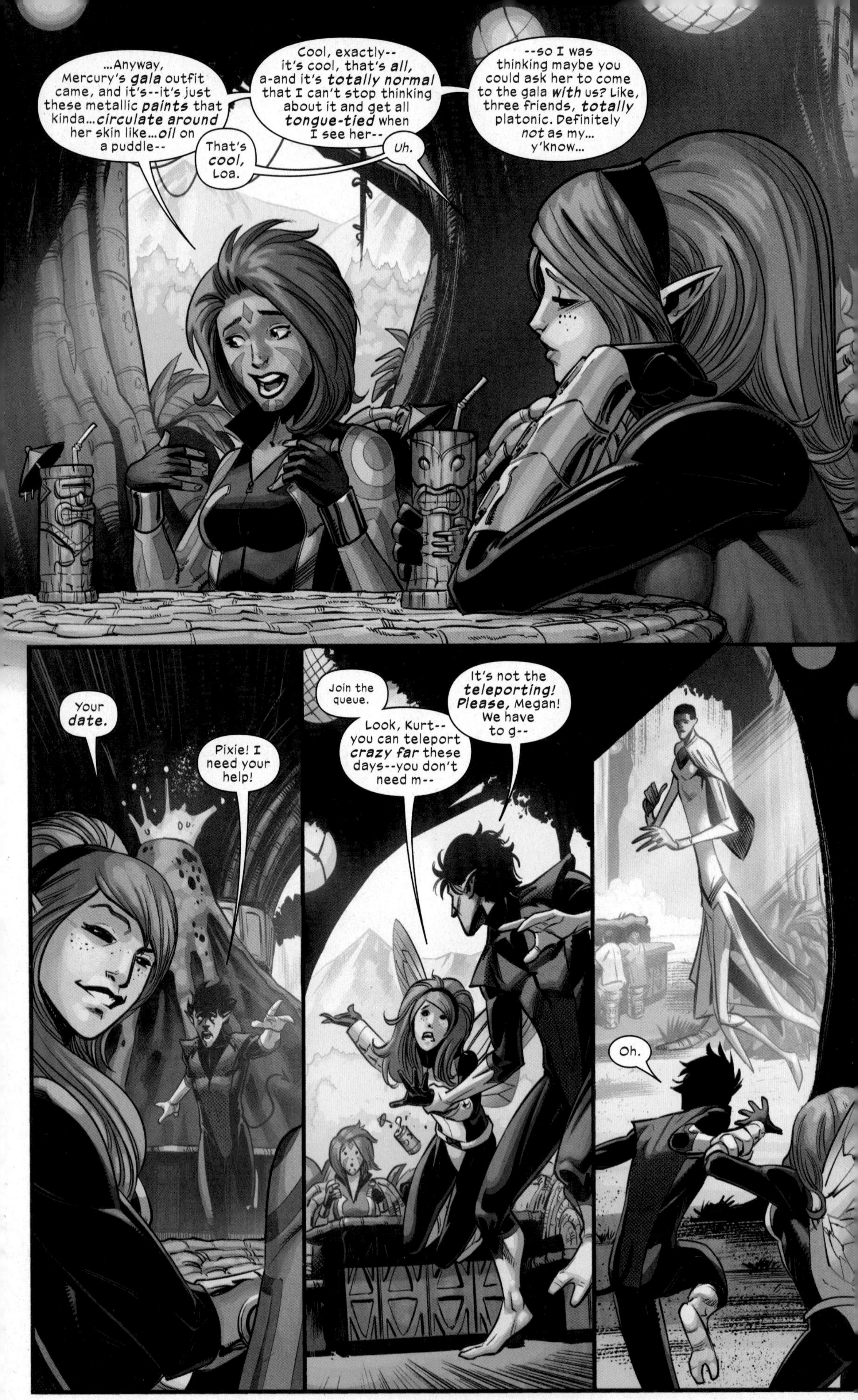

...Anyway, Mercury's *gala* outfit came, and it's--it's just these metallic *paints* that kinda...*circulate around* her skin like...*oil* on a puddle--
That's *cool,* Loa.
Cool, exactly-- it's cool, that's *all,* a-and it's *totally normal* that I can't stop thinking about it and get all *tongue-tied* when I see her--
Uh.
--so I was thinking maybe you could ask her to come to the gala *with* us? Like, three friends, *totally* platonic. Definitely *not* as my... y'know...
Your *date.*
Pixie! I need your help!
Join the queue.
Look, Kurt-- you can teleport *crazy far* these days--you don't need m--
It's not the *teleporting! Please,* Megan! We have to g--
Oh.

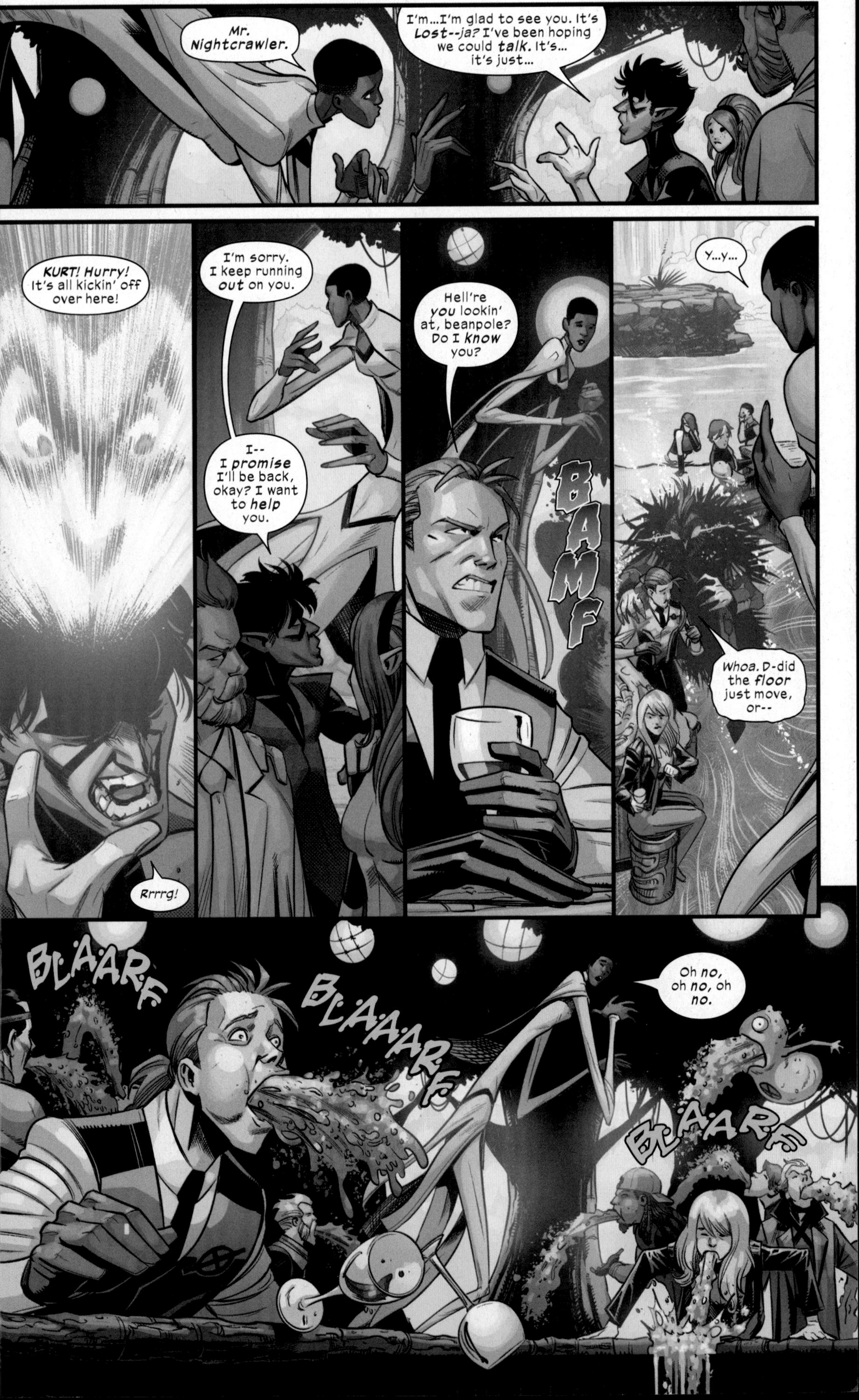

Mr. Nightcrawler.
I'm...I'm glad to see you. It's Lost--ja? I've been hoping we could talk. It's... it's just...
KURT! Hurry! It's all kickin' off over here!
Rrrrg!
I'm sorry. I keep running out on you.
I-- I promise I'll be back, okay? I want to help you.
Hell're you lookin' at, beanpole? Do I know you?
BAMF
Y...y...
Whoa. D-did the floor just move, or--
BLAARF
BLAAARF
Oh no, oh no, oh no.
BLAARF

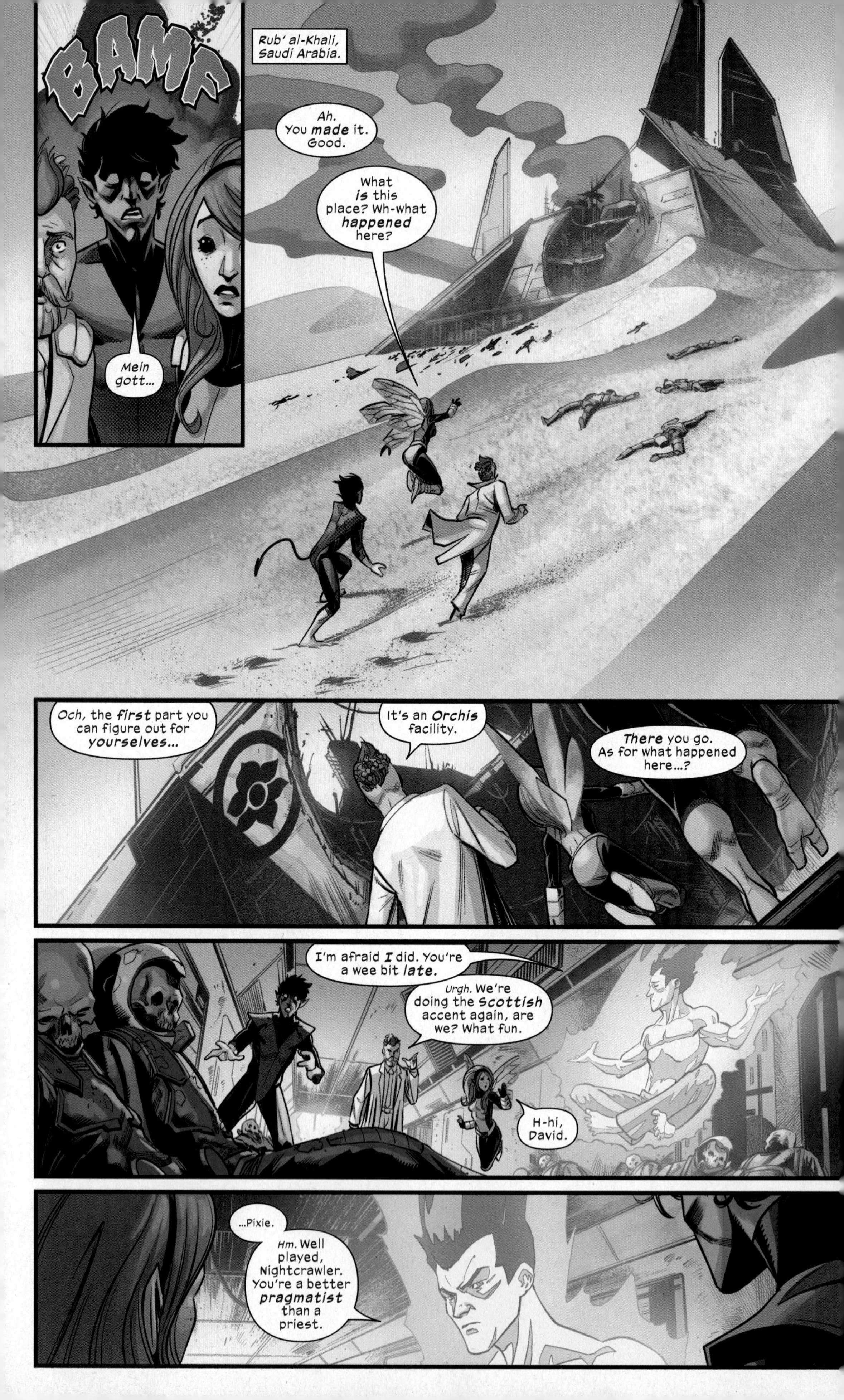
BAMF
Rub' al-Khali, Saudi Arabia.
Mein gott...
Ah. You made it. Good.
What is this place? Wh-what happened here?
Och, the first part you can figure out for yourselves...
It's an Orchis facility.
There you go. As for what happened here...?
I'm afraid I did. You're a wee bit late.
Urgh. We're doing the Scottish accent again, are we? What fun.
H-hi, David.
...Pixie.
Hm. Well played, Nightcrawler. You're a better pragmatist than a priest.

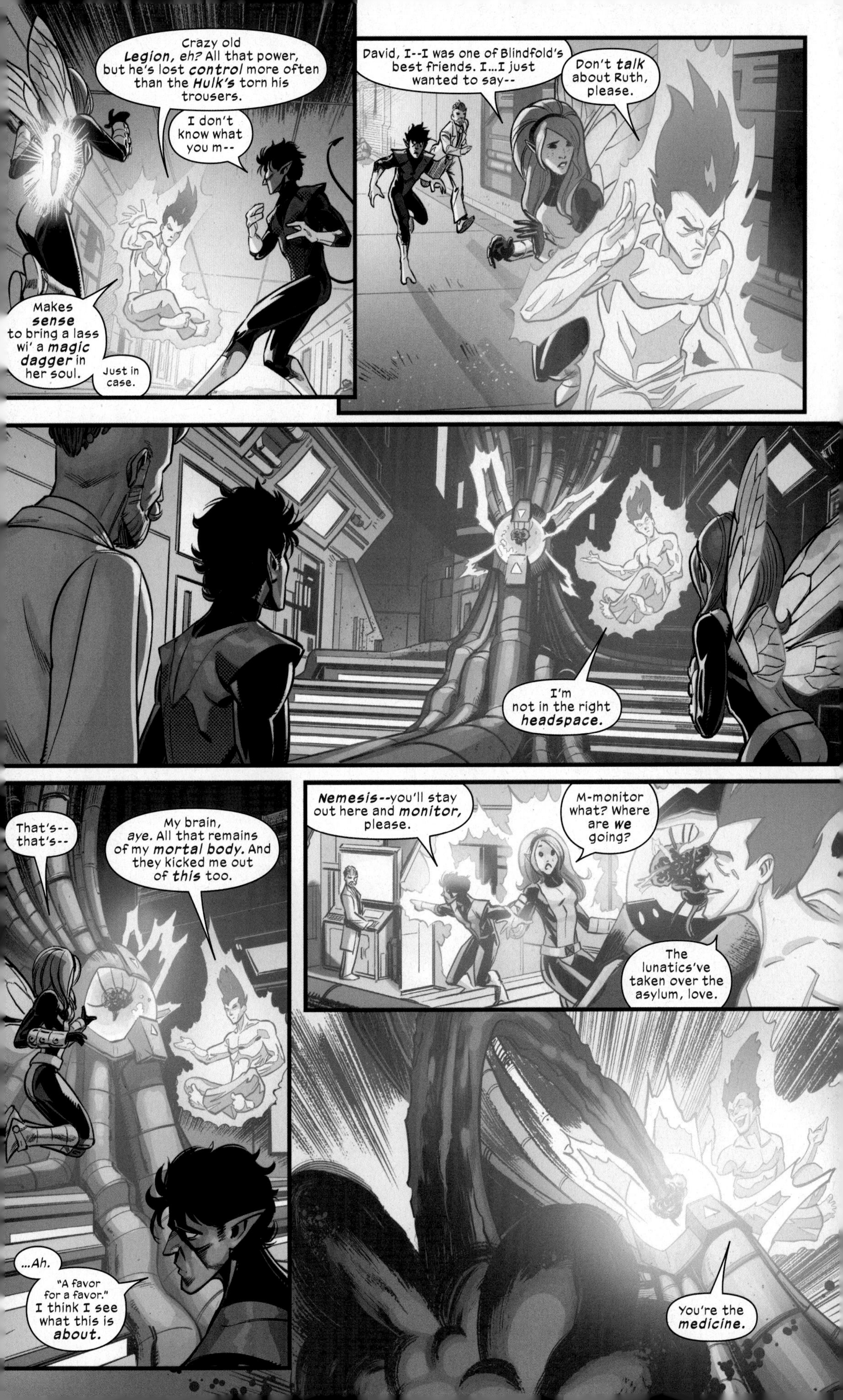

Crazy old Legion, eh? All that power, but he's lost control more often than the Hulk's torn his trousers.
I don't know what you m--
Makes sense to bring a lass wi' a magic dagger in her soul.
Just in case.
David, I--I was one of Blindfold's best friends. I...I just wanted to say--
Don't talk about Ruth, please.
I'm not in the right headspace.
That's--that's--
My brain, aye. All that remains of my mortal body. And they kicked me out of this too.
...Ah.
"A favor for a favor." I think I see what this is about.
Nemesis--you'll stay out here and monitor, please.
M-monitor what? Where are we going?
The lunatics've taken over the asylum, love.
You're the medicine.

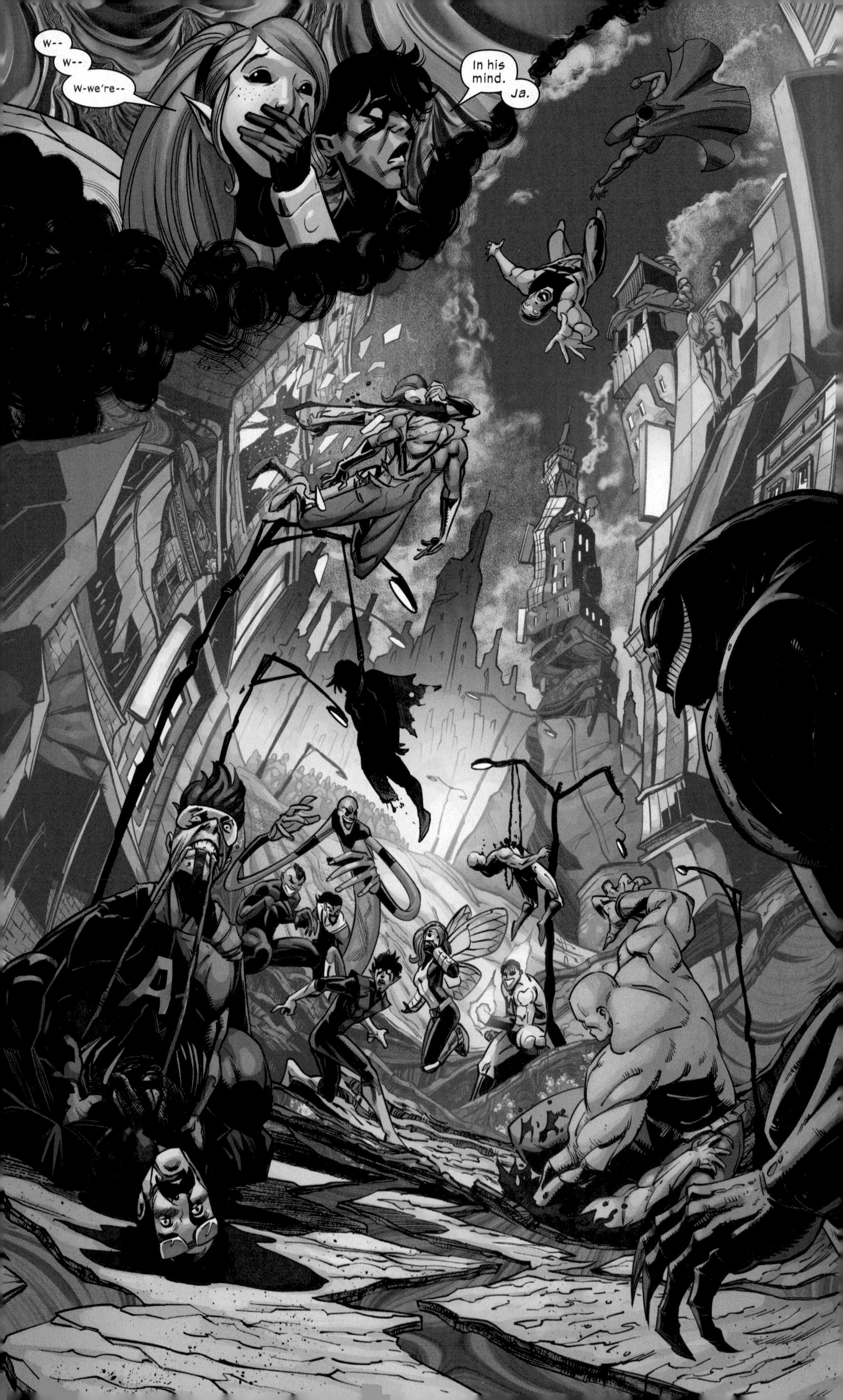
W--
W--
W-we're--
In his mind.
Ja.

ORCHIS PROTOCOL

SOCIOLOGY / MODELING DIVISION

[EYES ONLY: Fifth Petal Command]

INTERNAL COMMUNIQUÉ FROM THE DESK OF

[redacted]

Results at last.

The [redacted] Project has been a struggle from the start, politically speaking. Those crooks at Legacy House didn't realize what they were selling, but Gyrich and his flunkies in Second Petal absolutely did. We've been fending off his grabby hands from the moment we acquired the Asset. If the Central Column hadn't come out so strong in favor of our proposal, the richest research artifact in the mutant world would be liquifying on a shelf -- or, more likely, converted into some dreary sidearm.

Even with [redacted]'s backing, the pressure to demonstrate the value of the modeling facility in the Rub' al-Khali has been intense. I've been quietly informed of at least three attempts to requisition "the bell jar brain," as we've taken to calling it, for projects in more conventional fields.

But this month's introduction of the [redacted] has silenced all detractors. True, the autonomous entities that populate the psychic realm within the Asset were already degrading slowly into a state of antisocial stagnation (since we successfully excised the core personality and its capacity to pacify the rest). But within hours of the implantation, the decay had accelerated exponentially. A state of self-destructive violence was observed almost immediately and has only deepened since.

Two fields of immediate action emerge:

1. On a practical level, we must act swiftly to contain and mitigate the disquiet within the Asset. If we are to continue to benefit from the modeling resource it represents (and safeguard our personnel from potential externalizations), modes of reset are urgently required.

2. Naturally, the ultimate objective is the application of our results in practical, weaponized form against [redacted]. I'm happy to report that the Central Column has taken a direct leadership role in this endeavor, and I'm told a covert intervention analogous to our destabilizing implant is already being prepared by Sixth Petal personnel.

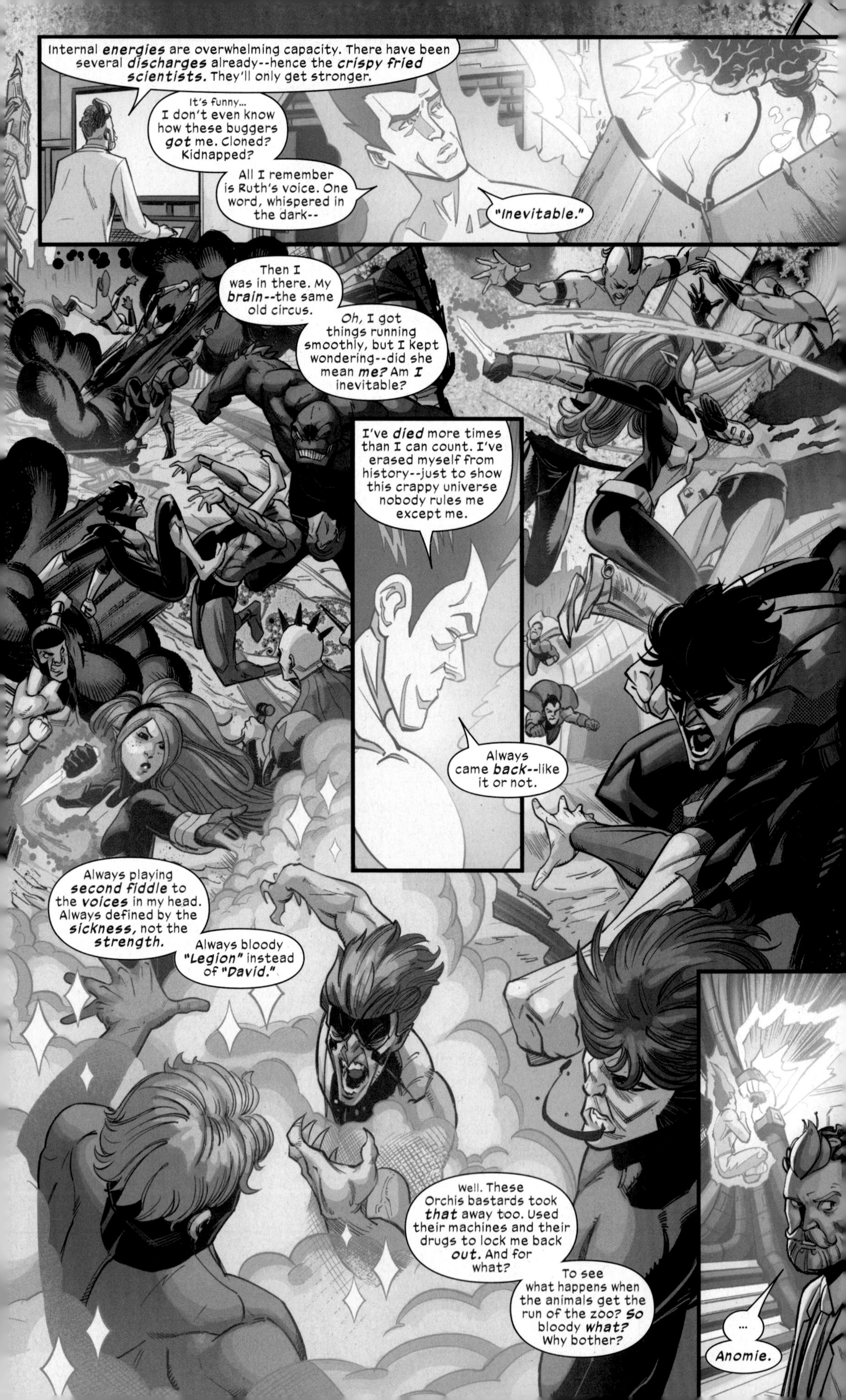

Internal energies are overwhelming capacity. There have been several discharges already--hence the crispy fried scientists. They'll only get stronger.
It's funny... I don't even know how these buggers got me. Cloned? Kidnapped?
All I remember is Ruth's voice. One word, whispered in the dark--
"Inevitable."
Then I was in there. My brain--the same old circus.
Oh, I got things running smoothly, but I kept wondering--did she mean me? Am I inevitable?
I've died more times than I can count. I've erased myself from history--just to show this crappy universe nobody rules me except me.
Always came back--like it or not.
Always playing second fiddle to the voices in my head. Always defined by the sickness, not the strength.
Always bloody "Legion" instead of "David."
Well. These Orchis bastards took that away too. Used their machines and their drugs to lock me back out. And for what?
To see what happens when the animals get the run of the zoo? So bloody what? Why bother?
...
Anomie.

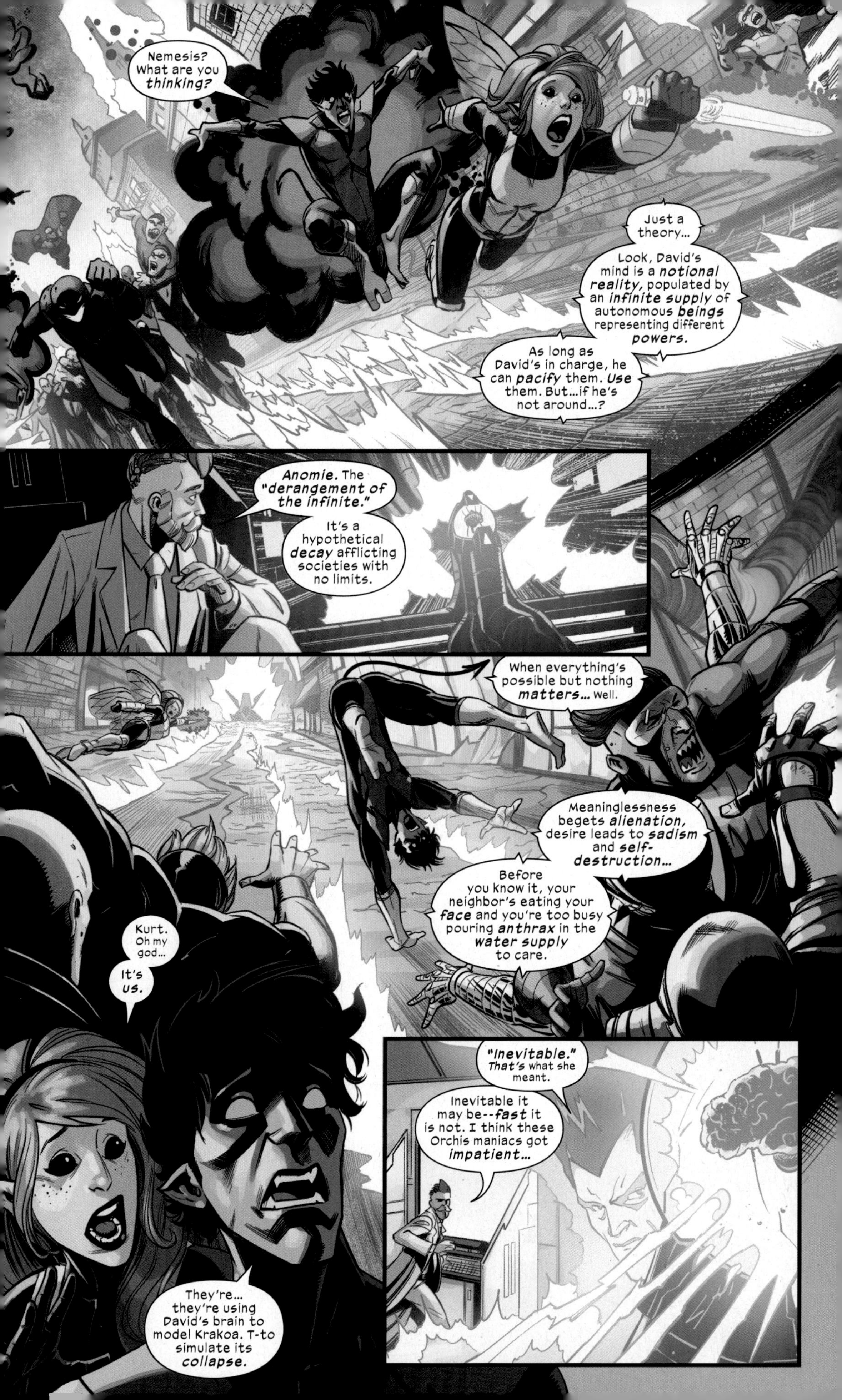

Nemesis? What are you *thinking?*
Just a theory...
Look, David's mind is a *notional reality,* populated by an *infinite supply* of autonomous *beings* representing different *powers.*
As long as David's in charge, he can *pacify* them. *Use* them. But...if he's not around...?
Anomie. The "*derangement of the infinite.*"
It's a hypothetical *decay* afflicting societies with no limits.
When everything's possible but nothing *matters...* Well.
Meaninglessness begets *alienation,* desire leads to *sadism* and *self-destruction...*
Before you know it, your neighbor's eating your *face* and you're too busy pouring *anthrax* in the *water supply* to care.
Kurt. Oh my god...
It's *us.*
They're... they're using David's brain to model Krakoa. T-to simulate its *collapse.*
"*Inevitable.*" *That's* what she meant.
Inevitable it may be--*fast* it is not. I think these Orchis maniacs got *impatient...*

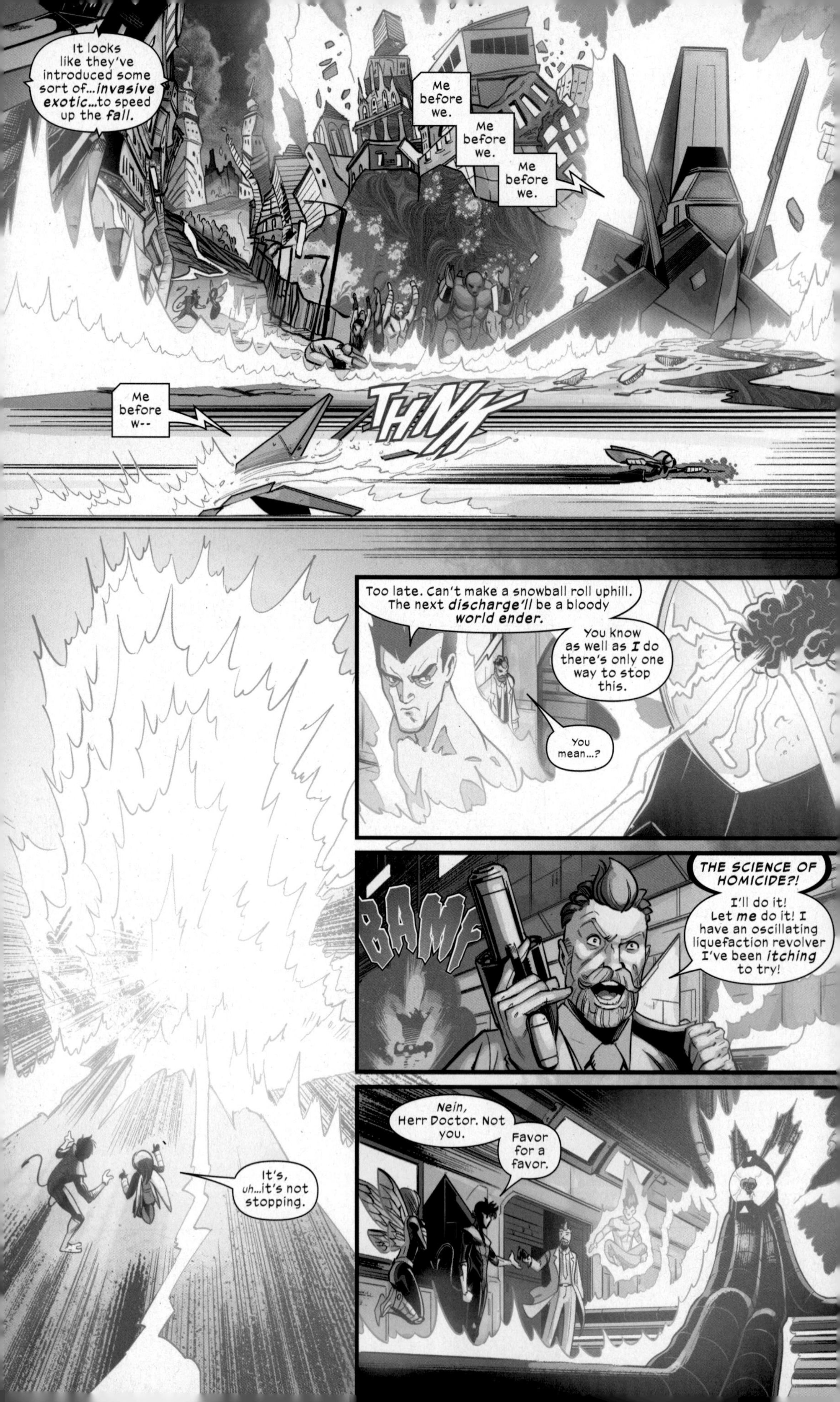

It looks like they've introduced some sort of...*invasive exotic*...to speed up the *fall.*
Me before we.
Me before we.
Me before we.
Me before w--
THINK
Too late. Can't make a snowball roll uphill. The next *discharge'll* be a bloody *world ender.*
You know as well as *I* do there's only one way to stop this.
You mean...?
BAMF
THE SCIENCE OF HOMICIDE?!
I'll do it! Let *me* do it! I have an oscillating liquefaction revolver I've been *itching* to try!
It's, *uh*...it's not stopping.
Nein, Herr Doctor. Not you.
Favor for a favor.

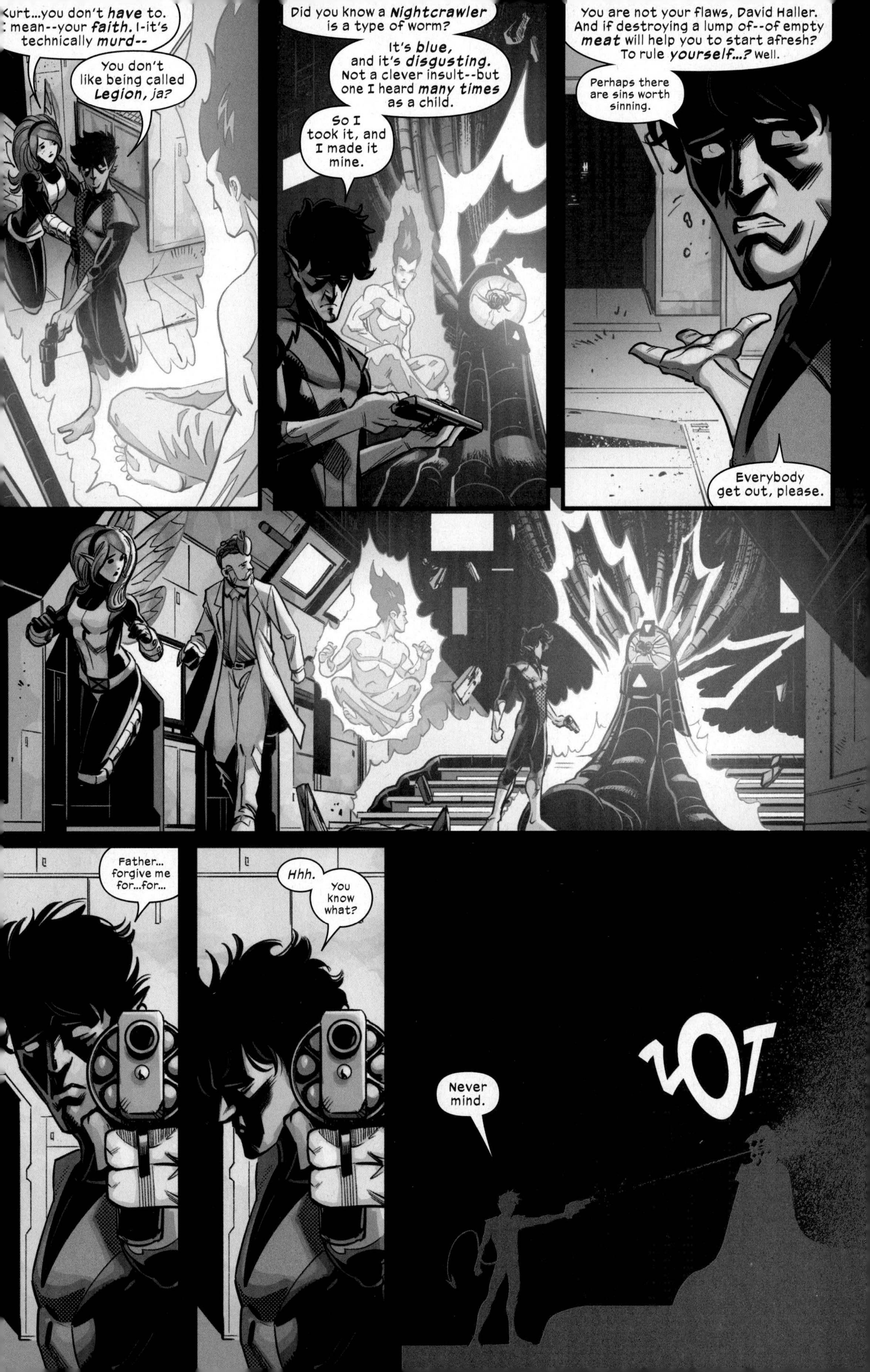
Kurt...you don't have to. I mean--your faith. I-it's technically murd--
You don't like being called Legion, ja?
Did you know a Nightcrawler is a type of worm?
It's blue, and it's disgusting. Not a clever insult--but one I heard many times as a child.
So I took it, and I made it mine.
You are not your flaws, David Haller. And if destroying a lump of--of empty meat will help you to start afresh? To rule yourself...? Well.
Perhaps there are sins worth sinning.
Everybody get out, please.
Father... forgive me for...for...
Hhh.
You know what?
Never mind.
ZOT

EXCERPT: THE BOOK OF ██████████

FIRST FLORILEGIUM
THE PRODIGAL SUN, 6:1-4

Reader, I killed him. By doing so, I permitted his rebirth.

That, I believe, was my first true step toward the Way. An ugly act -- an act that broke every piece of thoughtless conditioning I had ever accumulated, but which catalyzed an act of creation whose value I cannot now understate. A leap not of faith, but of painful empathy.

You must understand -- David is no god. No annointed messiah come to save us. He would laugh, or perhaps shudder, at the notion.

But I cannot deny that when we returned to Krakoa that day, unsure of what we had done, we each felt some dim understanding that something profound had changed. Something that spoke less to metaphysics and more to meaning.

It began with a silence...

...a silence like drums.

A rolling, stifling thunder of anti-noise, smothering songs, lifting eyes and minds from mundane matters.

In Arbor Magna, the Five fell still, as if each were struck by the same idea all at once.

Without a word spoken, they turned to a new task.

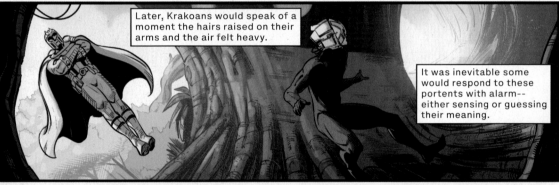

Later, Krakoans would speak of a moment the hairs raised on their arms and the air felt heavy.

It was inevitable some would respond to these portents with alarm-- either sensing or guessing their meaning.

While others were gripped by older instincts.

To witness. To protect.

To balance.

And with it? The unmistakable sensation of--

--something--

--descending.

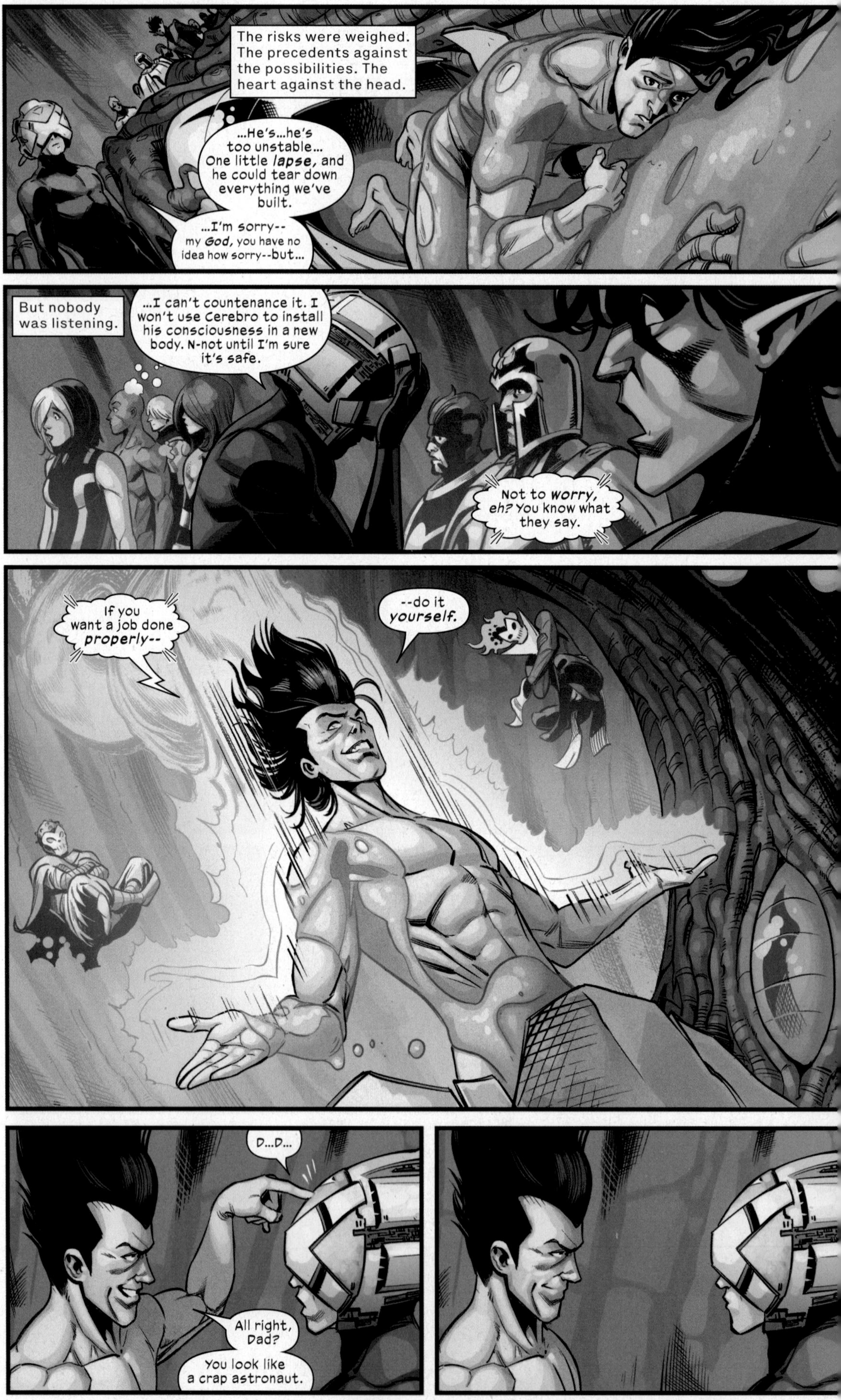

The risks were weighed. The precedents against the possibilities. The heart against the head.
...He's...he's too unstable... One little lapse, and he could tear down everything we've built.
...I'm sorry-- my God, you have no idea how sorry--but...
But nobody was listening.
...I can't countenance it. I won't use Cerebro to install his consciousness in a new body. N-not until I'm sure it's safe.
Not to worry, eh? You know what they say.
If you want a job done properly--
--do it yourself.
D...D...
All right, Dad?
You look like a crap astronaut.

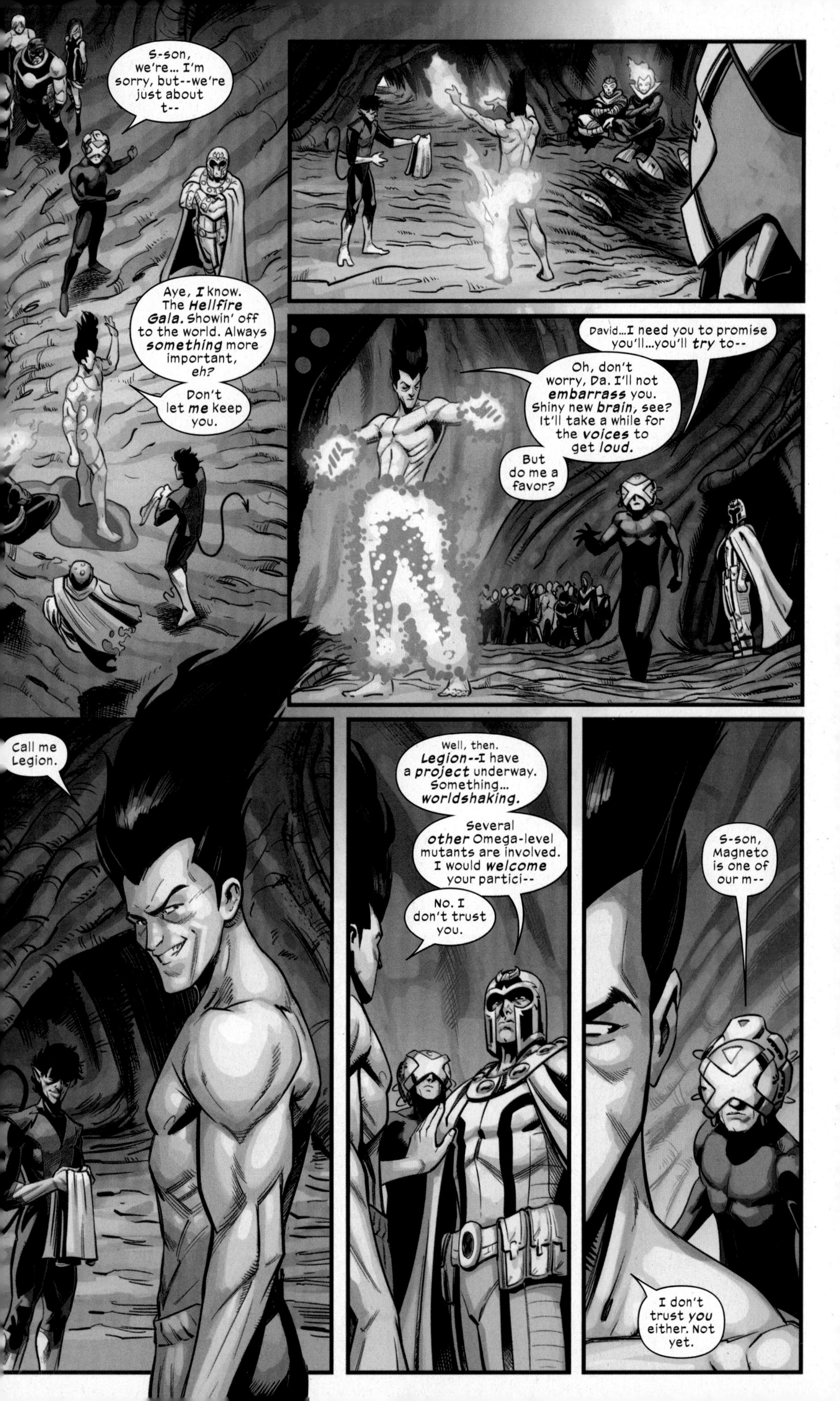

S-son, we're... I'm sorry, but--we're just about t--
Aye, *I* know. The *Hellfire Gala.* Showin' off to the world. Always *something* more important, *eh?*
Don't let *me* keep you.
David...I need you to promise you'll...you'll *try* to--
Oh, don't worry, Da. I'll not *embarrass* you. Shiny new *brain,* see? It'll take a while for the *voices* to get *loud.*
But do me a favor?
Call me Legion.
Well, then. *Legion--*I have a *project* underway. Something... *worldshaking.*
Several *other* Omega-level mutants are involved. I would *welcome* your partici--
No. I don't trust you.
S-son, Magneto is one of our m--
I don't trust *you* either. Not yet.

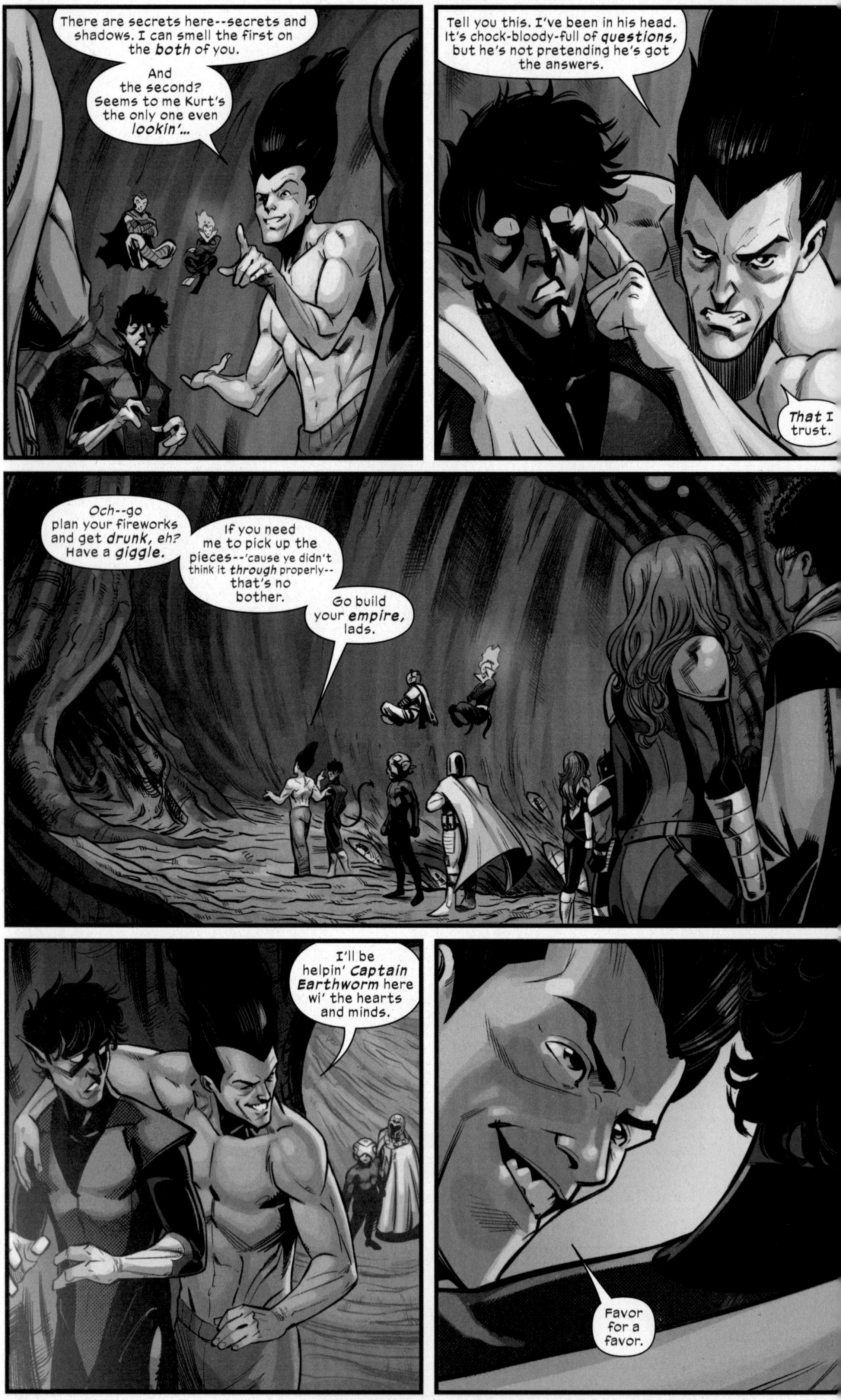

There are secrets here--secrets and shadows. I can smell the first on the both of you.
And the second? Seems to me Kurt's the only one even lookin'...
Tell you this. I've been in his head. It's chock-bloody-full of questions, but he's not pretending he's got the answers.
That I trust.
Och--go plan your fireworks and get drunk, eh? Have a giggle.
If you need me to pick up the pieces--'cause ye didn't think it through properly--that's no bother.
Go build your empire, lads.
I'll be helpin' Captain Earthworm here wi' the hearts and minds.
Favor for a favor.

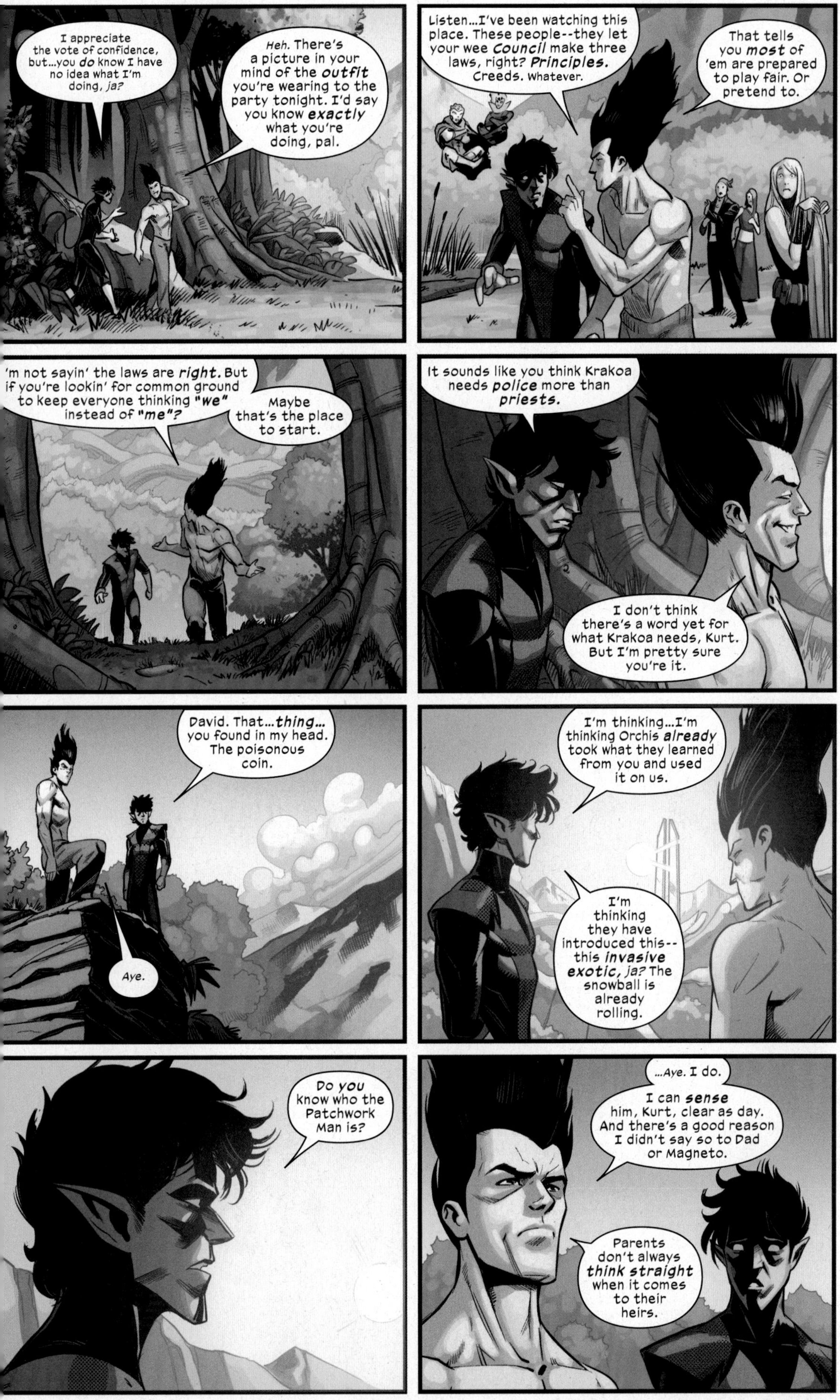

I appreciate the vote of confidence, but...you do know I have no idea what I'm doing, ja?
Heh. There's a picture in your mind of the outfit you're wearing to the party tonight. I'd say you know exactly what you're doing, pal.
Listen...I've been watching this place. These people--they let your wee Council make three laws, right? Principles. Creeds. Whatever.
That tells you most of 'em are prepared to play fair. Or pretend to.
'm not sayin' the laws are right. But if you're lookin' for common ground to keep everyone thinking "we" instead of "me"?
Maybe that's the place to start.
It sounds like you think Krakoa needs police more than priests.
I don't think there's a word yet for what Krakoa needs, Kurt. But I'm pretty sure you're it.
David. That...thing... you found in my head. The poisonous coin.
Aye.
I'm thinking...I'm thinking Orchis already took what they learned from you and used it on us.
I'm thinking they have introduced this--this invasive exotic, ja? The snowball is already rolling.
Do you know who the Patchwork Man is?
...Aye. I do.
I can sense him, Kurt, clear as day. And there's a good reason I didn't say so to Dad or Magneto.
Parents don't always think straight when it comes to their heirs.

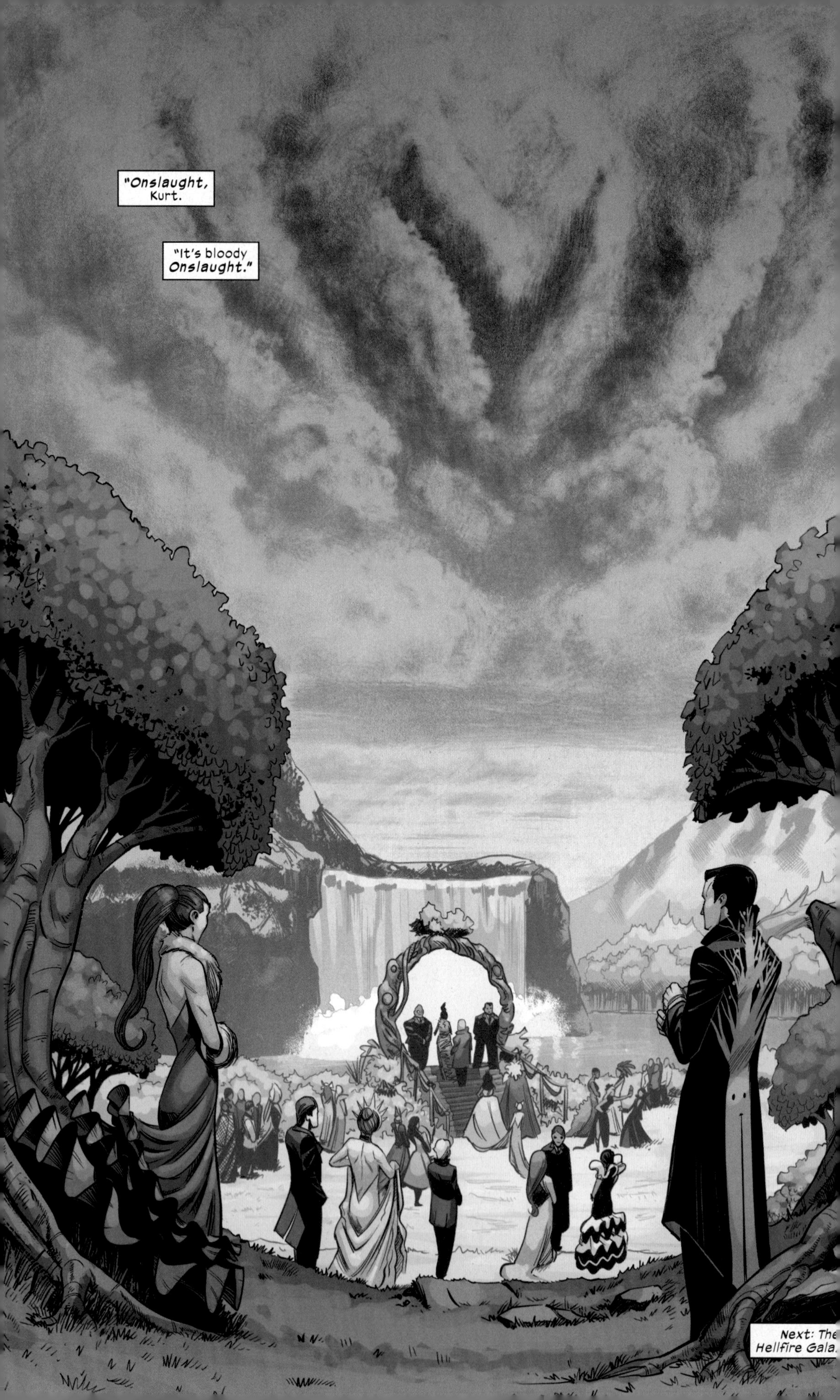
"Onslaught, Kurt.
"It's bloody Onslaught."
Next: The Hellfire Gala.

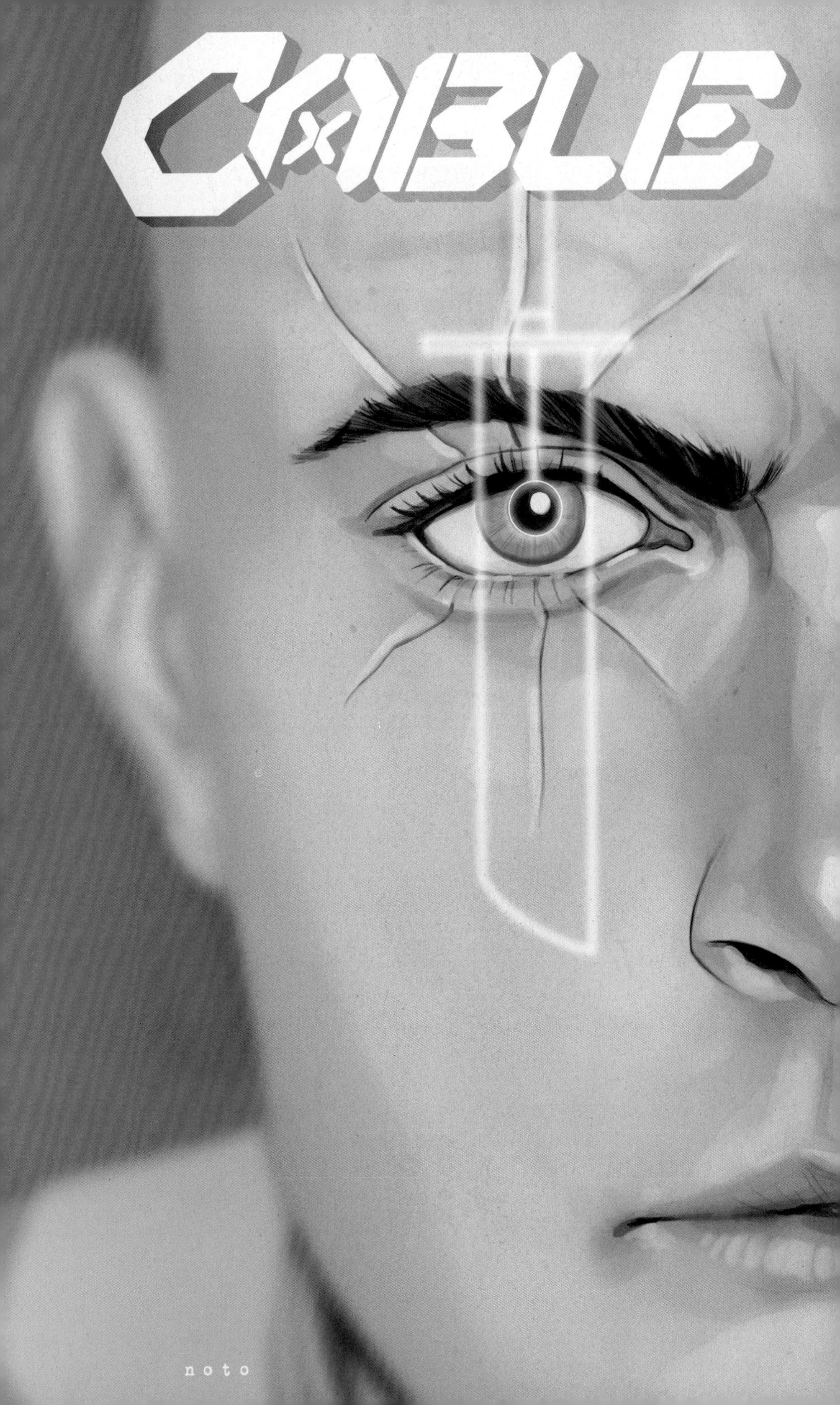
CABLE
noto

[ca__[0.11]
[ble_[0.11]

You know what's about to
happen, right?

-- CYCLOPS

[ca__[0.XX]
[ble_[0.XX]

[ca__[0.11]....]
[ble_[0.11]....]

[Cable_alpha.]

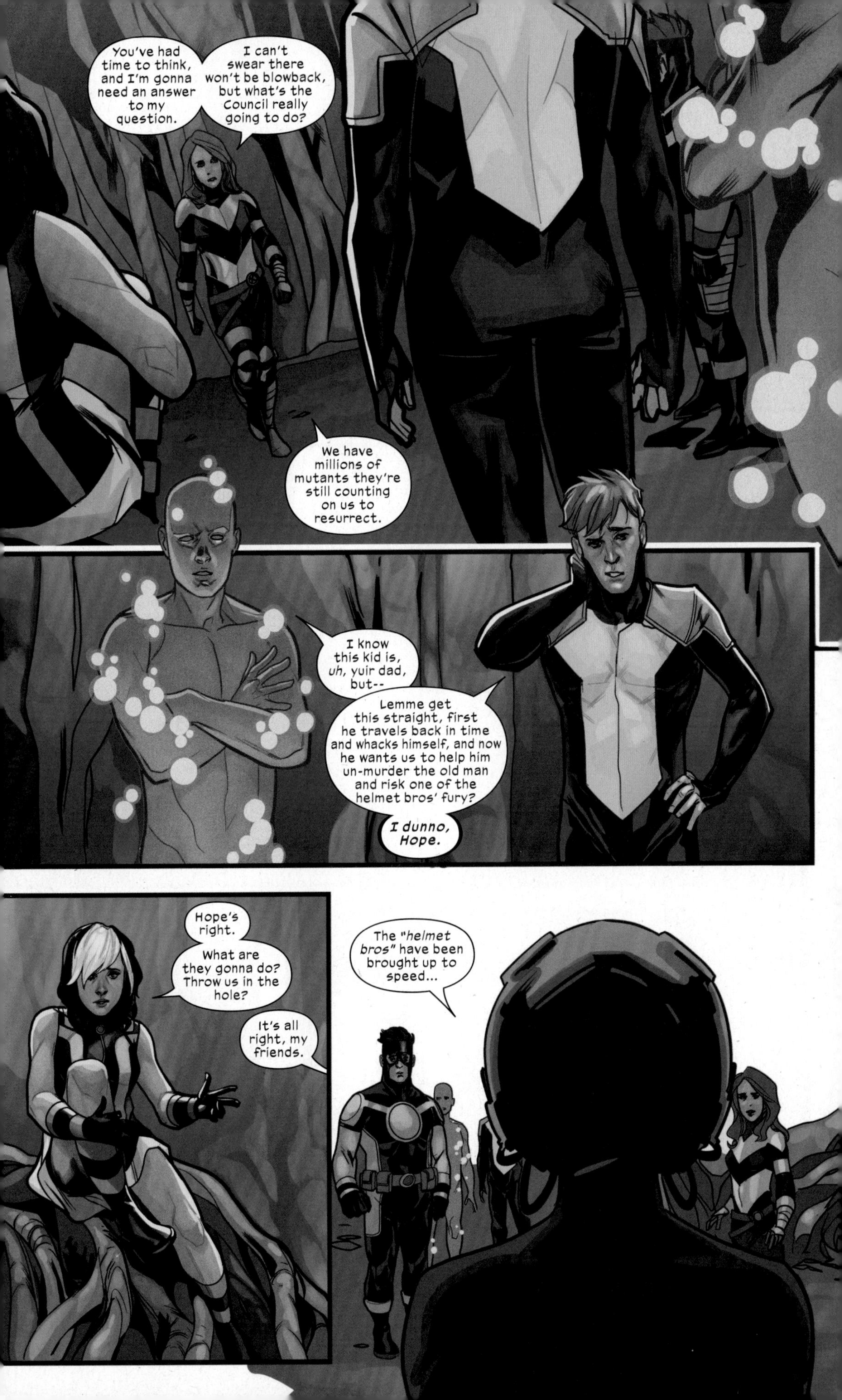
You've had time to think, and I'm gonna need an answer to my question.
I can't swear there won't be blowback, but what's the Council really going to do?
We have millions of mutants they're still counting on us to resurrect.
I know this kid is, *uh*, yuir dad, but--
Lemme get this straight, first he travels back in time and whacks himself, and now he wants us to help him un-murder the old man and risk one of the helmet bros' fury?
I dunno, Hope.
Hope's right.
What are they gonna do? Throw us in the hole?
It's all right, my friends.
The "*helmet bros*" have been brought up to speed...

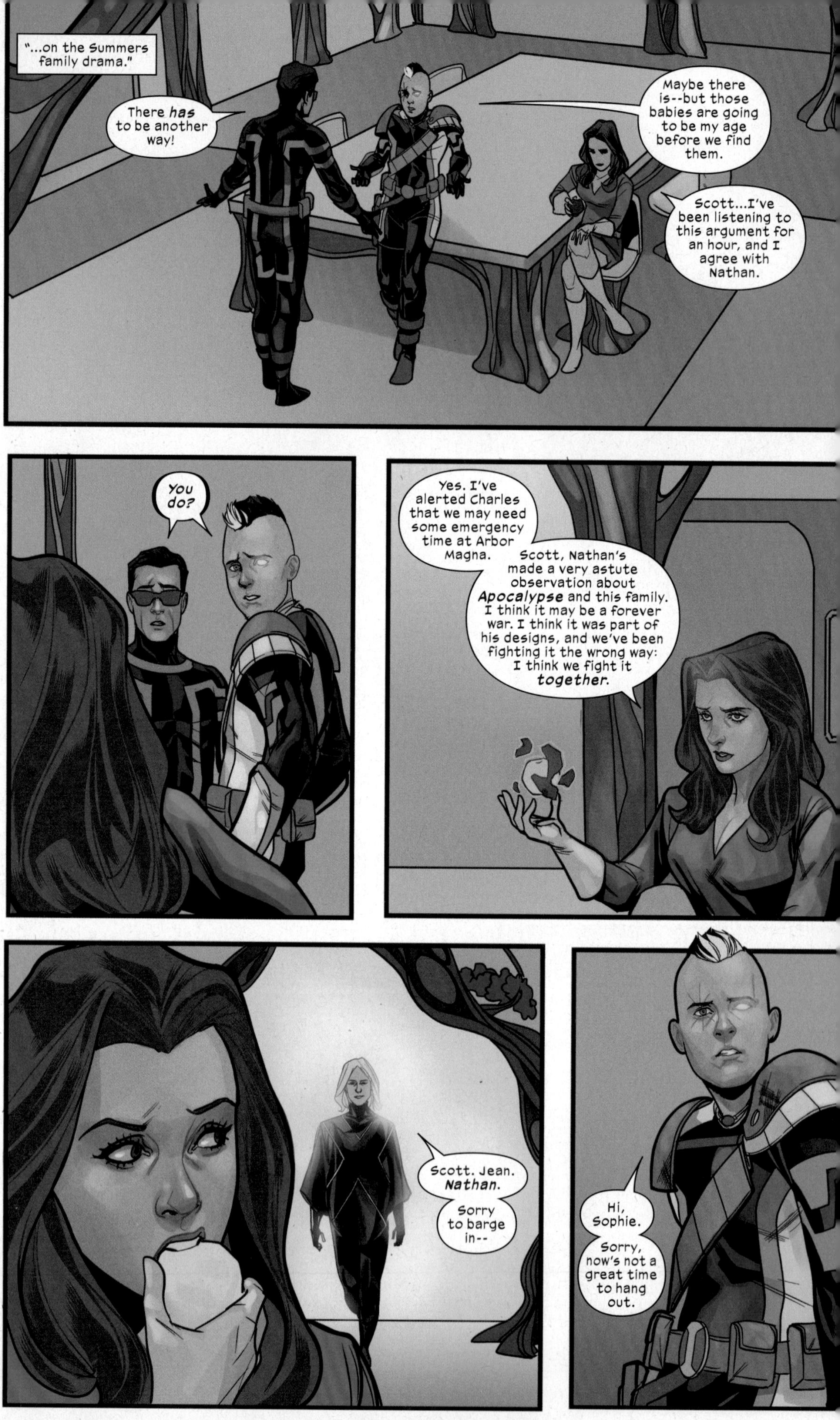
"...on the Summers family drama."
There *has* to be another way!
Maybe there is--but those babies are going to be my age before we find them.
Scott...I've been listening to this argument for an hour, and I agree with Nathan.
You do?
Yes. I've alerted Charles that we may need some emergency time at Arbor Magna.
Scott, Nathan's made a very astute observation about *Apocalypse* and this family. I think it may be a forever war. I think it was part of his designs, and we've been fighting it the wrong way: I think we fight it *together*.
Scott. Jean. *Nathan*.
Sorry to barge in--
Hi, Sophie.
Sorry, now's not a great time to hang out.

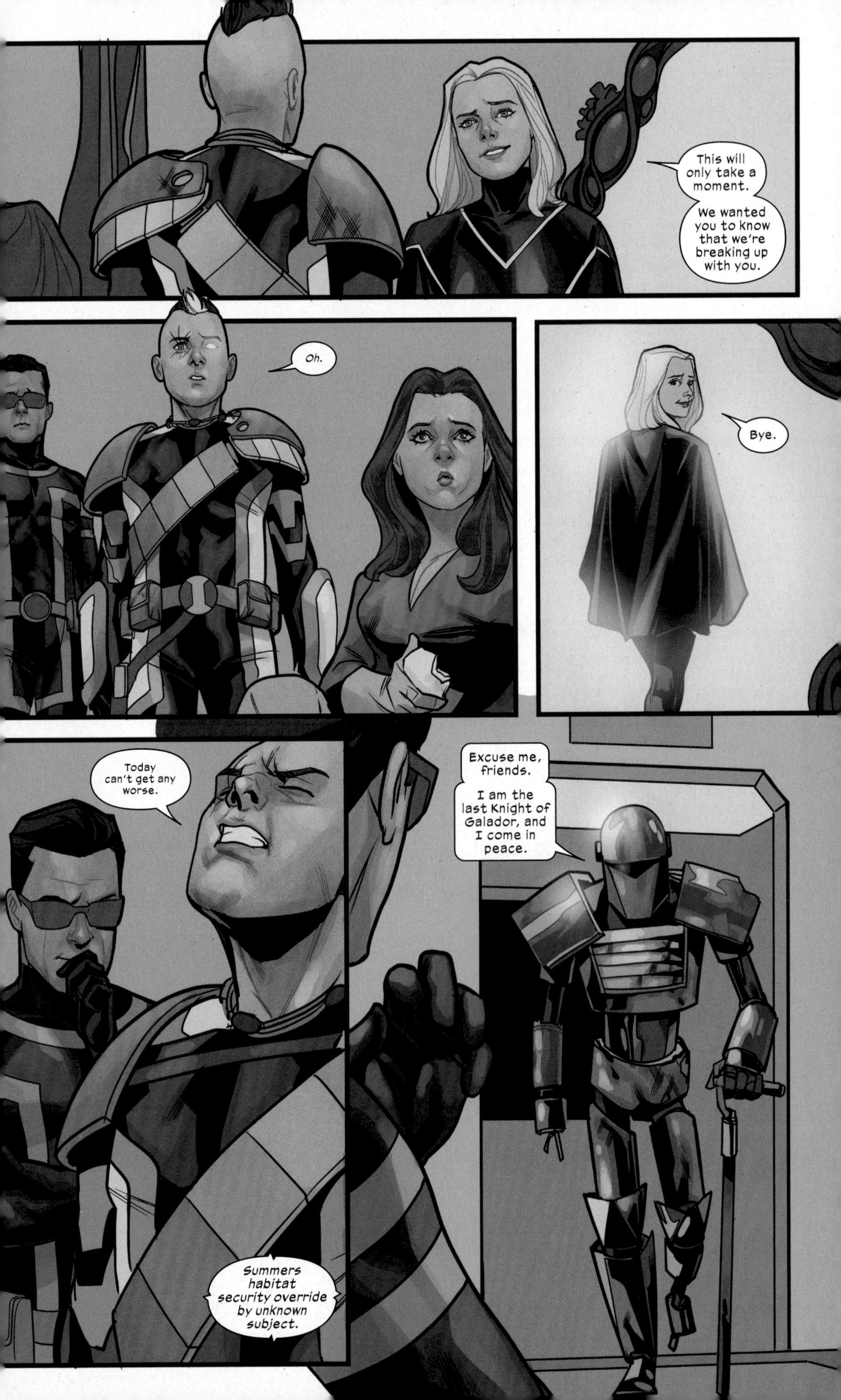
This will only take a moment.
We wanted you to know that we're breaking up with you.
Oh.
Bye.
Today can't get any worse.
Excuse me, friends.
I am the last Knight of Galador, and I come in peace.
Summers habitat security override by unknown subject.

TOGETHER

CABLE discovered that Stryfe, the enemy -- and clone -- of his older self, is alive and well. Increasingly convinced that he cannot defeat Stryfe, Cable has decided he must bring his older self -- yeah, the one he murdered a while ago -- back to the present.

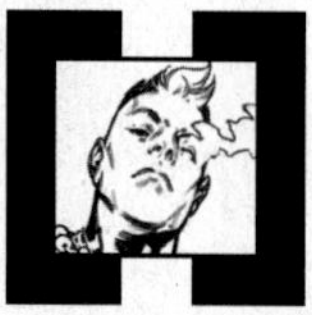

Cable

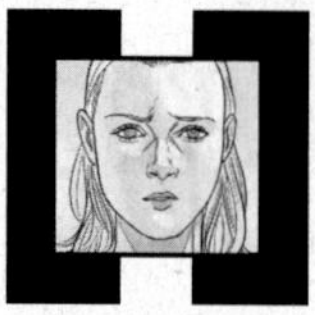

Esme Cuckoo

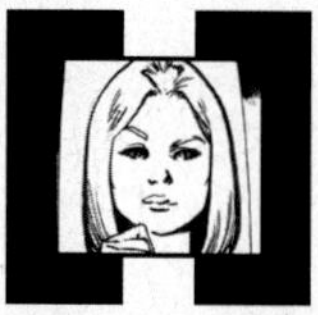

Emma Frost

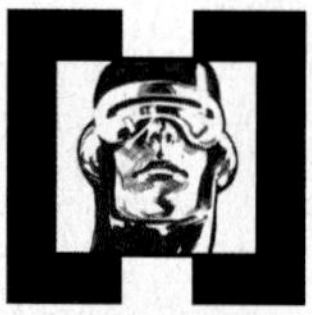

Cyclops

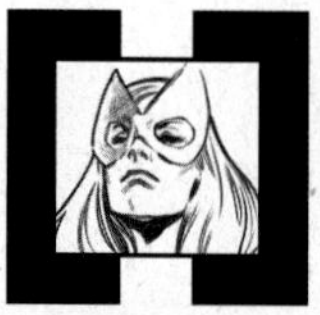

Jean Grey

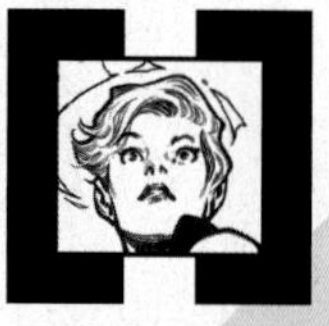

Rachel Summers

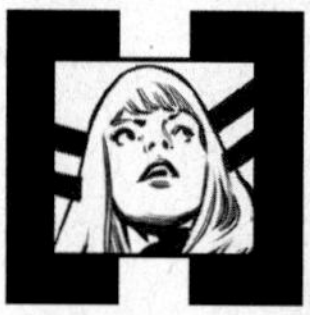

Magik

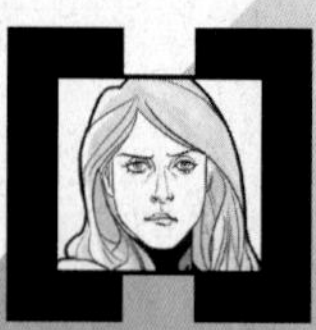

Hope Summers

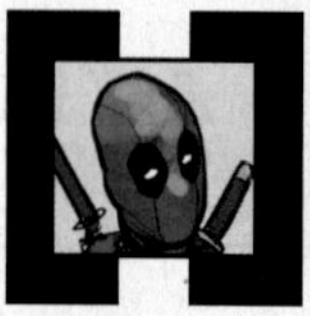

Deadpool

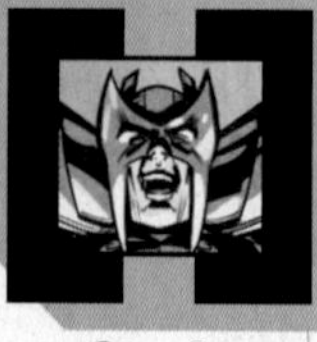

Stryfe

[00_Reign]
[00___ofX]

CABLE

[X_11]

[ISSUE ELEVEN].................... ACCEPTANCE

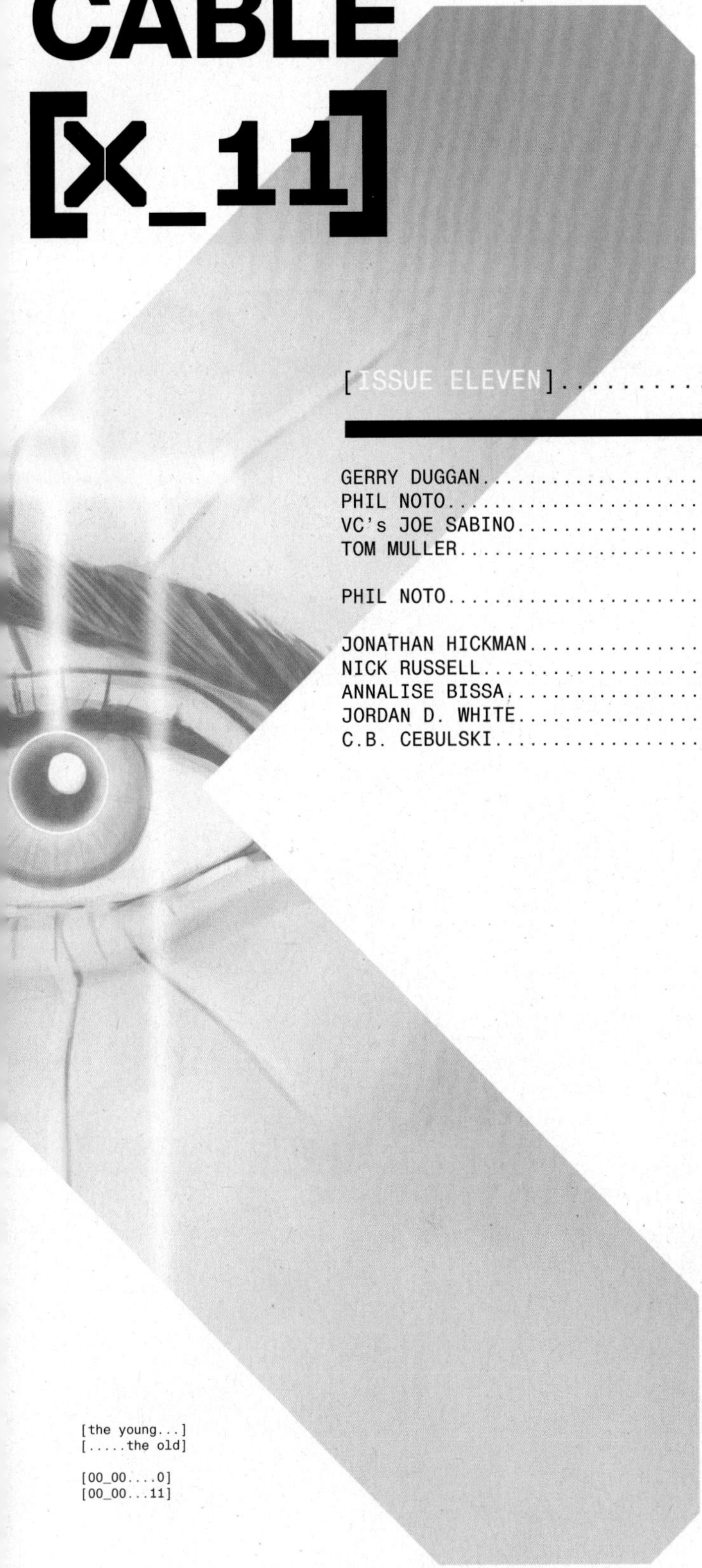

GERRY DUGGAN.................................... [WRITER]
PHIL NOTO....................................... [ARTIST]
VC's JOE SABINO................................ [LETTERER]
TOM MULLER...................................... [DESIGN]

PHIL NOTO................................ [COVER ARTIST]

JONATHAN HICKMAN............................ [HEAD OF X]
NICK RUSSELL............................... [PRODUCTION]
ANNALISE BISSA....................... [ASSOCIATE EDITOR]
JORDAN D. WHITE................................ [EDITOR]
C.B. CEBULSKI........................ [EDITOR IN CHIEF]

[the young...]
[.....the old]

[00_00....0]
[00_00...11]

[XX___past]
[00_______]

[00_______]

[future_XX]

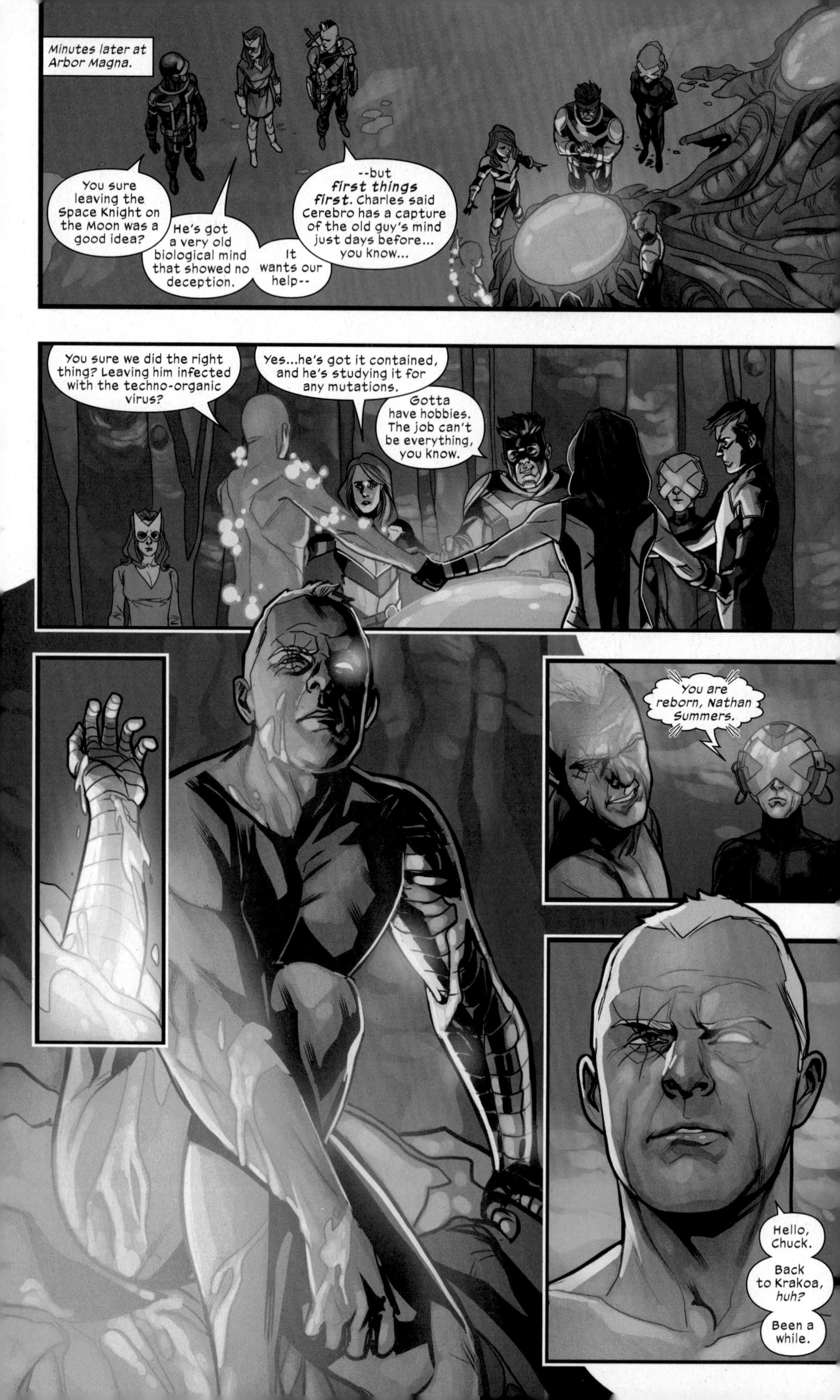
Minutes later at Arbor Magna.
You sure leaving the Space Knight on the Moon was a good idea?
He's got a very old biological mind that showed no deception.
It wants our help--
--but first things first. Charles said Cerebro has a capture of the old guy's mind just days before... you know...
You sure we did the right thing? Leaving him infected with the techno-organic virus?
Yes...he's got it contained, and he's studying it for any mutations.
Gotta have hobbies. The job can't be everything, you know.
You are reborn, Nathan Summers.
Hello, Chuck.
Back to Krakoa, huh?
Been a while.

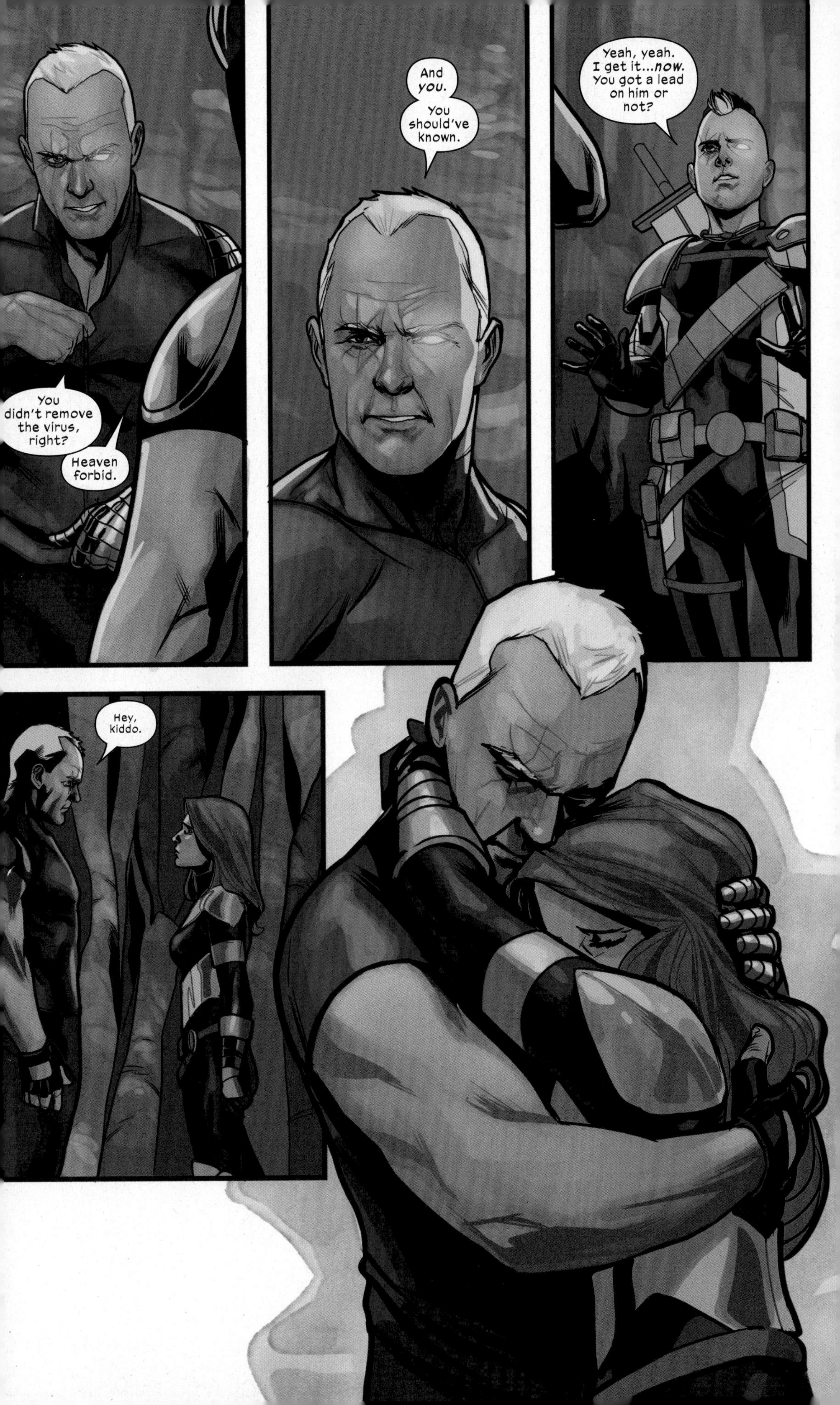
You didn't remove the virus, right?
Heaven forbid.
And *you*.
You should've known.
Yeah, yeah. I get it...*now*. You got a lead on him or not?
Hey, kiddo.

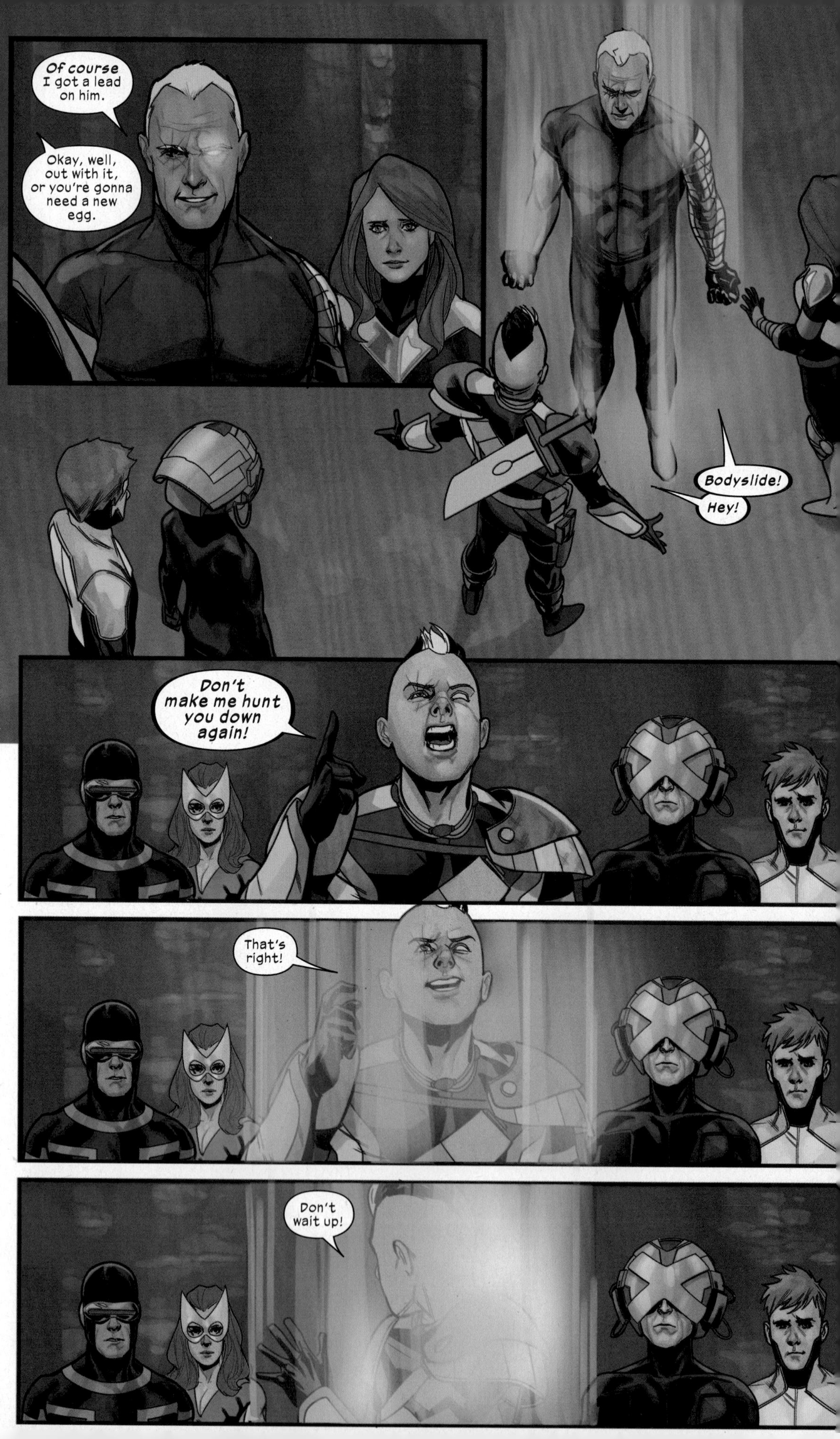
Of course I got a lead on him.
Okay, well, out with it, or you're gonna need a new egg.
Bodyslide!
Hey!
Don't make me hunt you down again!
That's right!
Don't wait up!

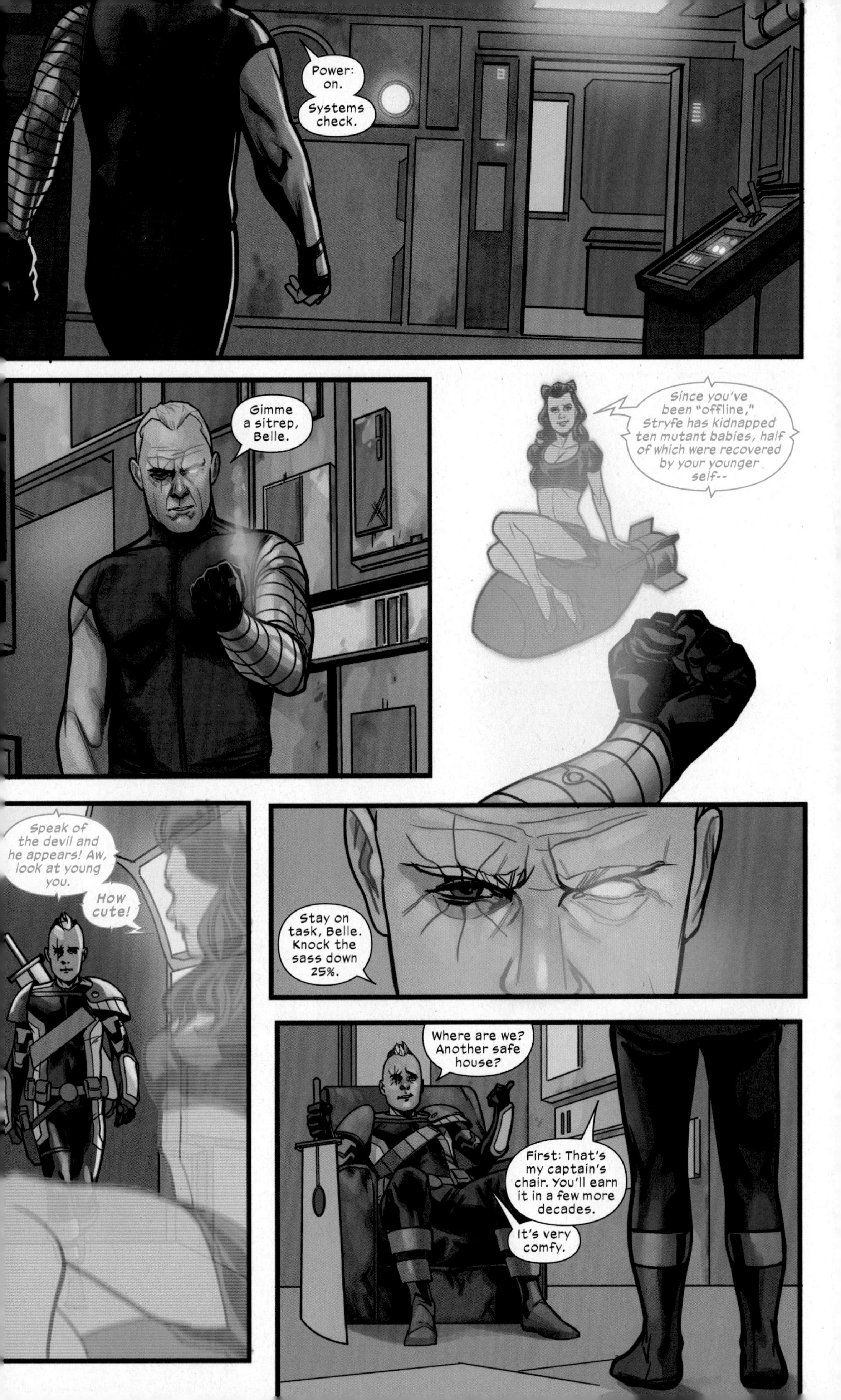
Power: on. Systems check.
Gimme a sitrep, Belle.
Since you've been "offline," Stryfe has kidnapped ten mutant babies, half of which were recovered by your younger self--
Speak of the devil and he appears! Aw, look at young you.
How cute!
Stay on task, Belle. Knock the sass down 25%.
Where are we? Another safe house?
First: That's my captain's chair. You'll earn it in a few more decades.
It's very comfy.

Welcome to *Graymalkin II*. A salvage job from late in the next century. We're cloaked above Earth.

Now get out of my chair unless you wanna wake up crawling out of an egg.

I'm not gonna apologize for what I did.

I don't care. You did what you thought you had to do.

I only give a damn that you grew up a bit.

The idea that you thought you'd grow up to be "*the protector of the timeline*" or something?

I never met a timeline I didn't #@%# up for my benefit.

We're still on the TVA's watch list--and don't think they'll give you a pass for my crimes.

I'm gonna borrow this pig-sticker. If I get into trouble, they won't see it coming.

So where is he?

Belle?

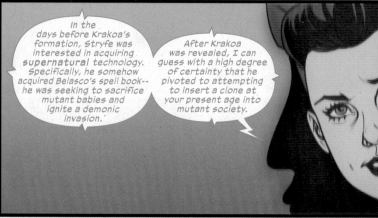

In the days before Krakoa's formation, Stryfe was interested in acquiring *supernatural* technology. Specifically, he somehow acquired Belasco's spell book-- he was seeking to sacrifice mutant babies and ignite a demonic invasion.

After Krakoa was revealed, I can guess with a high degree of certainty that he pivoted to attempting to insert a clone at your present age into mutant society.

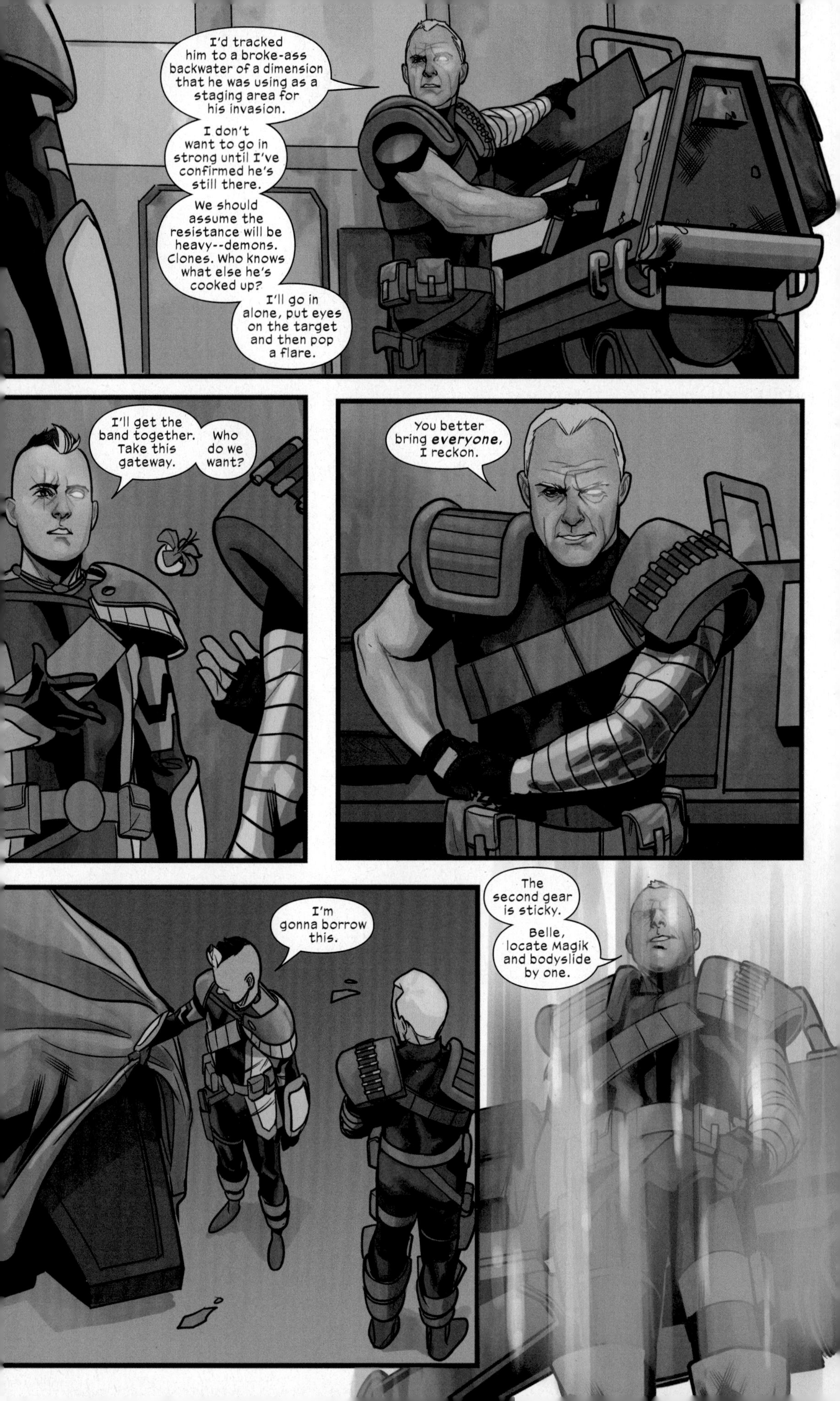
I'd tracked him to a broke-ass backwater of a dimension that he was using as a staging area for his invasion.
I don't want to go in strong until I've confirmed he's still there.
We should assume the resistance will be heavy--demons. Clones. Who knows what else he's cooked up?
I'll go in alone, put eyes on the target and then pop a flare.
I'll get the band together. Take this gateway.
Who do we want?
You better bring *everyone*, I reckon.
I'm gonna borrow this.
The second gear is sticky.
Belle, locate Magik and bodyslide by one.

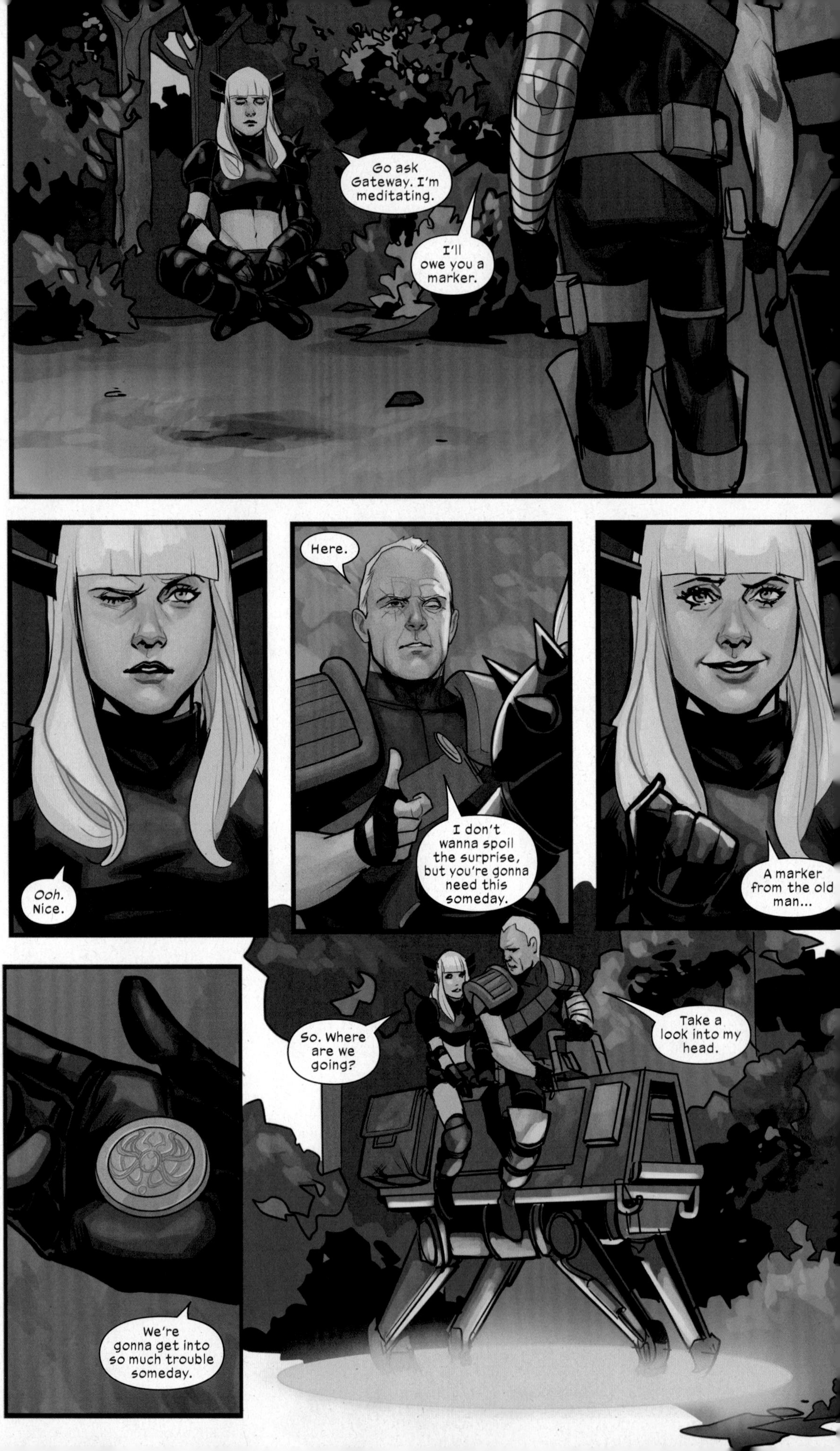
Go ask Gateway. I'm meditating.
I'll owe you a marker.
Ooh. Nice.
Here.
I don't wanna spoil the surprise, but you're gonna need this someday.
A marker from the old man...
We're gonna get into so much trouble someday.
So. Where are we going?
Take a look into my head.

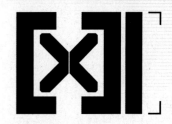

CABLE'S WAR WAGON
DEPLOYMENT LOG

1992: The War Wagon was constructed.

2021: "The Summers War" in the demon lands against Stryfe.

2023: ▮▮▮▮▮▮▮.

1918: Tunguska racing catastrophe.

2901: Impounded during the attack on a corrupt Time Variance Authority.

1978: NYC blackout caused by assault on Stryfe in the Bronx.

2099: War Wagon II debuts, with a new AI selected from a contest in the Mojoverse.

2015: Secret War Wagons. Admittedly, this was more of a Deadpool story.

All events are untold tales in chronological order. All of this has happened already, you just don't know it yet.

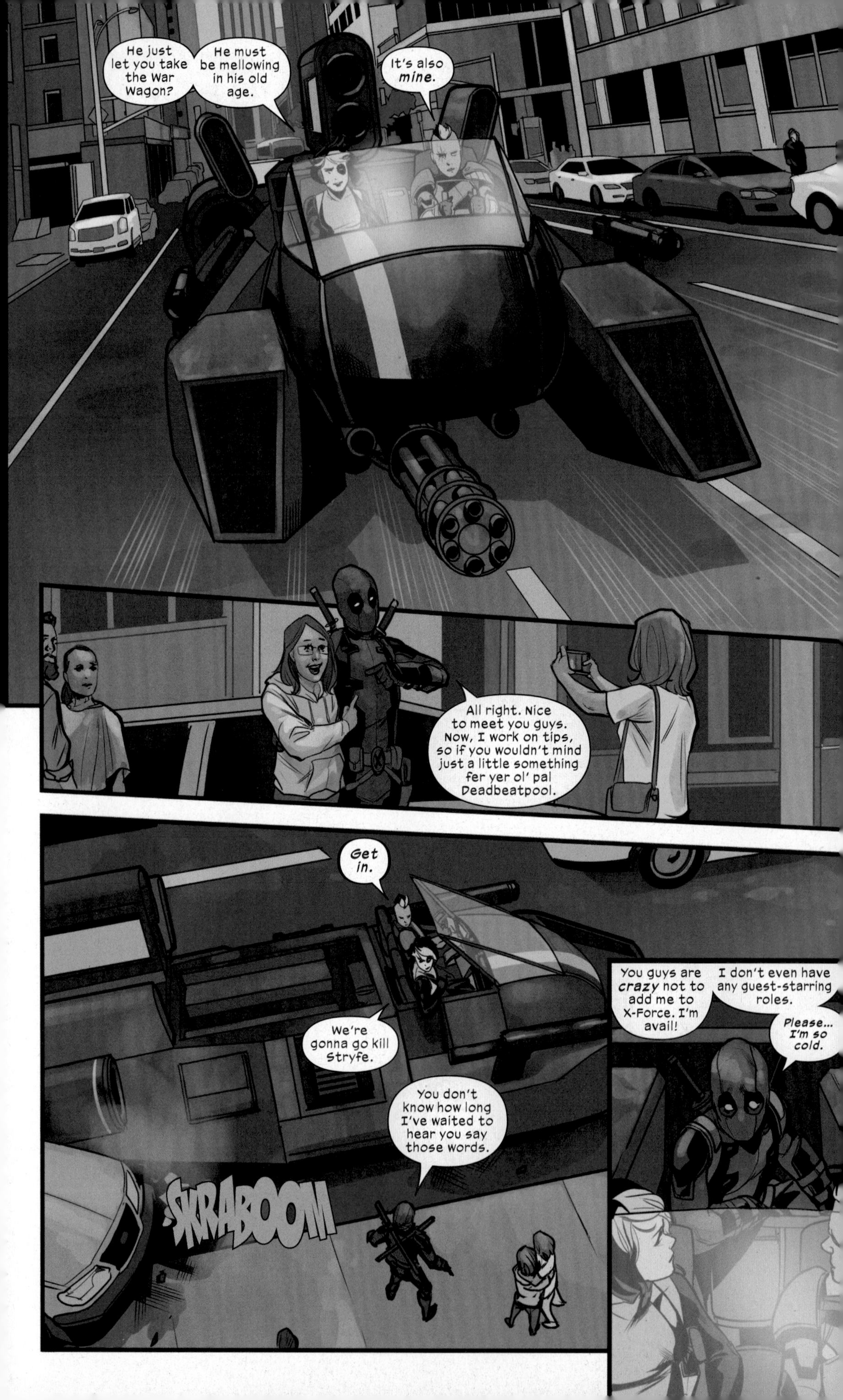
He just let you take the War Wagon?
He must be mellowing in his old age.
It's also *mine*.
All right. Nice to meet you guys. Now, I work on tips, so if you wouldn't mind just a little something fer yer ol' pal Deadbeatpool.
Get in.
We're gonna go kill Stryfe.
You don't know how long I've waited to hear you say those words.
SKRABOOM
You guys are *crazy* not to add me to X-Force. I'm avail!
I don't even have any guest-starring roles.
Please... I'm so cold.

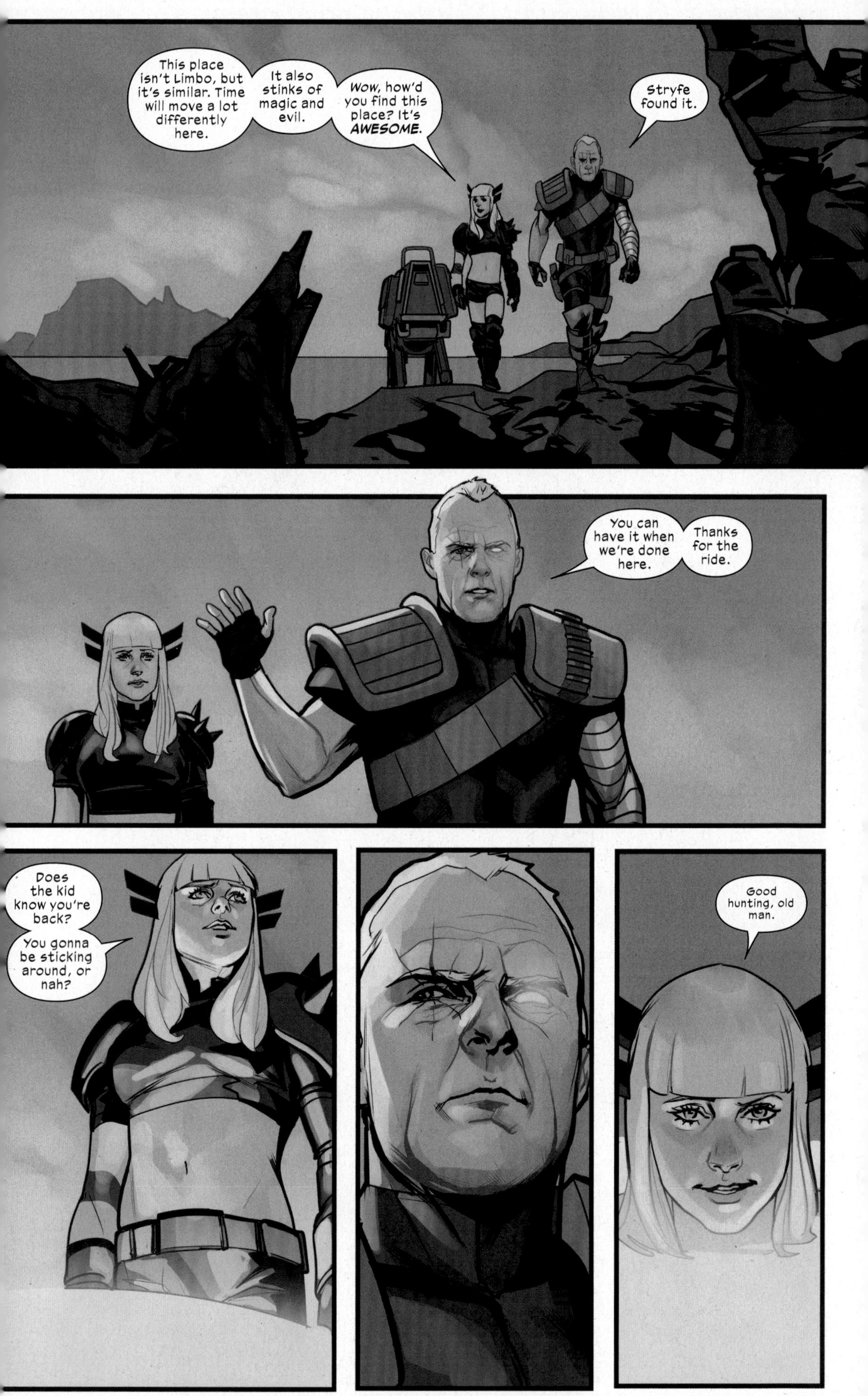

This place isn't Limbo, but it's similar. Time will move a lot differently here.
It also stinks of magic and evil.
Wow, how'd you find this place? It's AWESOME.
Stryfe found it.
You can have it when we're done here.
Thanks for the ride.
Does the kid know you're back?
You gonna be sticking around, or nah?
Good hunting, old man.

Scott, Jean--got time for a quick mission?

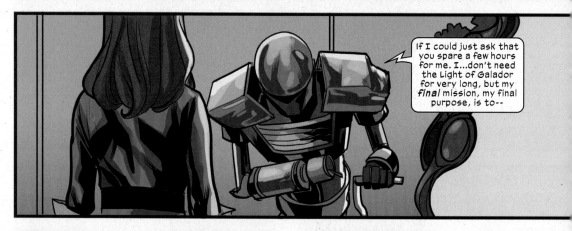

Of course, Cable.

And you, good Sir Knight of Galador.

You're welcome to stay as long as you want.

If I could just ask that you spare a few hours for me. I...don't need the Light of Galador for very long, but my *final* mission, my final purpose, is to--

Hold that thought. The Light of Galador is in good hands...my other hands.

I'll be back with the sword for you soon--I *promise.*

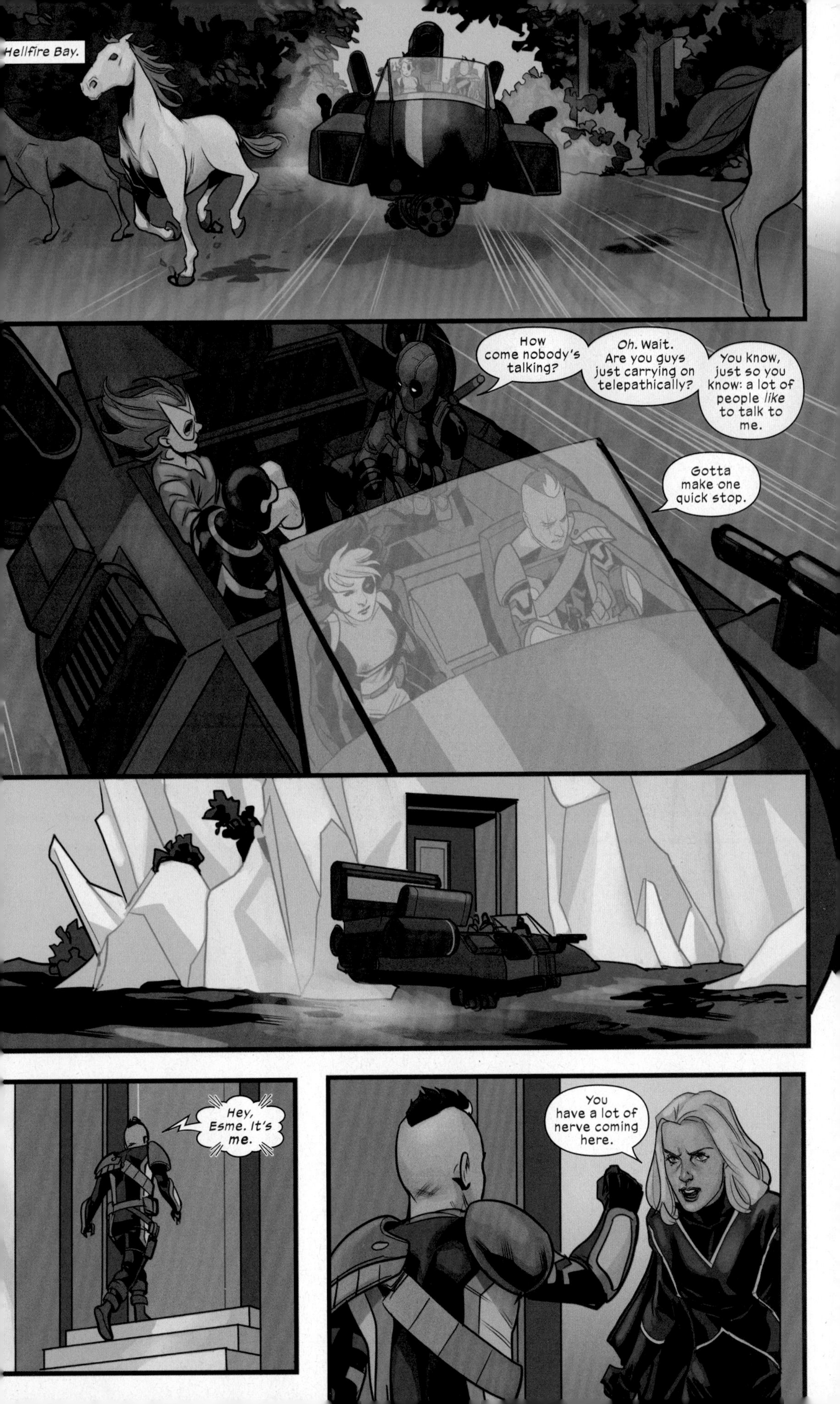

Hellfire Bay.
How come nobody's talking?
Oh. Wait. Are you guys just carrying on telepathically?
You know, just so you know: a lot of people like to talk to me.
Gotta make one quick stop.
Hey, Esme. It's me.
You have a lot of nerve coming here.

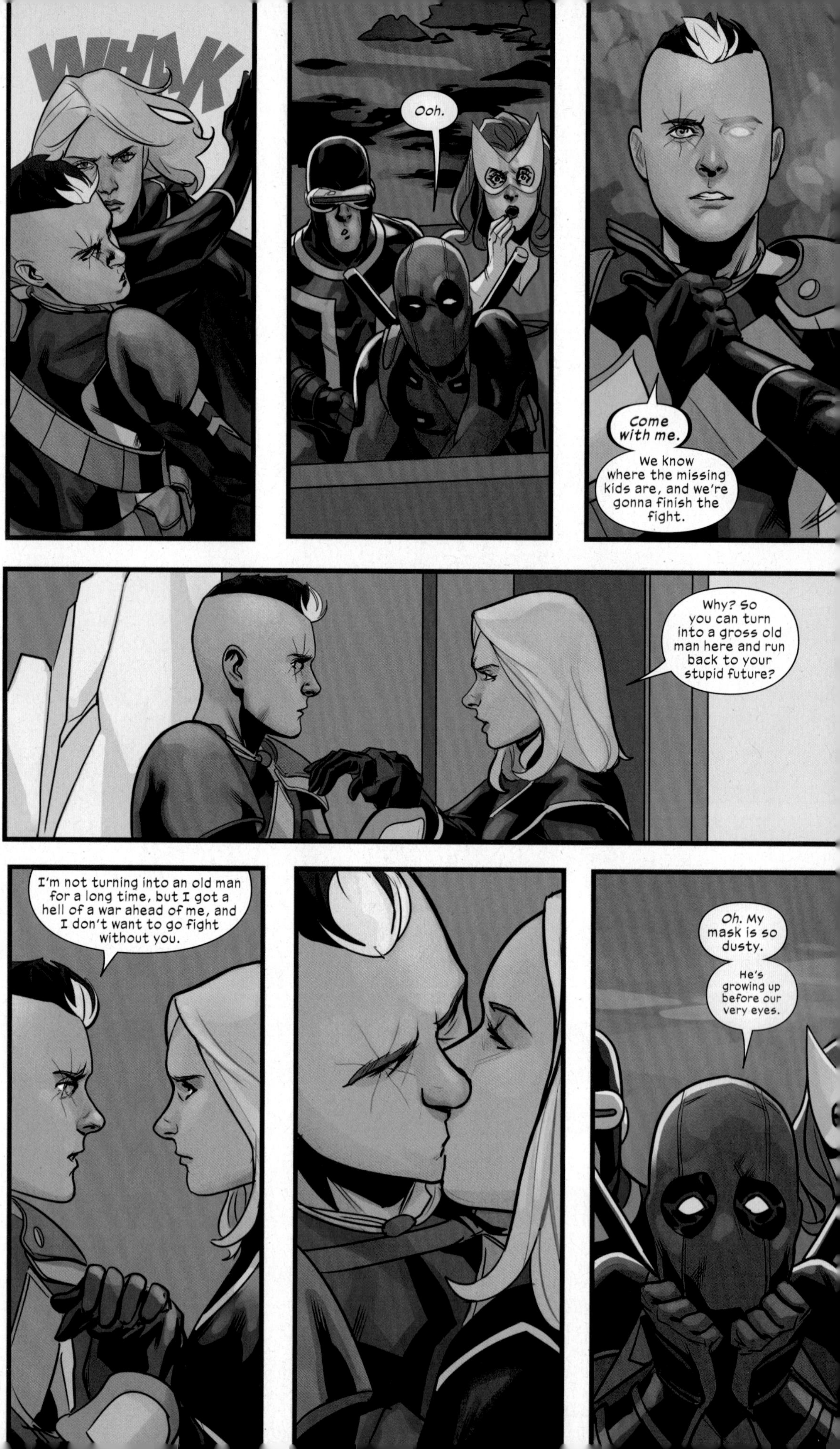
WHAK
Ooh.
Come with me.
We know where the missing kids are, and we're gonna finish the fight.
Why? So you can turn into a gross old man here and run back to your stupid future?
I'm not turning into an old man for a long time, but I got a hell of a war ahead of me, and I don't want to go fight without you.
Oh. My mask is so dusty.
He's growing up before our very eyes.

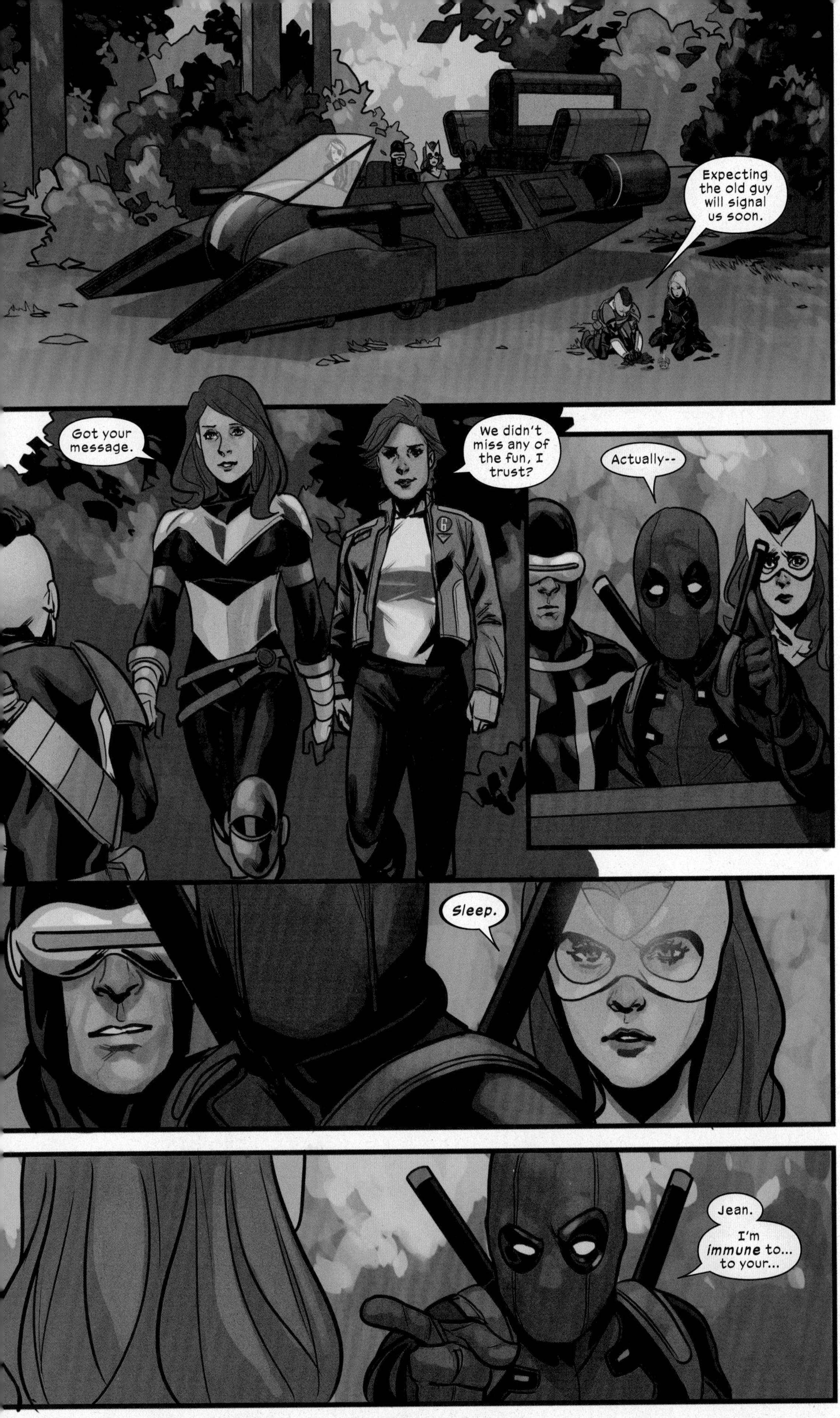

Expecting the old guy will signal us soon.
Got your message.
We didn't miss any of the fun, I trust?
Actually--
Sleep.
Jean.
I'm *immune* to... to your...

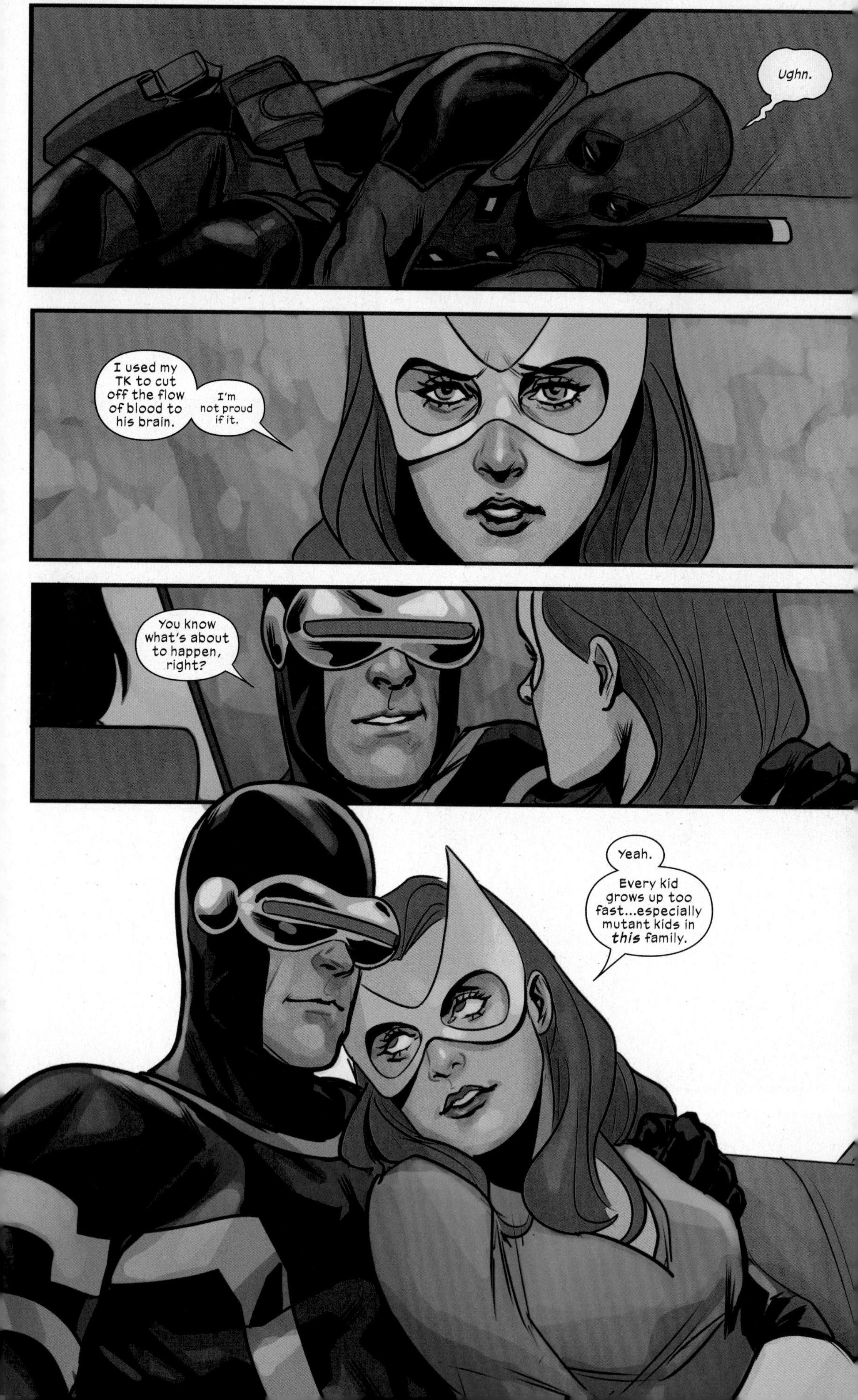
Ughn.
I used my TK to cut off the flow of blood to his brain.
I'm not proud if it.
You know what's about to happen, right?
Yeah.
Every kid grows up too fast...especially mutant kids in *this* family.

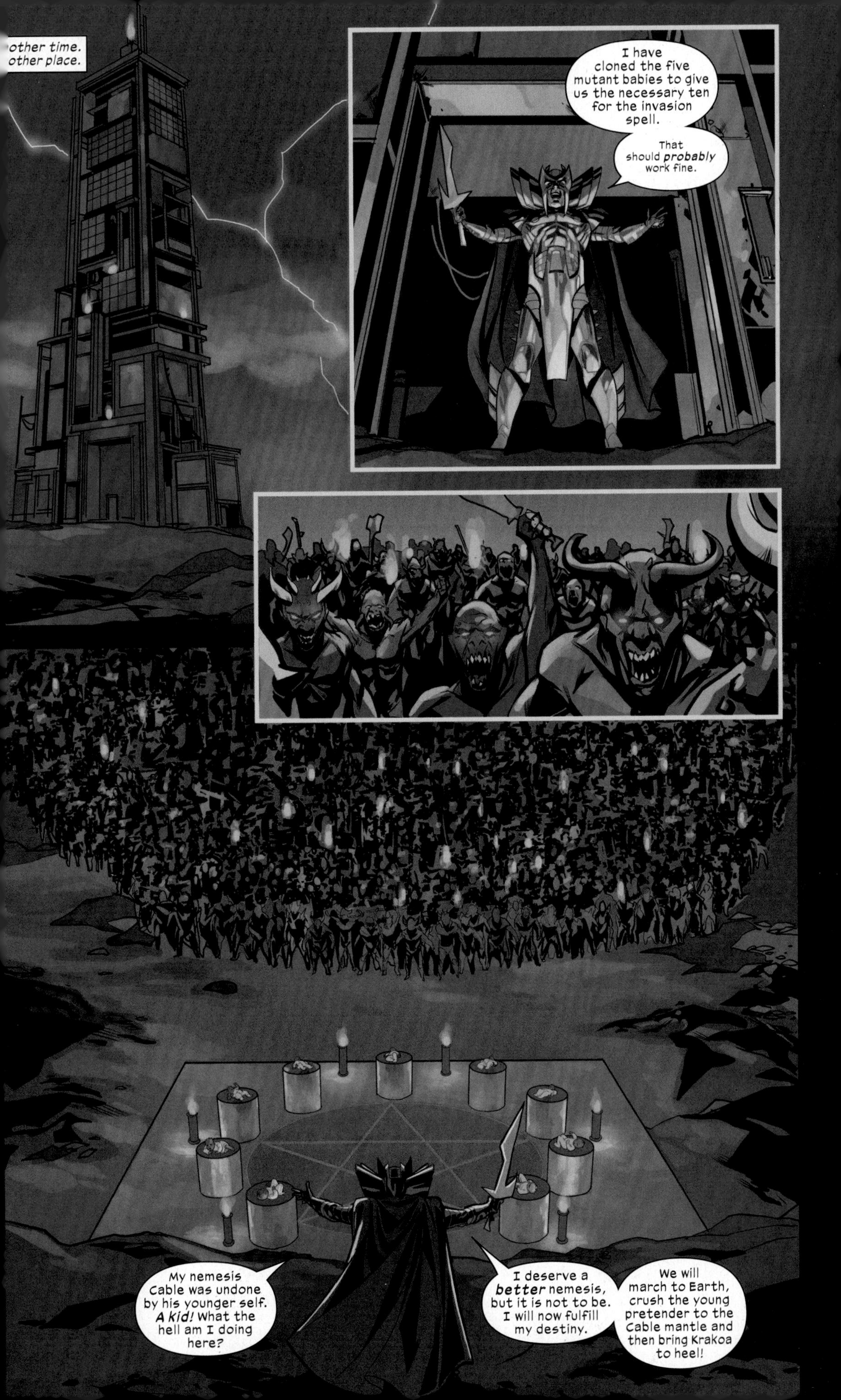

other time.
other place.
I have cloned the five mutant babies to give us the necessary ten for the invasion spell.
That should *probably* work fine.
My nemesis Cable was undone by his younger self. *A kid!* What the hell am I doing here?
I deserve a *better* nemesis, but it is not to be. I will now fulfill my destiny.
We will march to Earth, crush the young pretender to the Cable mantle and then bring Krakoa to heel!

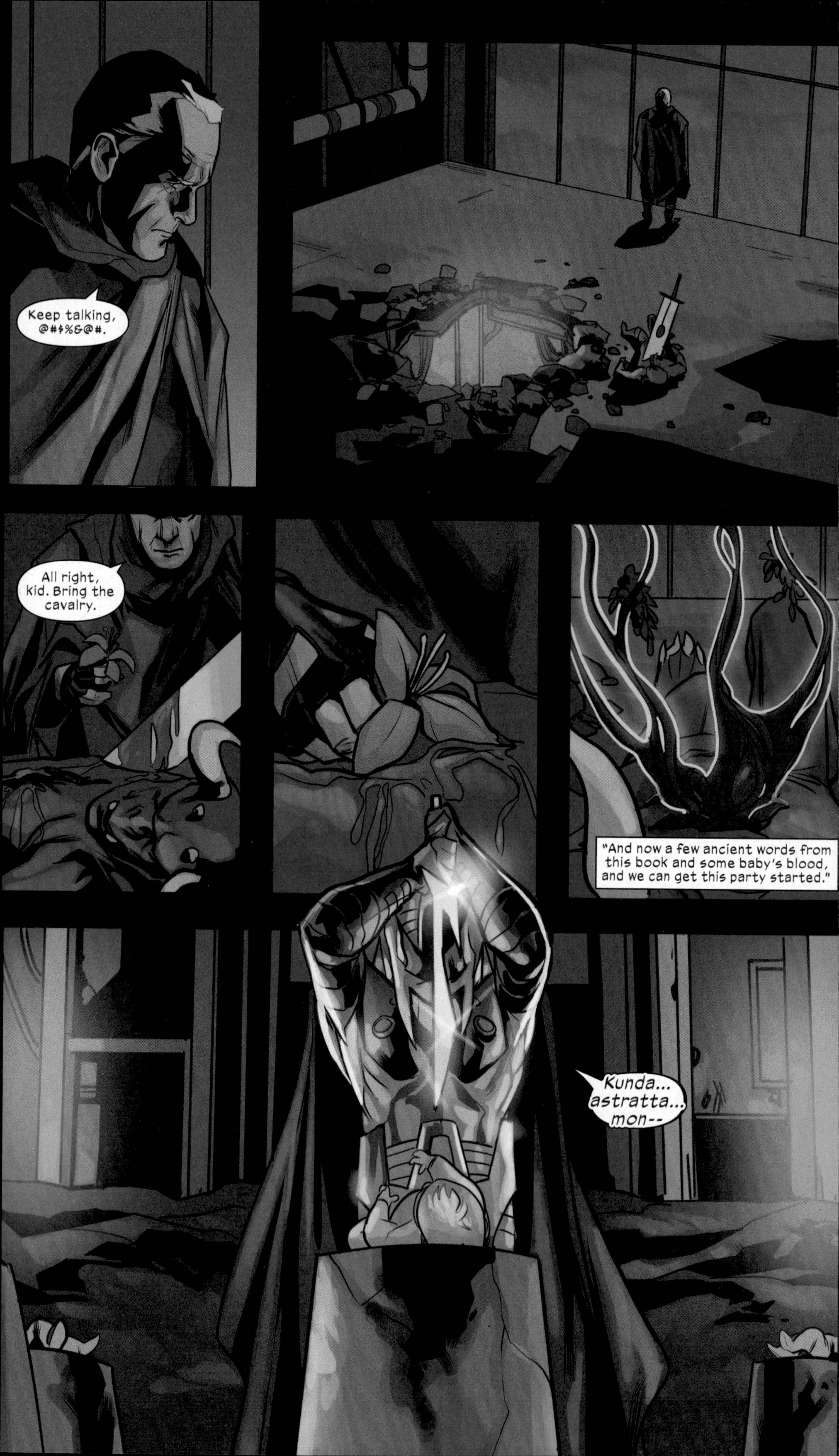

Keep talking, @#$%&@#.
All right, kid. Bring the cavalry.
"And now a few ancient words from this book and some baby's blood, and we can get this party started."
Kunda... astratta... mon--

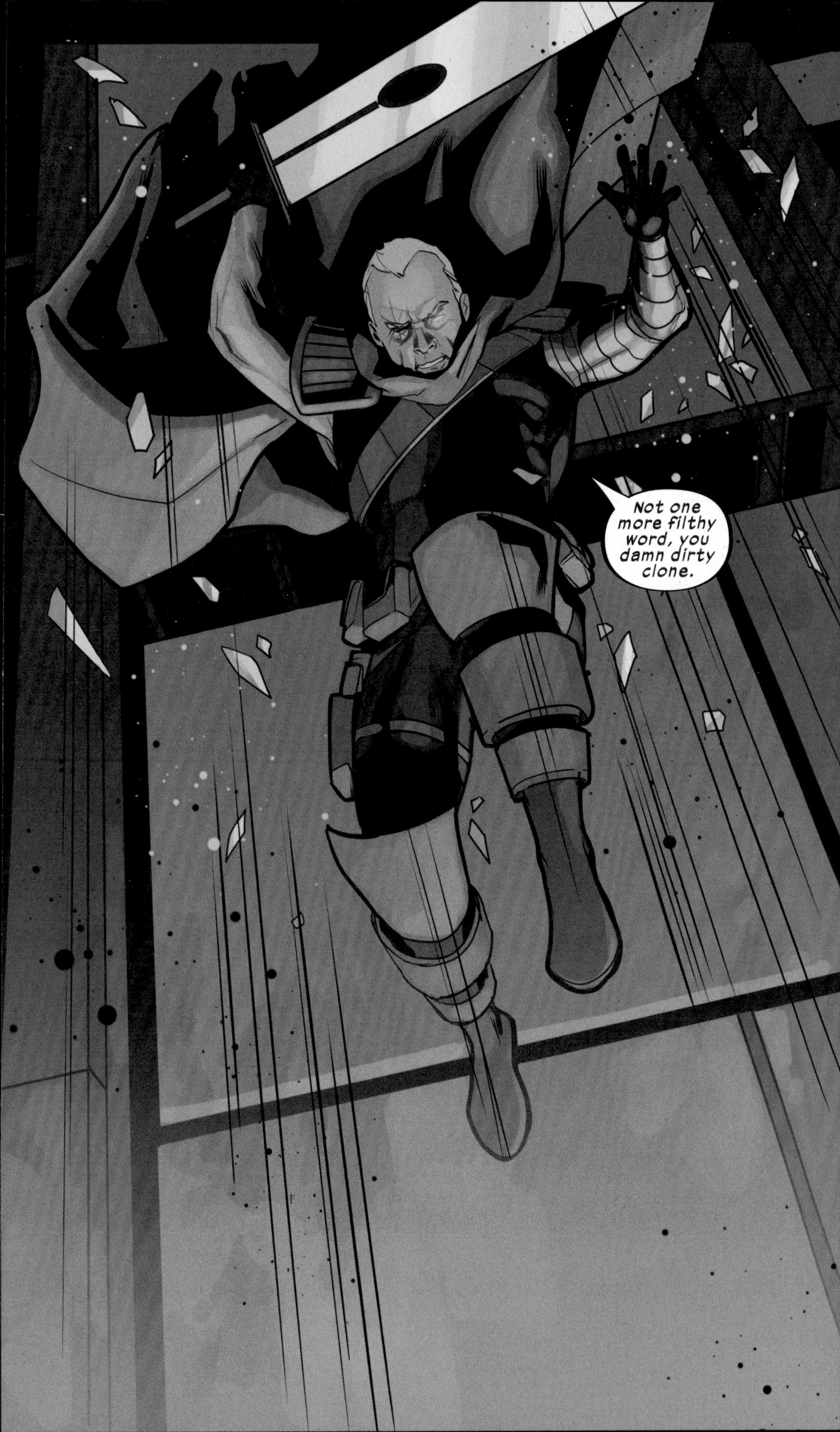
Not one more filthy word, you damn dirty clone.

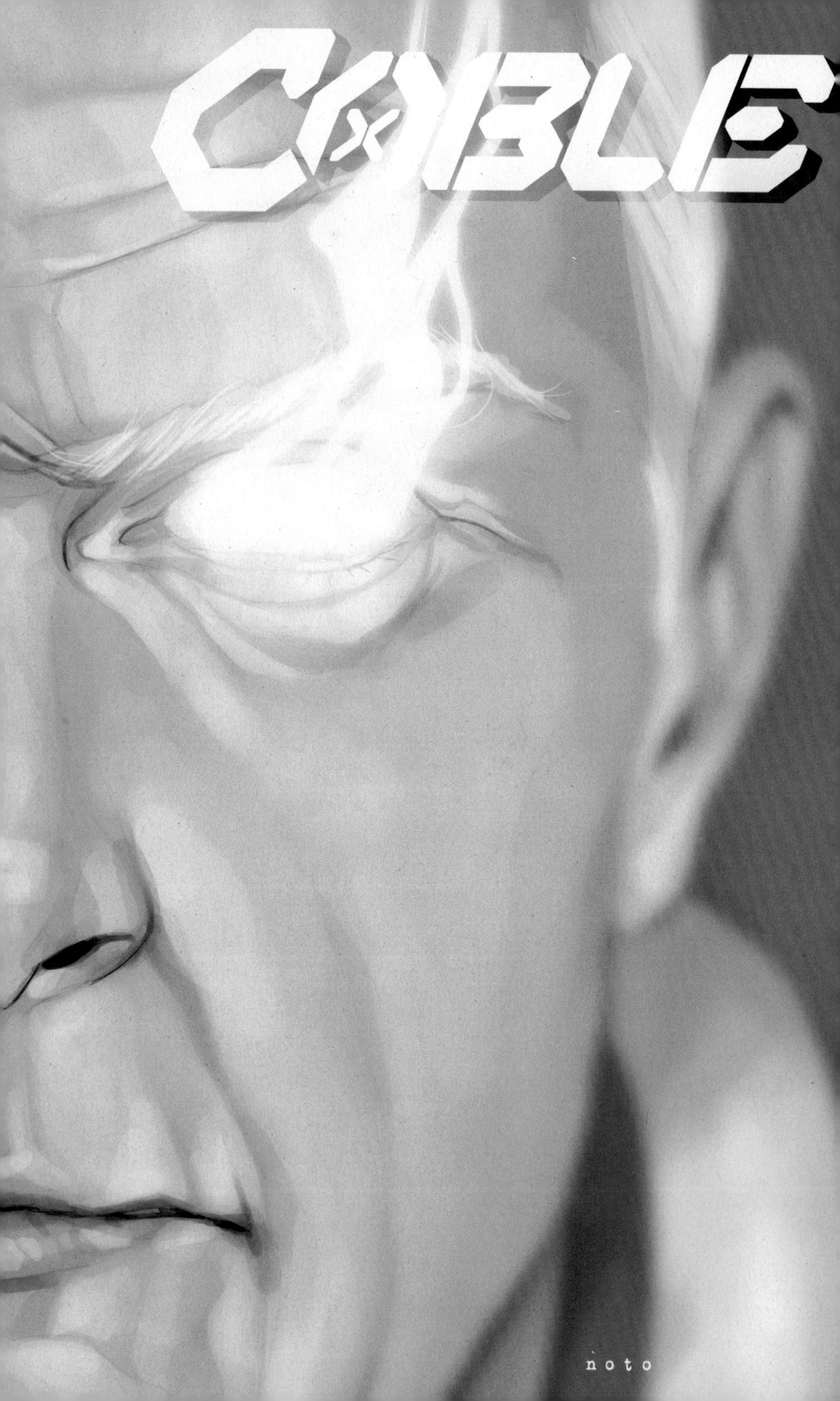
CABLE
noto

[ca__[0.12]
[ble_[0.12]

Cable...*you're relieved of your duty.*

-- CABLE

[ca__[0.XX]
[ble_[0.XX]

[ca__[0.12]....]
[ble_[0.12]....]

[Cable_alpha.]

SUMMERS END

Young Cable came to a decision -- he might be having the time of his life as part of a proper family on Krakoa, but he isn't the Cable that the present needs. He's ceded his resurrections privileges to his older self -- the one he killed a while back -- and pledged to go back to the future to do some growing up. But first...one last mission to stop Stryfe with a little help from his friends.

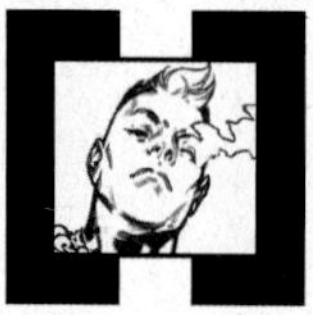
Cable

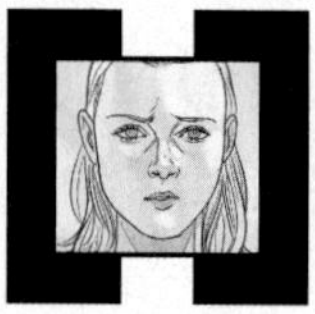
Esme Cuckoo

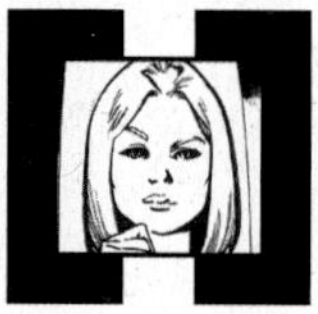
Emma Frost

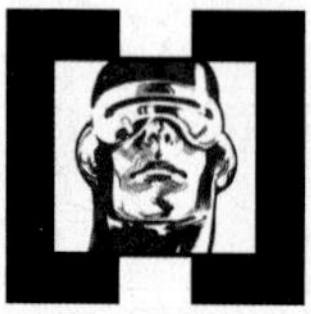
Cyclops

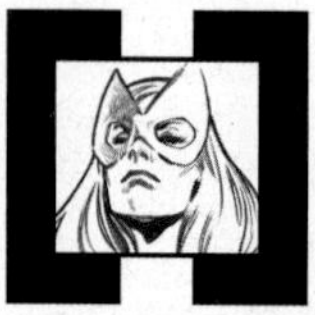
Jean Grey

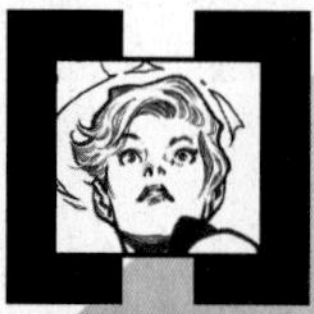
Rachel Summers

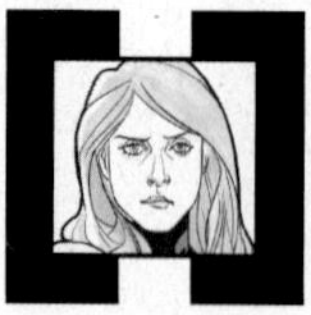
Hope Summers

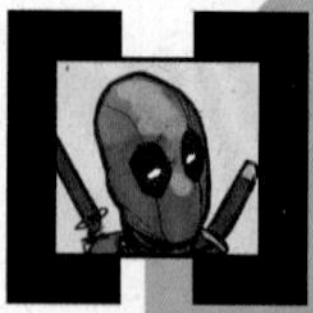
Deadpool

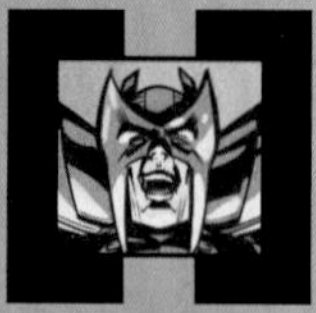
Stryfe

CABLE
[X_12]

[ISSUE TWELVE].............................
...................SHAKESPEARE IN THE ZARK

GERRY DUGGAN...[WRITER]
PHIL NOTO...[ARTIST]
VC's JOE SABINO..[LETTERER]
TOM MULLER...[DESIGN]

PHIL NOTO..[COVER ARTIST]

ERNANDA SOUZA.....................................[VARIANT COVER ARTIST]

JONATHAN HICKMAN..[HEAD OF X]
NICK RUSSELL..[PRODUCTION]
ANNALISE BISSA...[ASSOCIATE EDITOR]
JORDAN D. WHITE..[EDITOR]
C.B. CEBULSKI...[EDITOR IN CHIEF]

[the young...]
[.....the old]

[00_00....0]
[00_00...12]

[XX___past]
[00_____]

[00_____]

[future_XX]

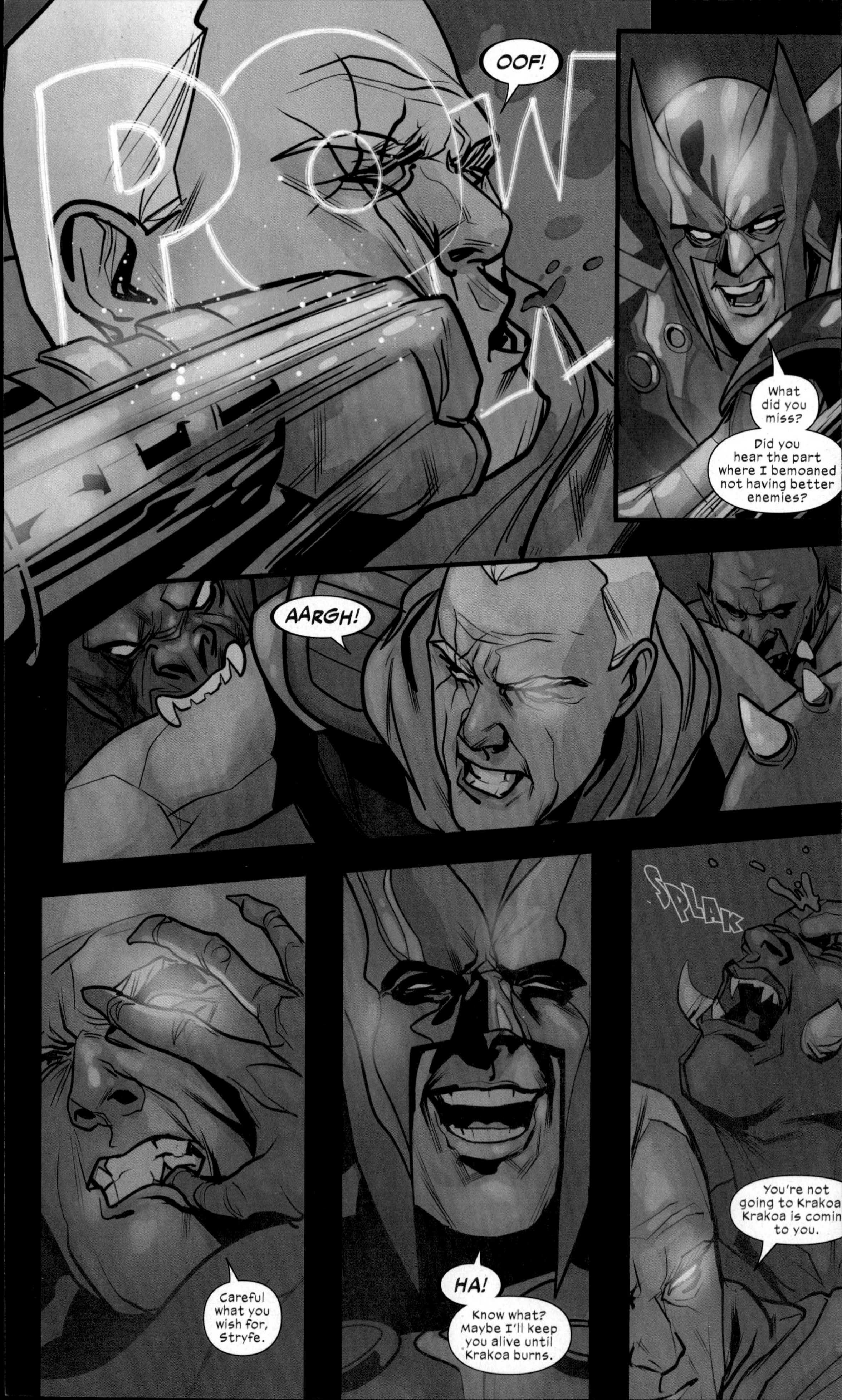

POW
OOF!
What did you miss?
Did you hear the part where I bemoaned not having better enemies?
AARGH!
Careful what you wish for, Stryfe.
HA!
Know what? Maybe I'll keep you alive until Krakoa burns.
SPLAK
You're not going to Krakoa. Krakoa is comin to you.

Let the old bastard go.

Heeeey! Now I'll get to kill you both!

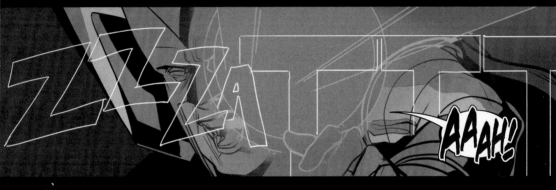

ZZZATTTT

AAAH!

Call it.

Jam Stryfe, and get the babies away from him.

Nice. I'll handle the babies.

Aw! I guess the old man and the kid thought they needed a little help.

Or a lot of help.

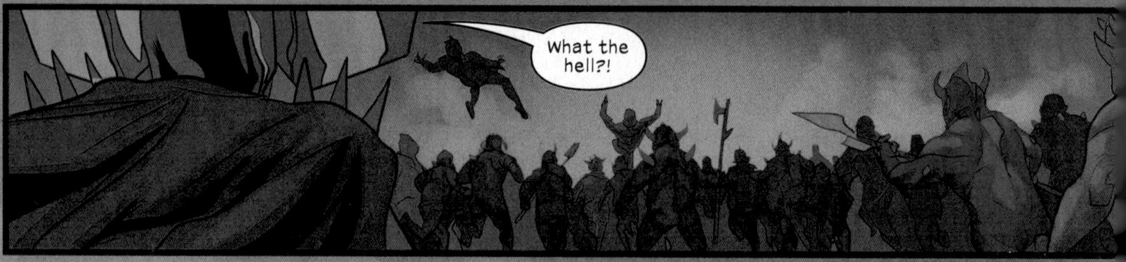
What the hell?!

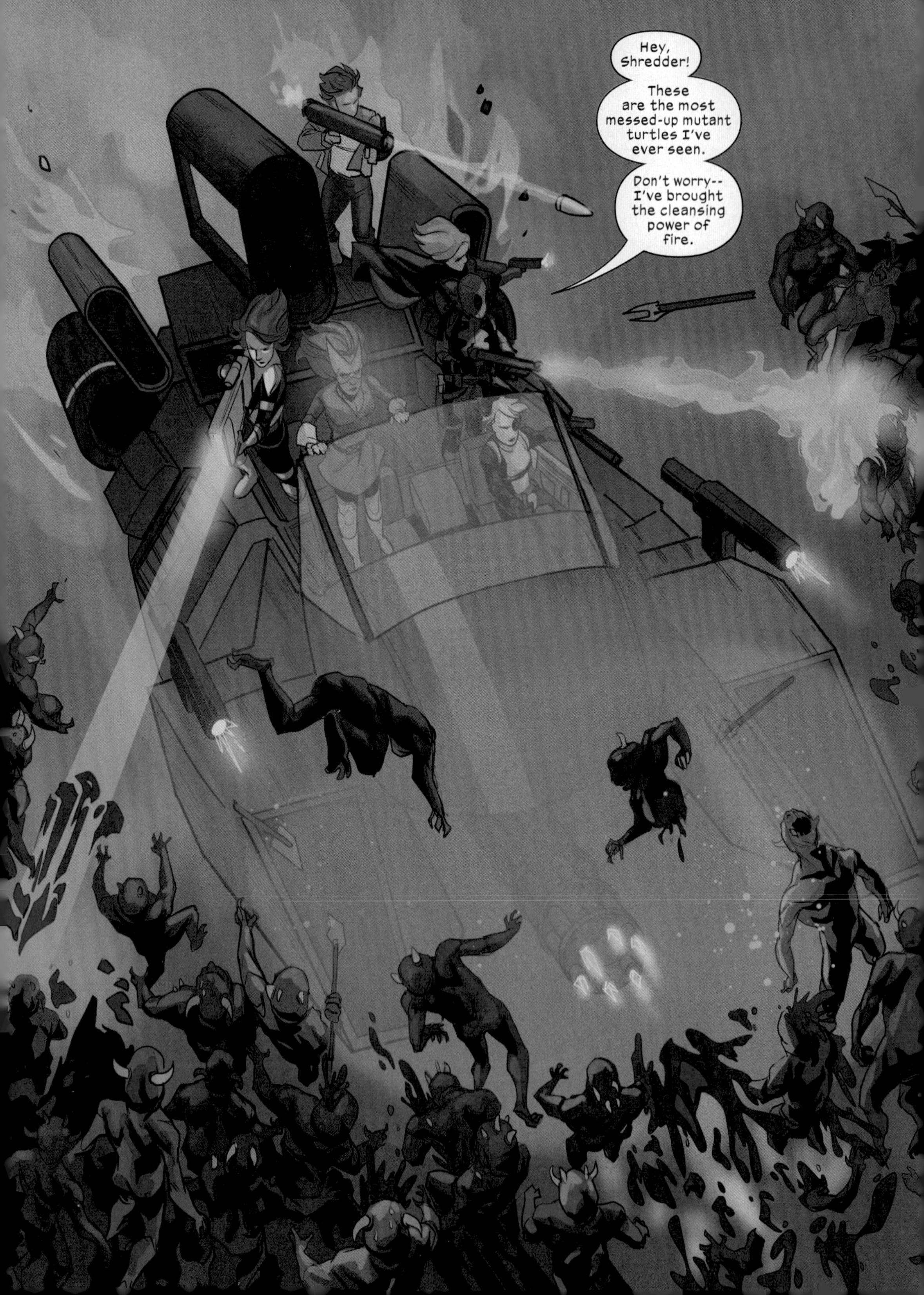
Hey, Shredder!
These are the most messed-up mutant turtles I've ever seen.
Don't worry-- I've brought the cleansing power of fire.

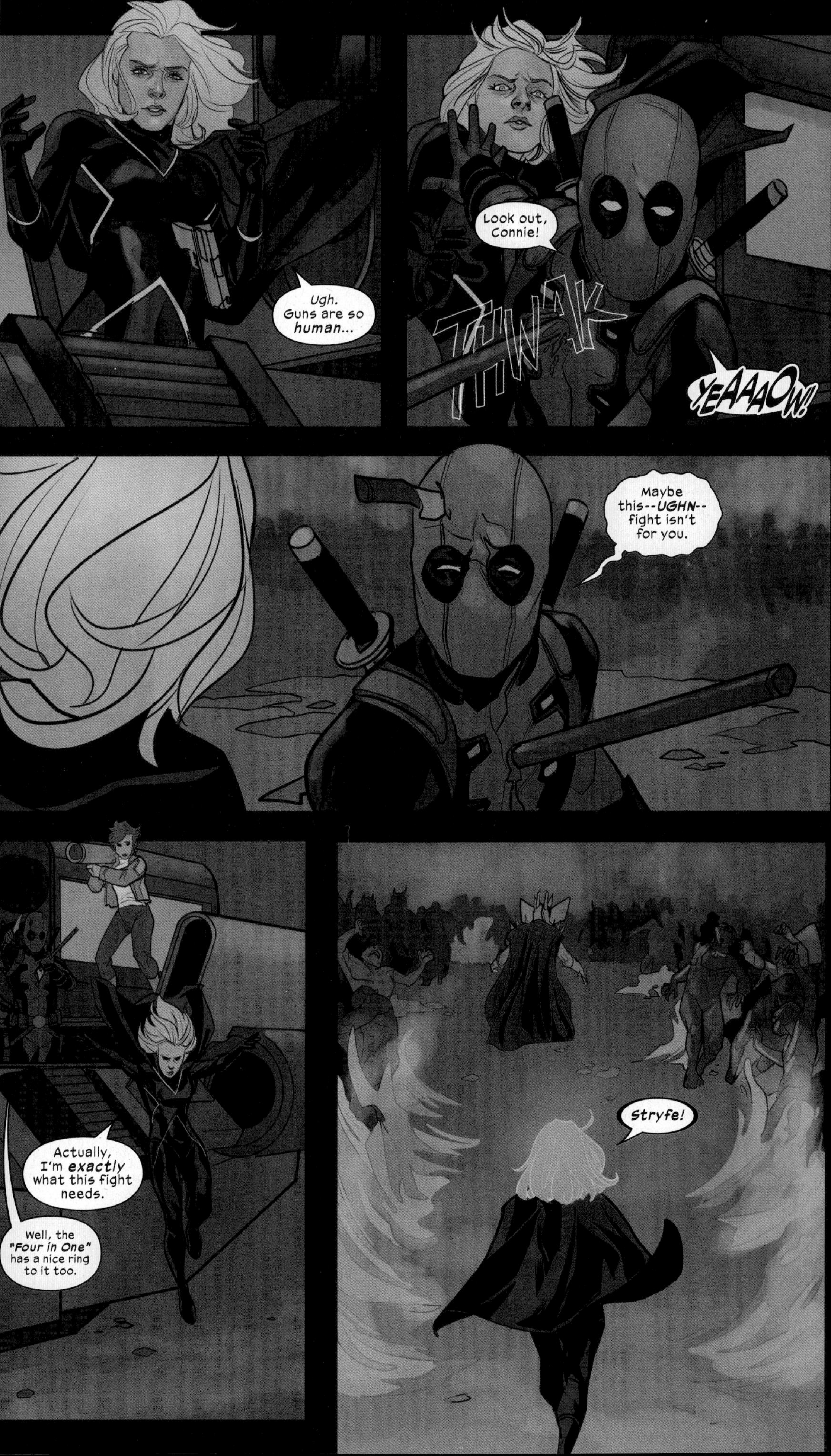
Ugh. Guns are so *human*...
Look out, Connie!
THWAK
YEAAAOW!
Maybe this--*UGHN*--fight isn't for you.
Actually, I'm *exactly* what this fight needs.
Well, the *"Four in One"* has a nice ring to it too.
Stryfe!

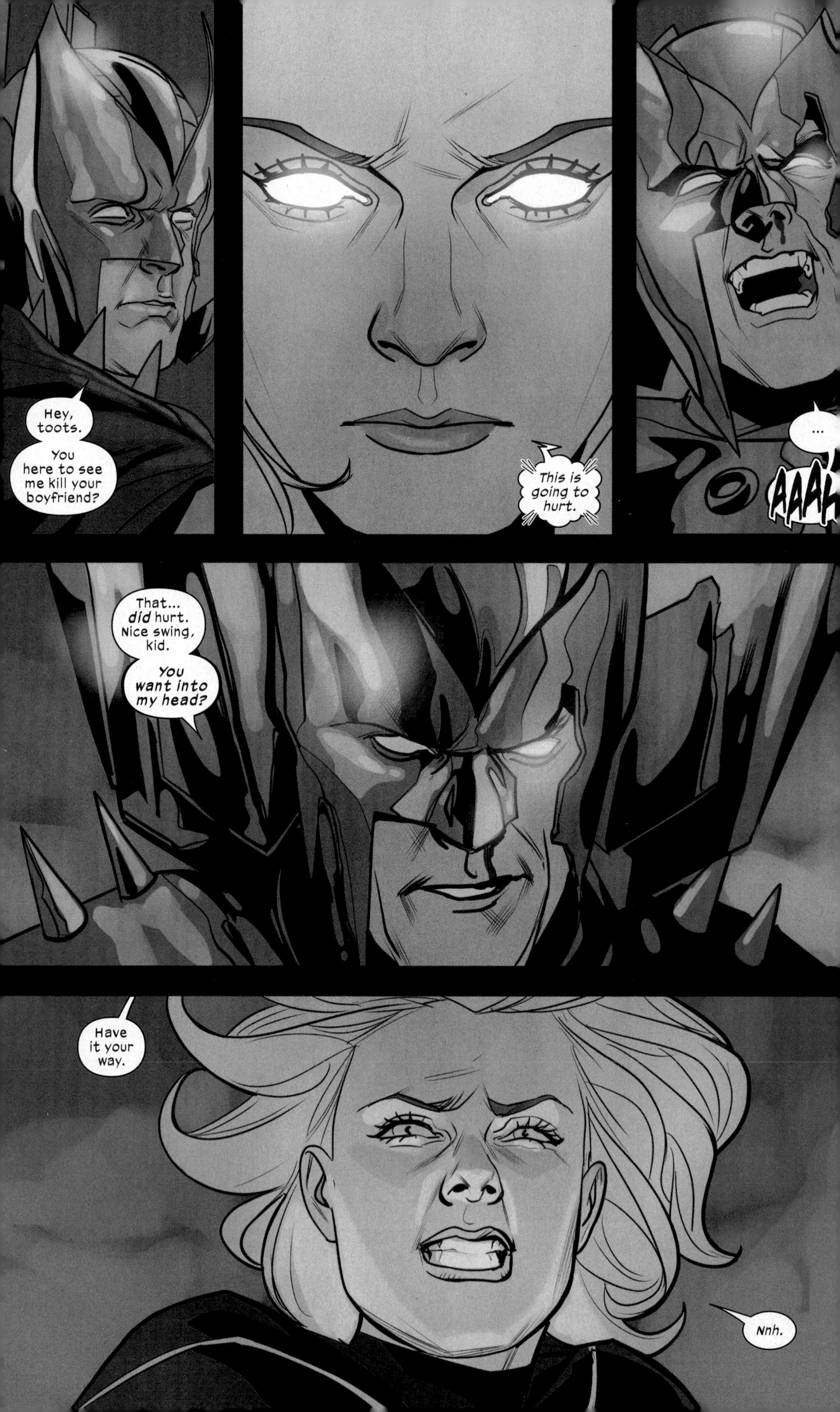

Hey, toots.
You here to see me kill your boyfriend?
This is going to hurt.
...
AAAH
That... *did* hurt. Nice swing, kid.
You want into my head?
Have it your way.
Nnh.

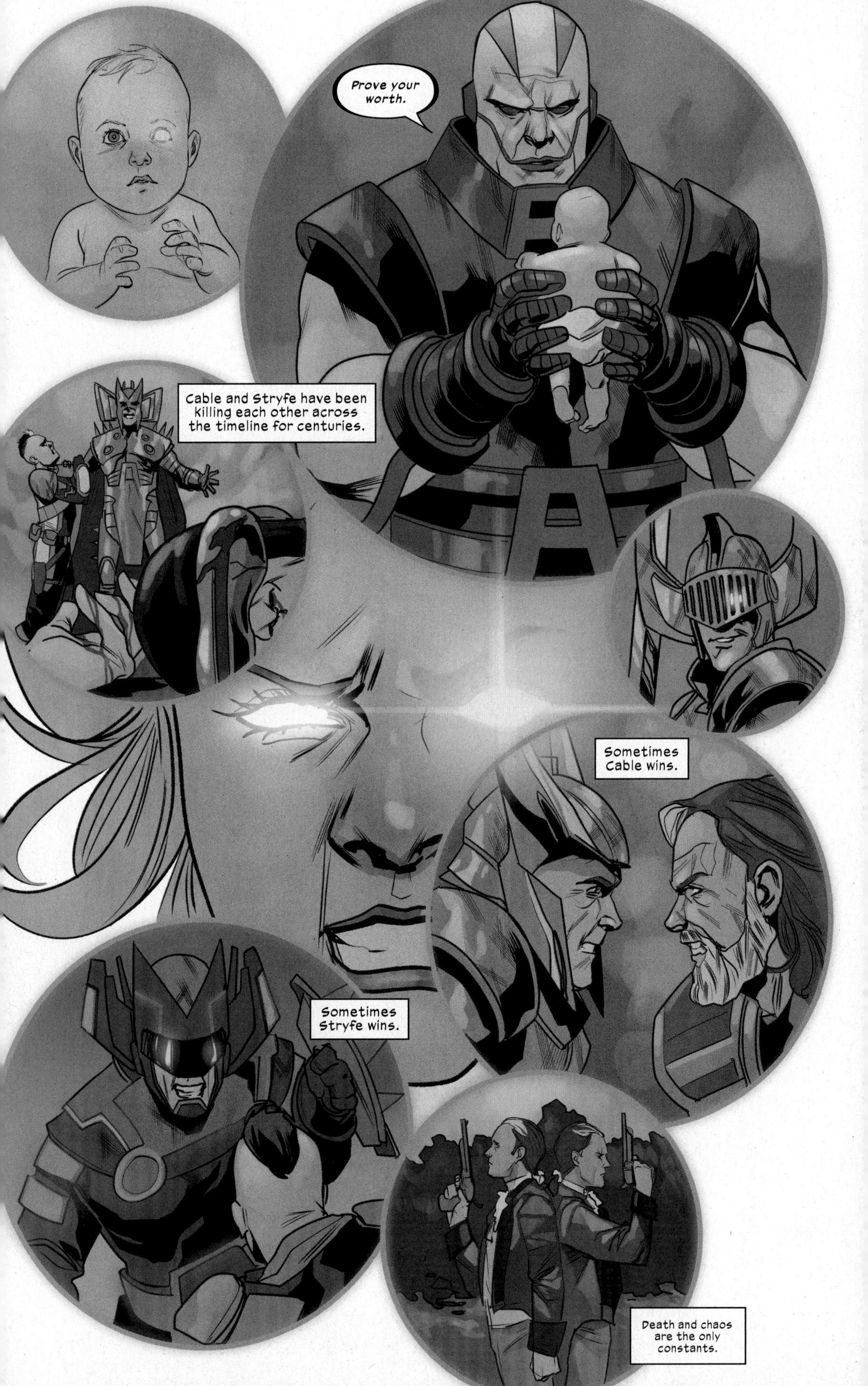
Prove your worth.
Cable and Stryfe have been killing each other across the timeline for centuries.
Sometimes Cable wins.
Sometimes Stryfe wins.
Death and chaos are the only constants.

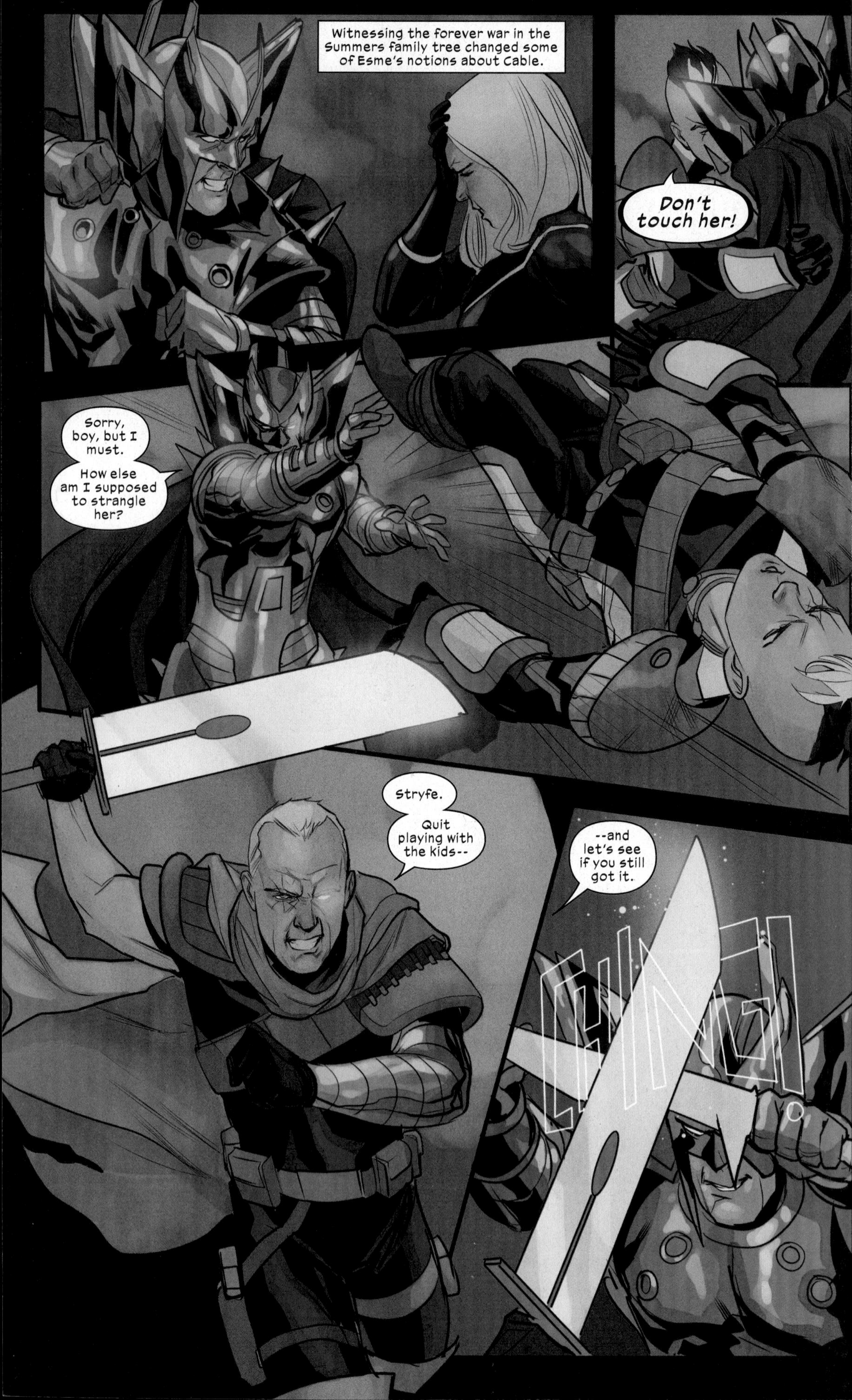
Witnessing the forever war in the Summers family tree changed some of Esme's notions about Cable.
Don't touch her!
Sorry, boy, but I must.
How else am I supposed to strangle her?
Stryfe.
Quit playing with the kids--
--and let's see if you still got it.
CHING!

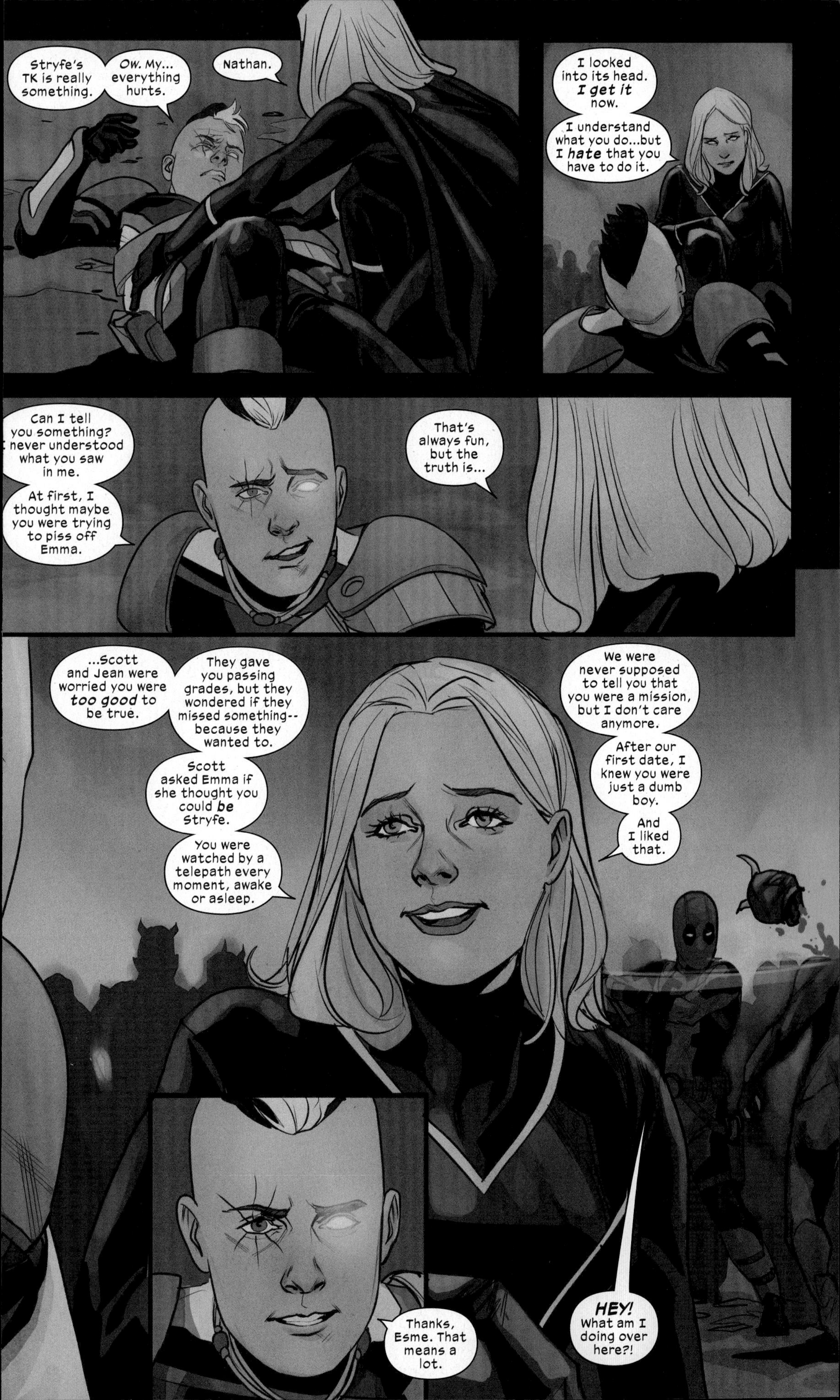
Stryfe's TK is really something.
Ow. My... everything hurts.
Nathan.
I looked into its head. I get it now.
I understand what you do...but I hate that you have to do it.
Can I tell you something? I never understood what you saw in me.
At first, I thought maybe you were trying to piss off Emma.
That's always fun, but the truth is...
...Scott and Jean were worried you were too good to be true.
They gave you passing grades, but they wondered if they missed something--because they wanted to.
Scott asked Emma if she thought you could be Stryfe.
You were watched by a telepath every moment, awake or asleep.
We were never supposed to tell you that you were a mission, but I don't care anymore.
After our first date, I knew you were just a dumb boy.
And I liked that.
Thanks, Esme. That means a lot.
HEY! What am I doing over here?!

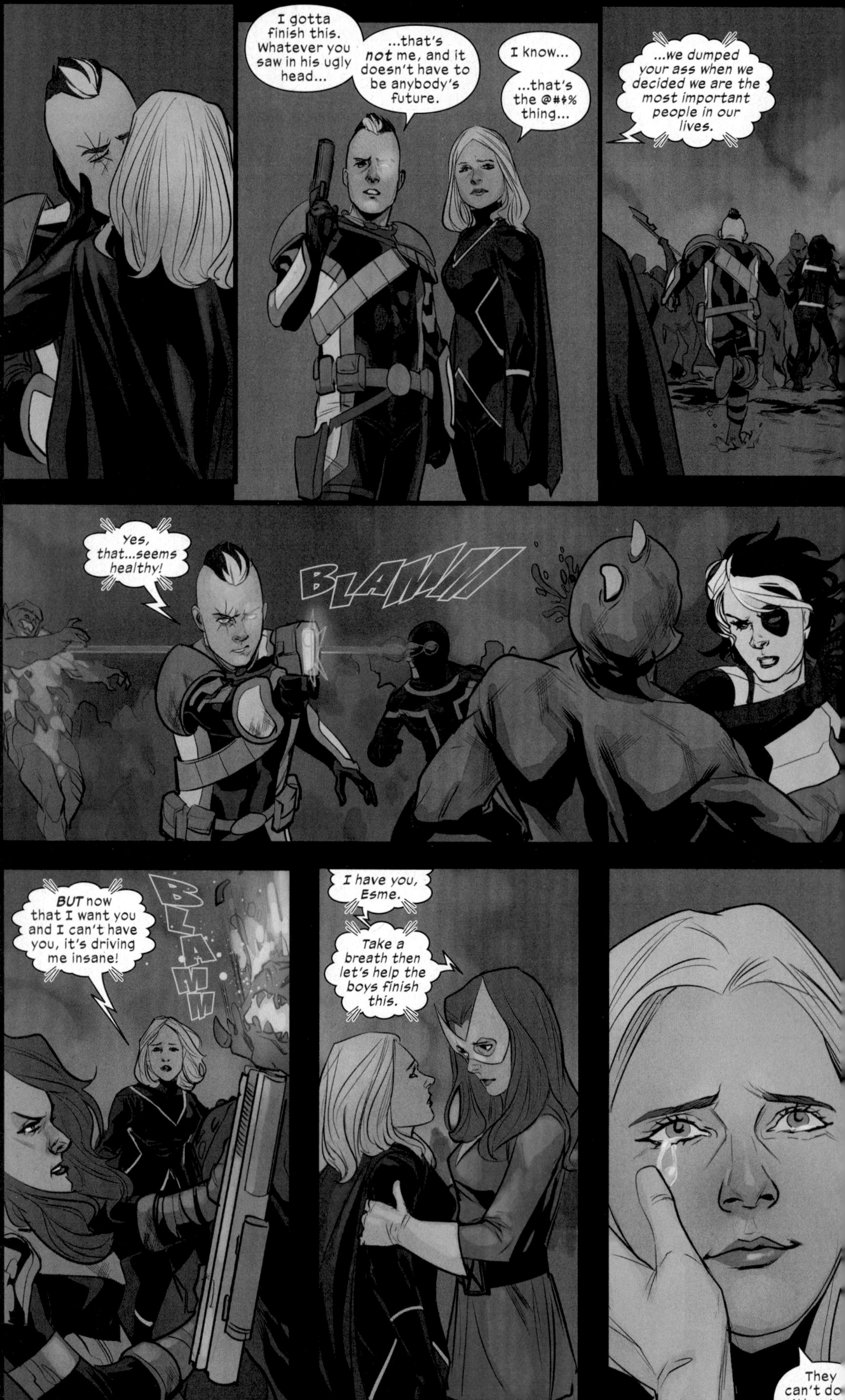

I gotta finish this. Whatever you saw in his ugly head...
...that's not me, and it doesn't have to be anybody's future.
I know...
...that's the @#$% thing...
...we dumped your ass when we decided we are the most important people in our lives.
Yes, that...seems healthy!
BLAMM
BUT now that I want you and I can't have you, it's driving me insane!
BLAMM
I have you, Esme.
Take a breath then let's help the boys finish this.
They can't do without

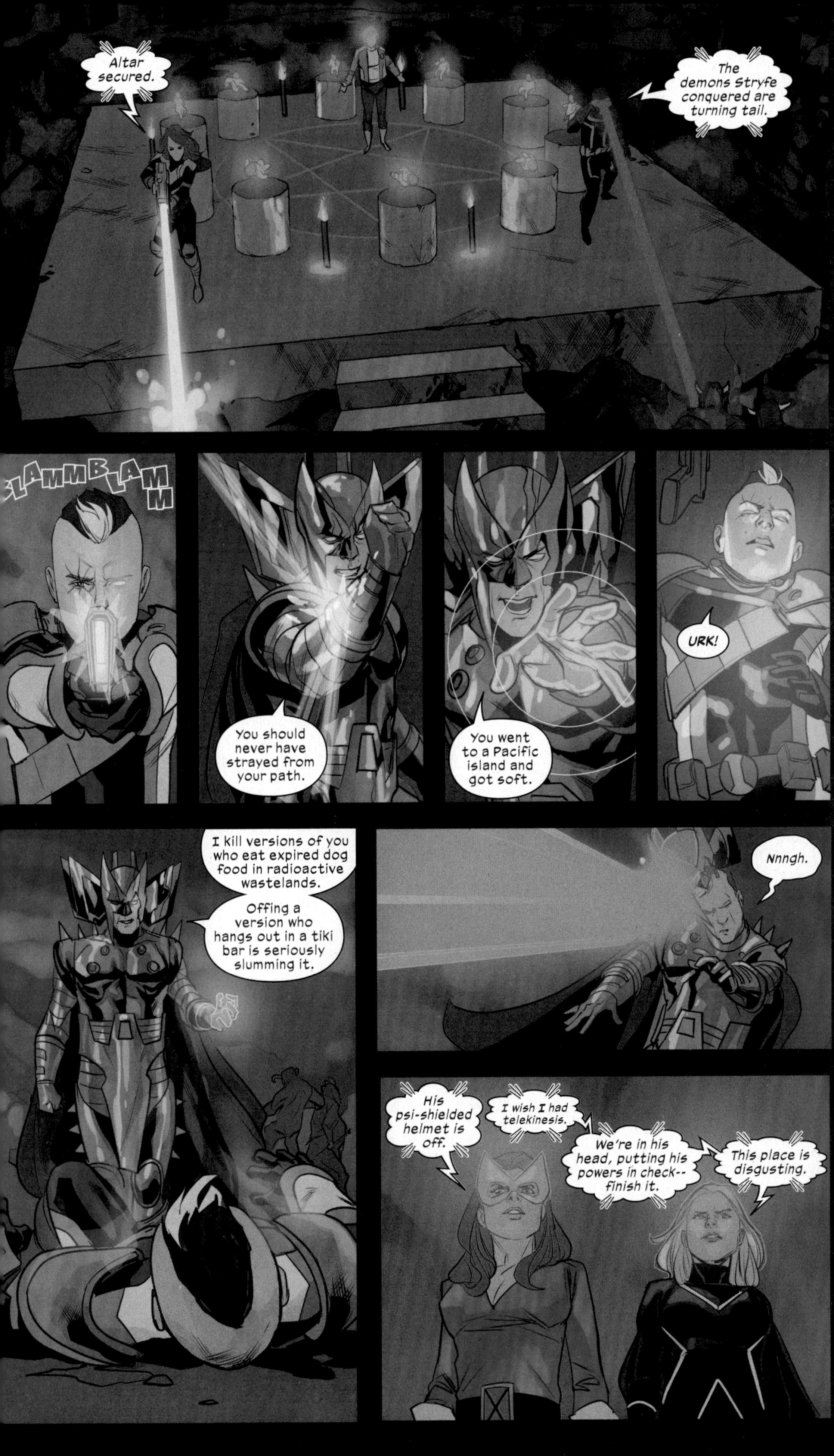
Altar secured.
The demons Stryfe conquered are turning tail.
SLAMMBLAMM
You should never have strayed from your path.
You went to a Pacific island and got soft.
URK!
I kill versions of you who eat expired dog food in radioactive wastelands.
Offing a version who hangs out in a tiki bar is seriously slumming it.
Nnngh.
His psi-shielded helmet is off.
I wish I had telekinesis.
We're in his head, putting his powers in check--finish it.
This place is disgusting.

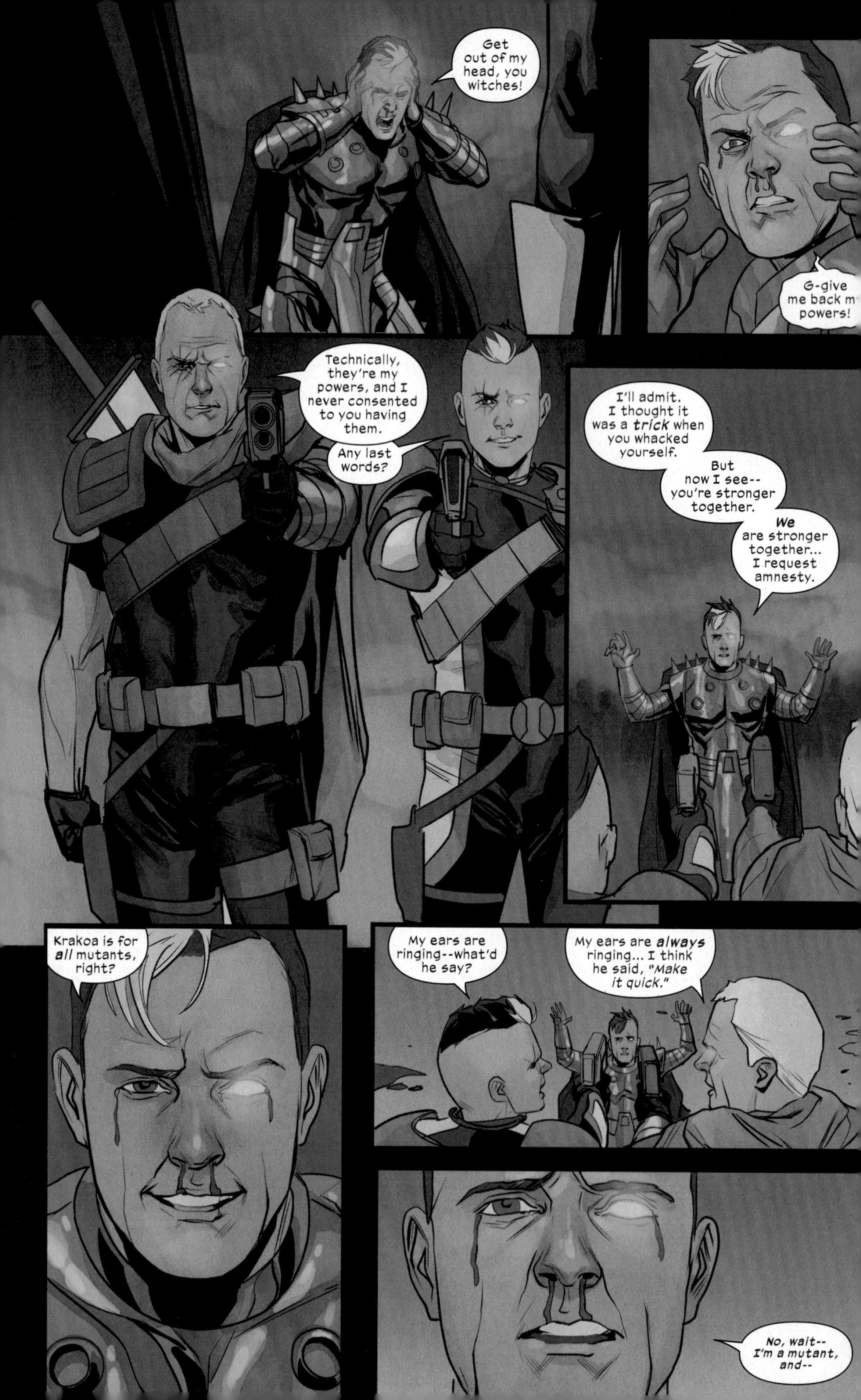
Get out of my head, you witches!
G-give me back my powers!
Technically, they're my powers, and I never consented to you having them.
Any last words?
I'll admit. I thought it was a *trick* when you whacked yourself.
But now I see-- you're stronger together.
We are stronger together... I request amnesty.
Krakoa is for *all* mutants, right?
My ears are ringing--what'd he say?
My ears are *always* ringing... I think he said, "*Make it quick.*"
No, wait-- I'm a mutant, and--

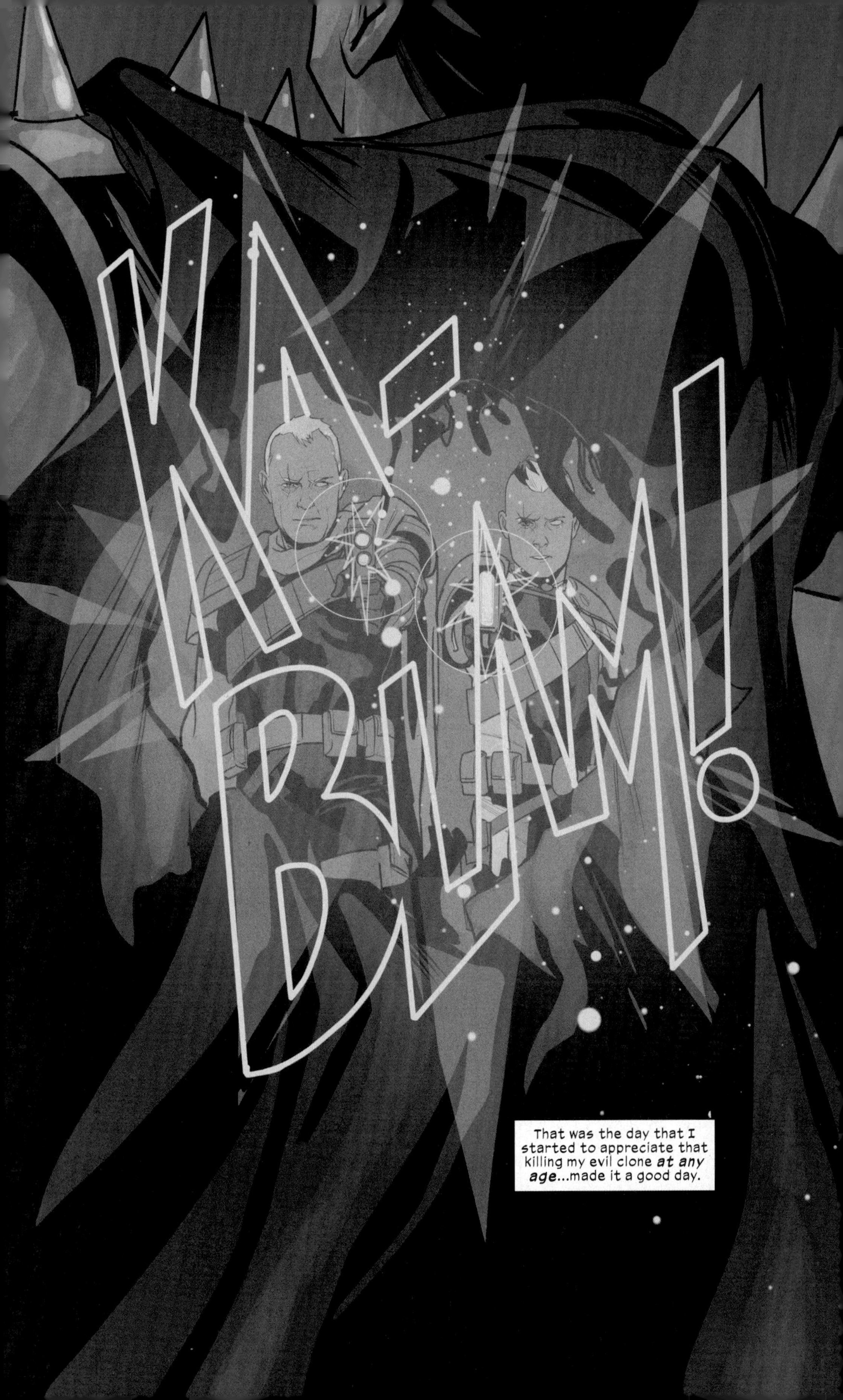
KA-BLAM!
That was the day that I started to appreciate that killing my evil clone *at any age*...made it a good day.

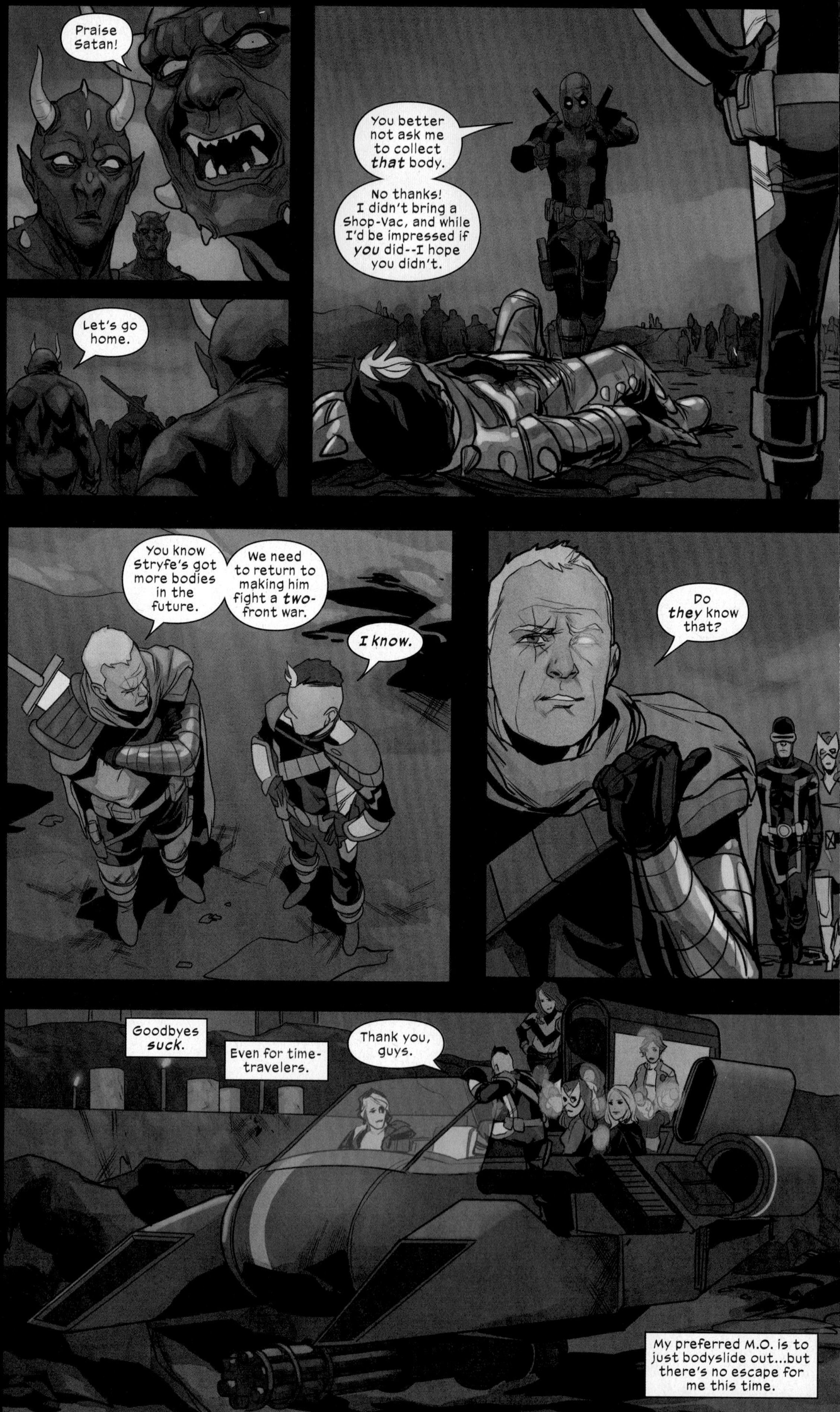

Praise Satan!
Let's go home.
You better not ask me to collect *that* body.
No thanks! I didn't bring a Shop-Vac, and while I'd be impressed if *you* did--I hope you didn't.
You know Stryfe's got more bodies in the future.
We need to return to making him fight a *two*-front war.
I know.
Do *they* know that?
Goodbyes *suck*.
Even for time-travelers.
Thank you, guys.
My preferred M.O. is to just bodyslide out...but there's no escape for me this time.

Dealing with the Galadorian Knight was easy.

Hmm. My chronometers must be failing...I didn't realize you were gone so long.

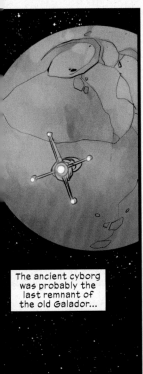

The ancient cyborg was probably the last remnant of the old Galador...

...his dying body was transformed by the sword's energy.

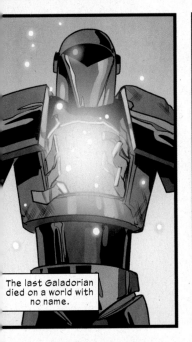

The last Galadorian died on a world with no name.

But with patience and time, that barren rock might be the cradle of a new Galadorian civilization...

...someday.

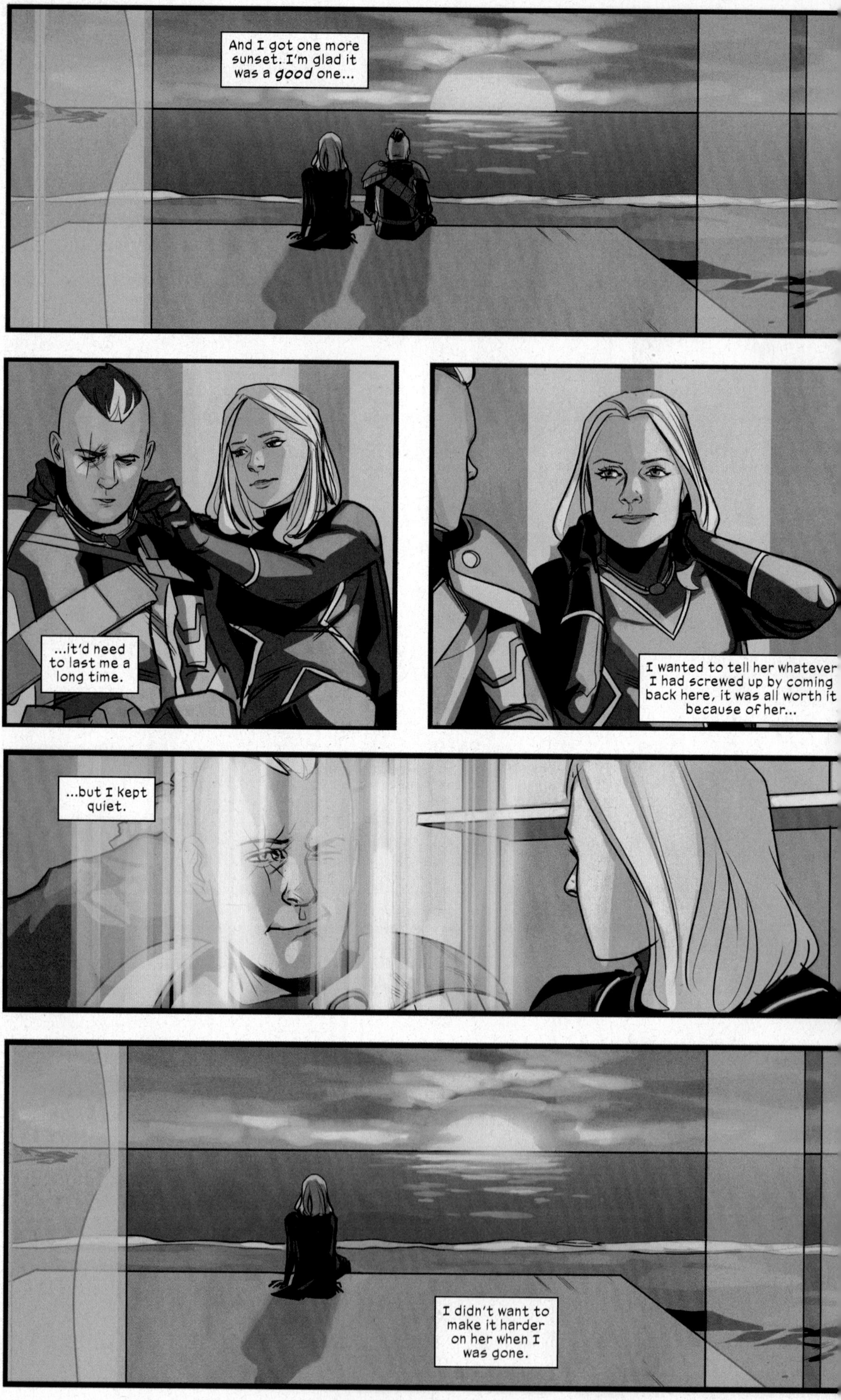

And I got one more sunset. I'm glad it was a *good* one...
...it'd need to last me a long time.
I wanted to tell her whatever I had screwed up by coming back here, it was all worth it because of her...
...but I kept quiet.
I didn't want to make it harder on her when I was gone.

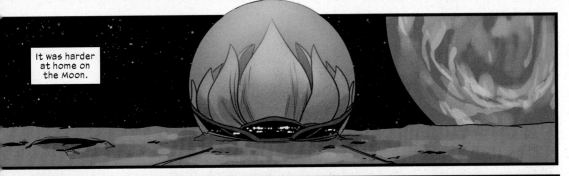

It was harder at home on the Moon.

You know when to find me if you need me.

What do we do to win?

Whatever it takes.

You make me proud at any age.

Go give 'em hell.

Thanks.

Bodyslide by one.

I call in the marker Logan owes me from our fight back in the Quarry. Logan's had enough hard goodbyes to last ten lifetimes. He'll get them through it.

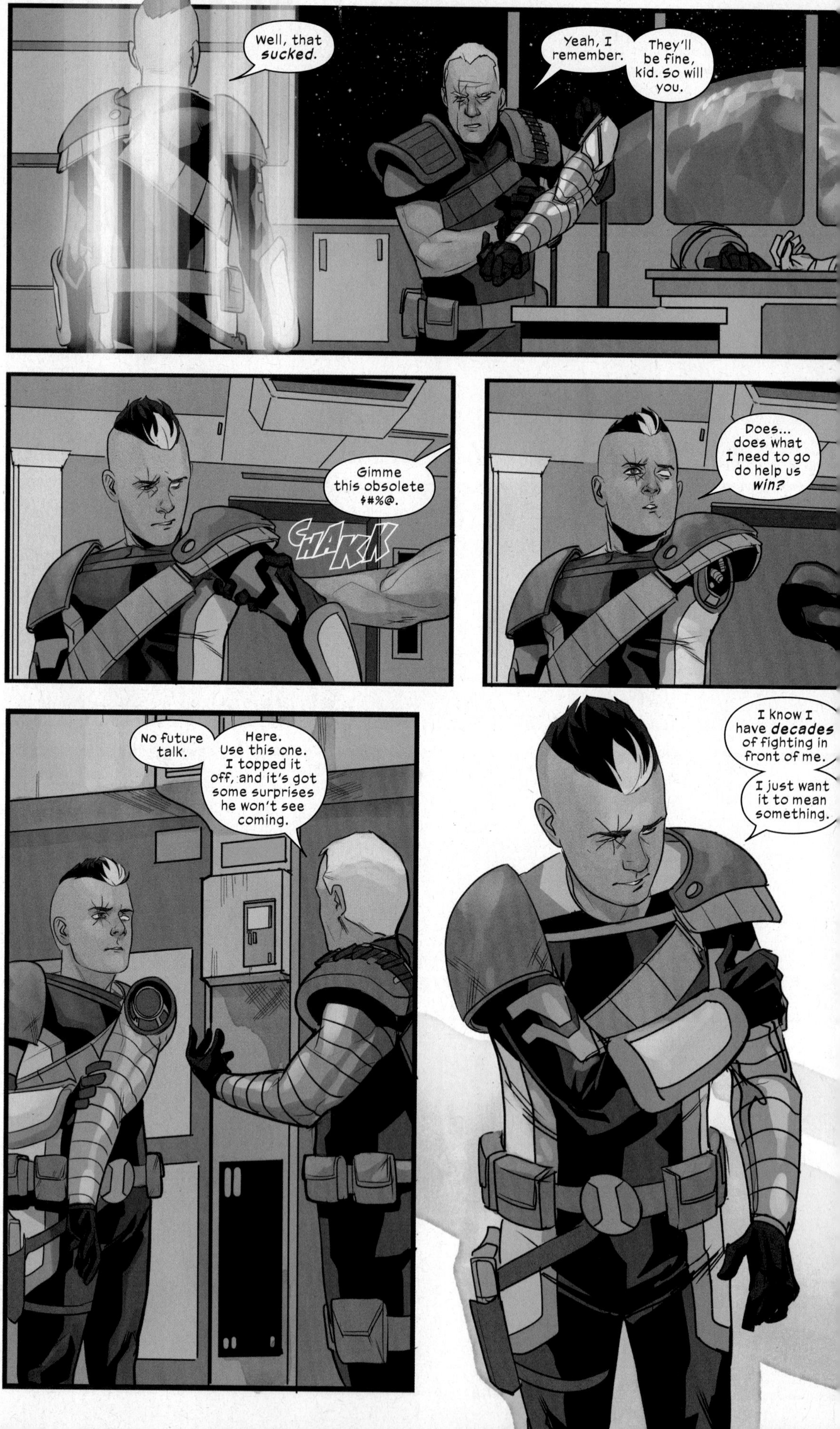

Well, that *sucked.*
Yeah, I remember.
They'll be fine, kid. So will you.
Gimme this obsolete $#%@.
CHAKK
Does... does what I need to go do help us *win?*
No future talk.
Here. Use this one. I topped it off, and it's got some surprises he won't see coming.
I know I have *decades* of fighting in front of me.
I just want it to mean something.

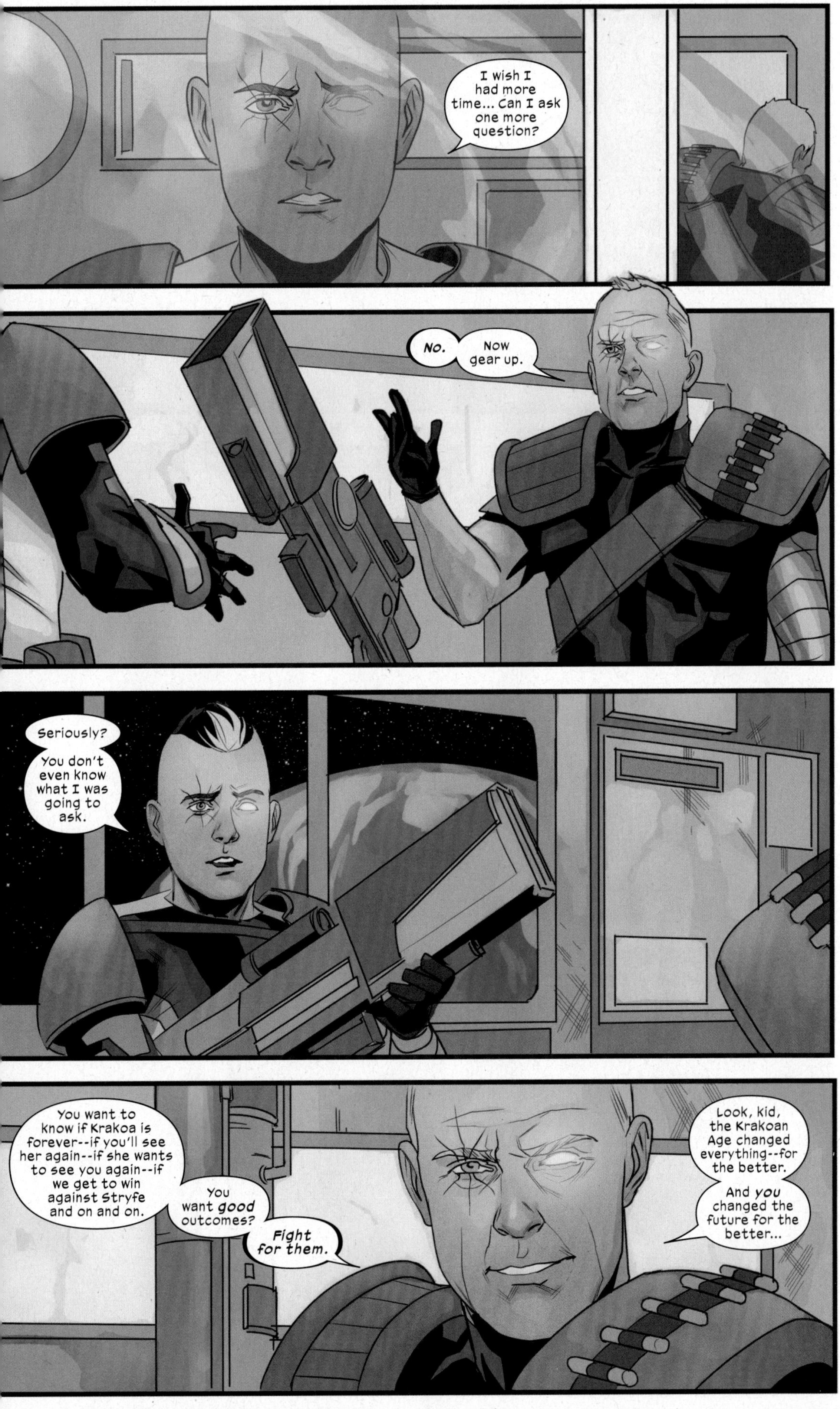
I wish I had more time... Can I ask one more question?
No.
Now gear up.
Seriously?
You don't even know what I was going to ask.
You want to know if Krakoa is forever--if you'll see her again--if she wants to see you again--if we get to win against Stryfe and on and on.
You want *good* outcomes?
Fight for them.
Look, kid, the Krakoan Age changed everything--for the better.
And *you* changed the future for the better...

"...we all have more, but now we have more to *lose* if we slip up."

Stupid little @#$%.

Go easy on that kid, old man.

He's got a soft spot in my heart.

Have fun dying.

I always do.

See you on the other side.

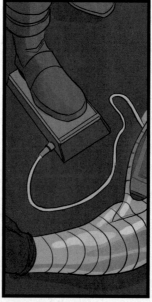

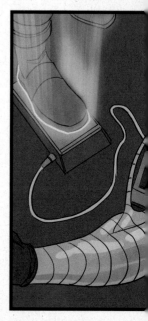

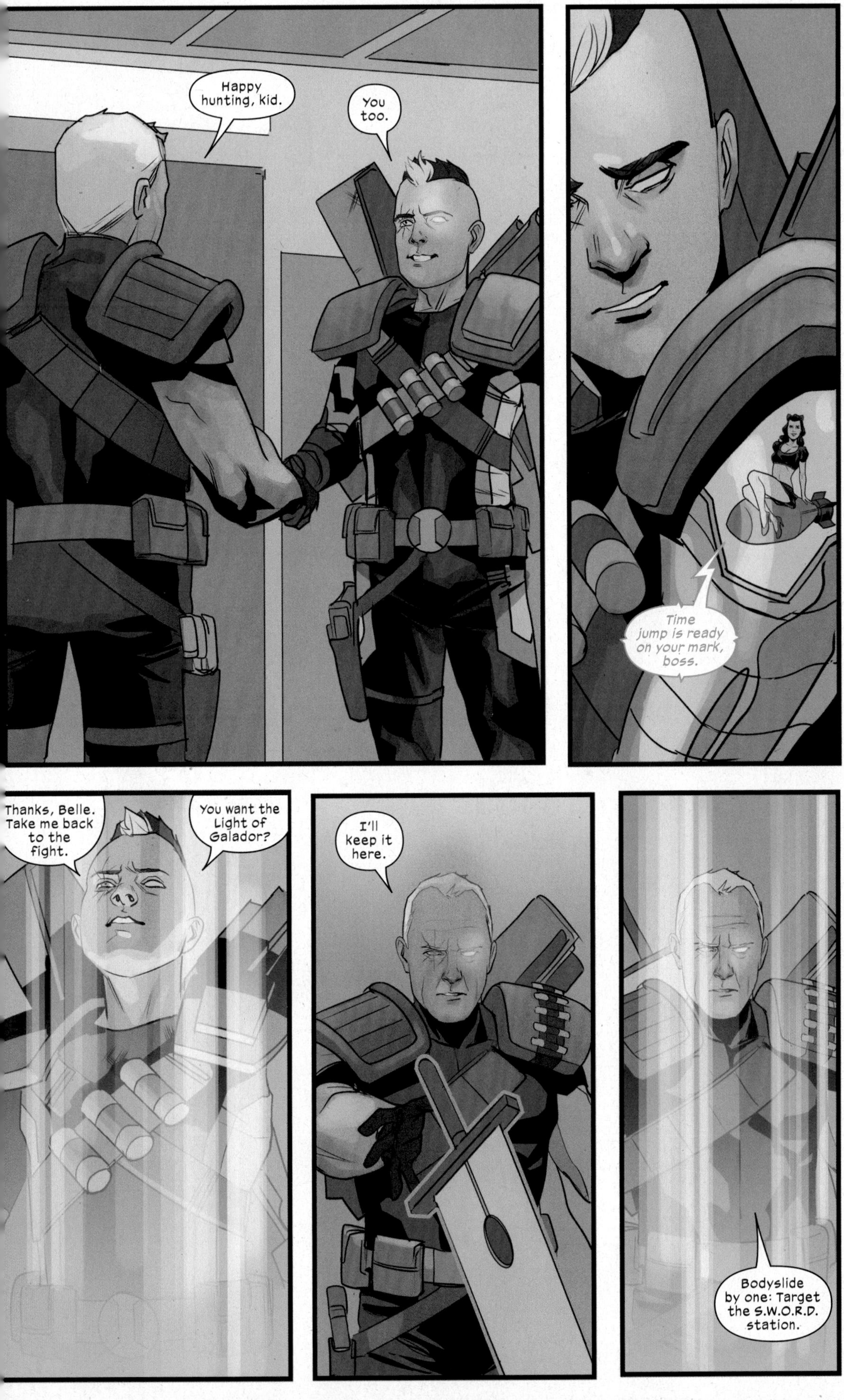

Happy hunting, kid.
You too.
Time jump is ready on your mark, boss.
Thanks, Belle. Take me back to the fight.
You want the Light of Galador?
I'll keep it here.
Bodyslide by one: Target the S.W.O.R.D. station.

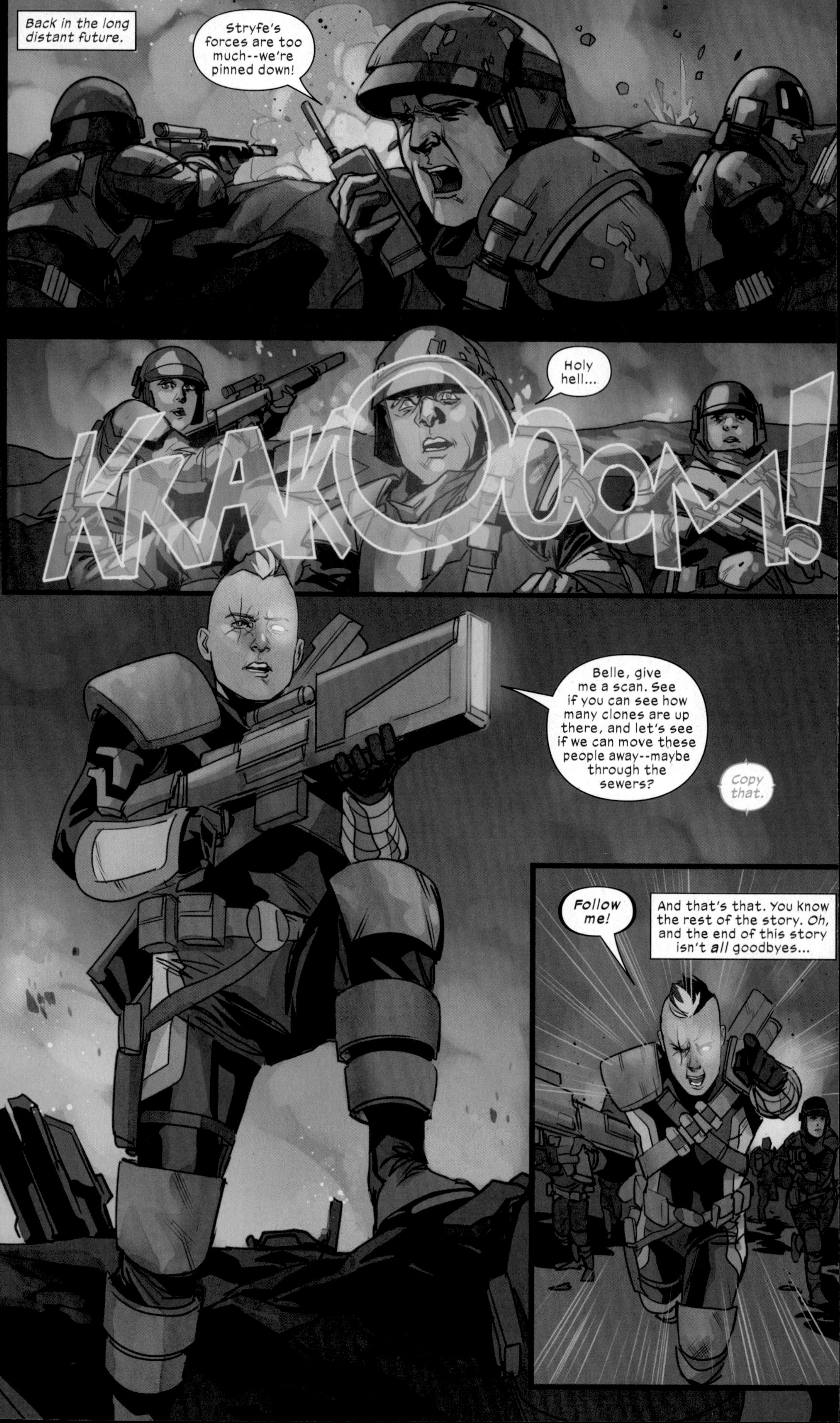
Back in the long distant future.
Stryfe's forces are too much--we're pinned down!
Holy hell...
KRAKOOOOM!
Belle, give me a scan. See if you can see how many clones are up there, and let's see if we can move these people away--maybe through the sewers?
Copy that.
Follow me!
And that's that. You know the rest of the story. Oh, and the end of this story isn't all goodbyes...

The five mutant families were reunited with their kidnapped children. And their new twins.

It was awful losing the baby for as long as we did...

...but I don't mind the sudden addition. They'll be able to keep each other company.

They'll always have each other.

Strange things seem to happen to mutant families.

Sometimes your one baby gets kidnapped and two of them return to you...

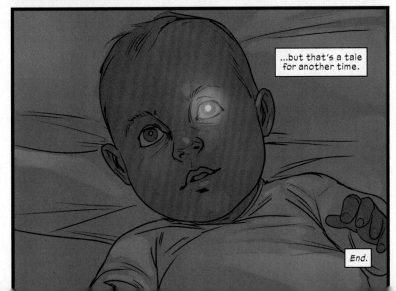

...but that's a tale for another time.

End.

[reign_of_x]

[kra_]
[koa_]

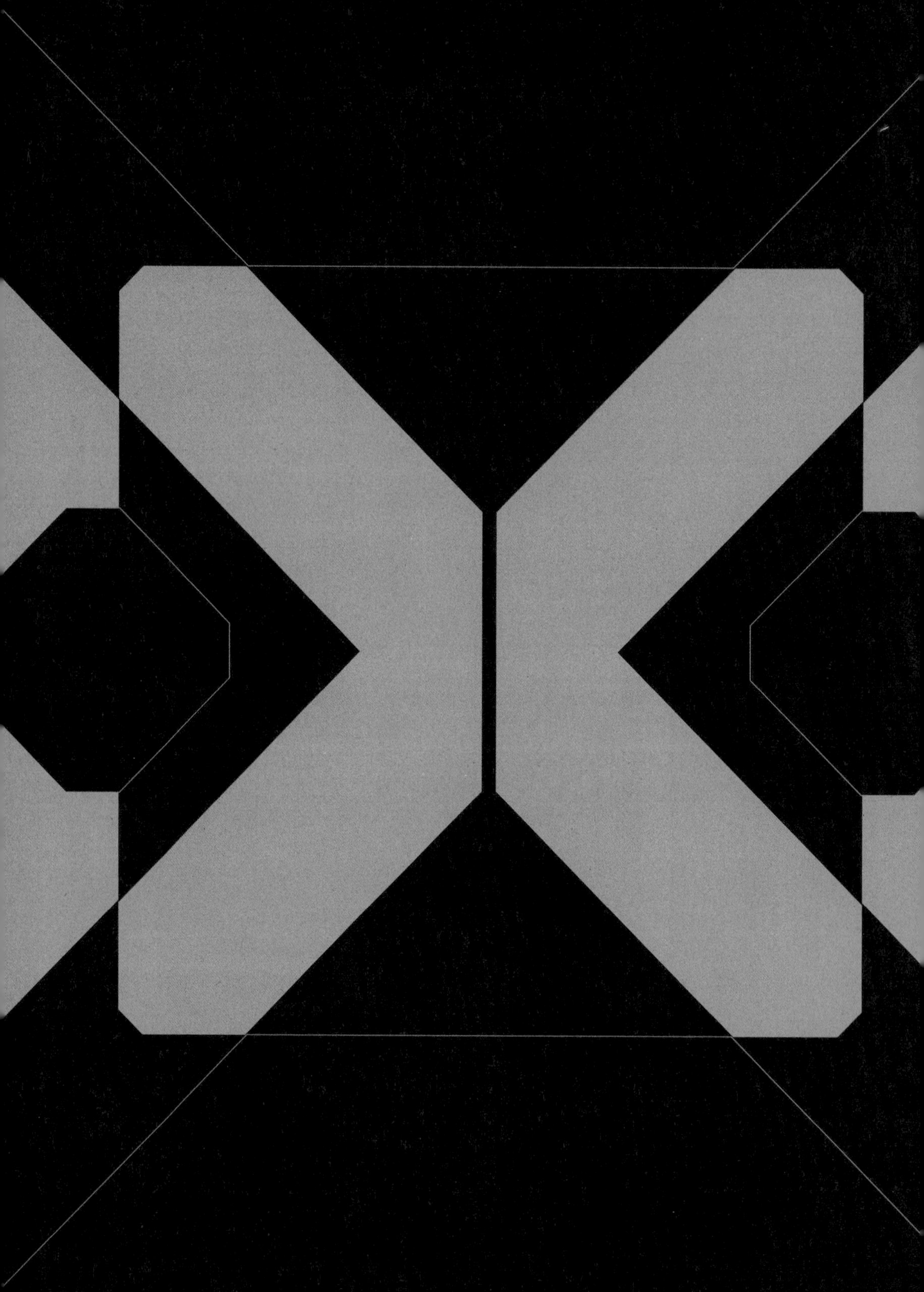

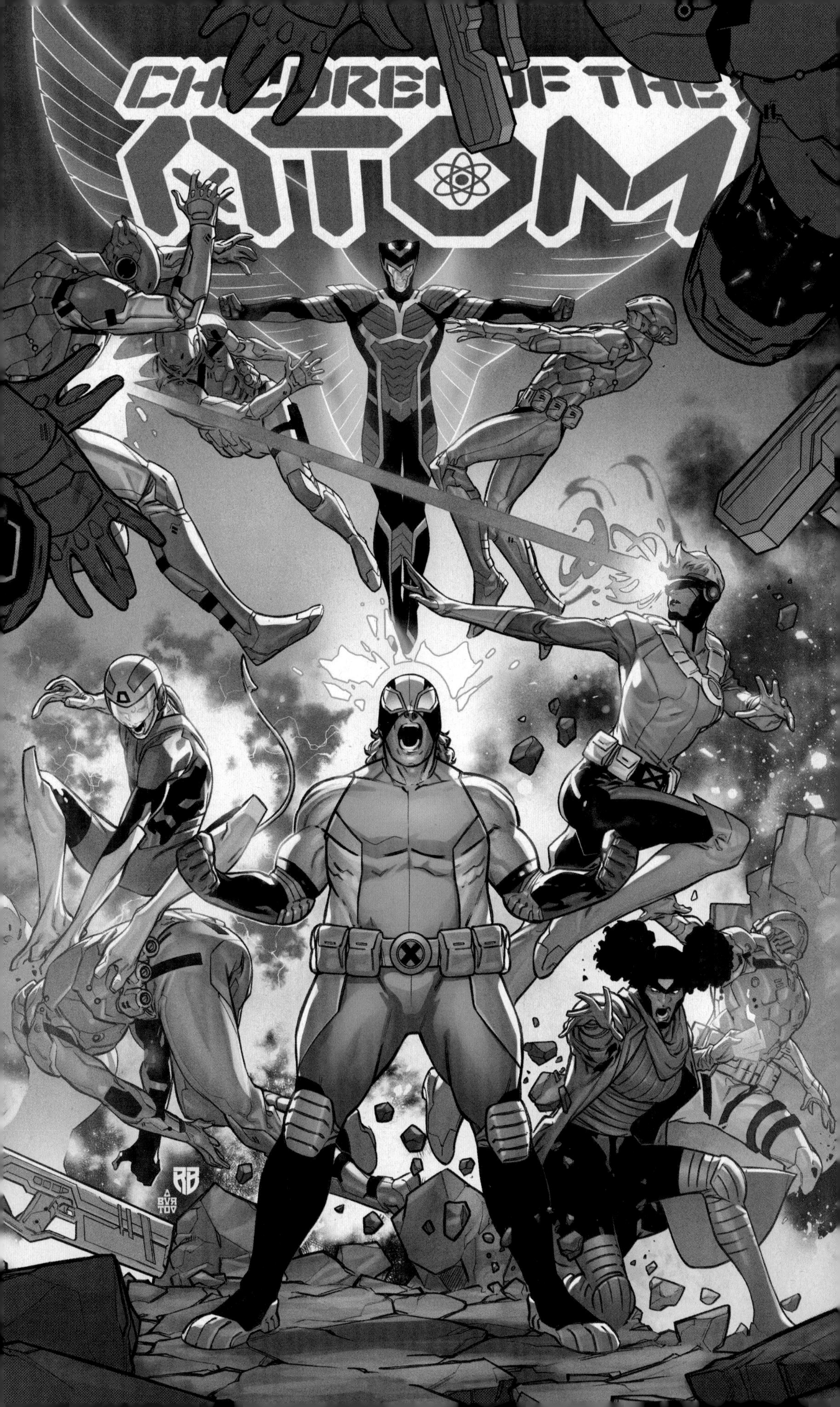

CHILDREN OF THE
ATOM

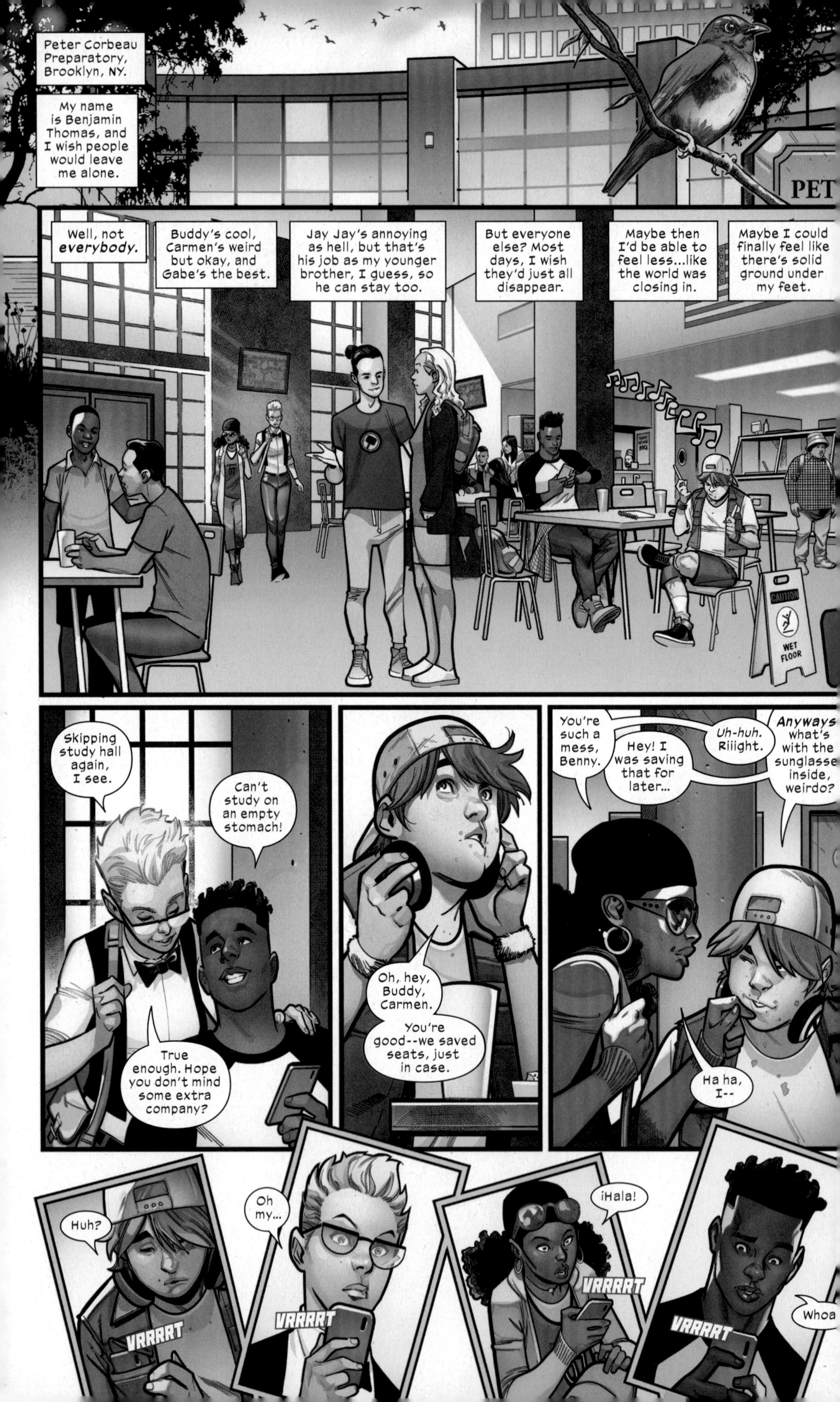
Peter Corbeau Preparatory, Brooklyn, NY.
My name is Benjamin Thomas, and I wish people would leave me alone.
PET
Well, not *everybody.*
Buddy's cool, Carmen's weird but okay, and Gabe's the best.
Jay Jay's annoying as hell, but that's his job as my younger brother, I guess, so he can stay too.
But everyone else? Most days, I wish they'd just all disappear.
Maybe then I'd be able to feel less...like the world was closing in.
Maybe I could finally feel like there's solid ground under my feet.
CAUTION
WET FLOOR
Skipping study hall again, I see.
Can't study on an empty stomach!
True enough. Hope you don't mind some extra company?
Oh, hey, Buddy, Carmen.
You're good--we saved seats, just in case.
You're such a mess, Benny.
Hey! I was saving that for later...
Uh-huh. Riiight.
Anyways what's with the sunglasse inside, weirdo?
Ha ha, I--
Huh?
VRRRRT
Oh my...
VRRRRT
¡Hala!
VRRRRT
VRRRRT
Whoa

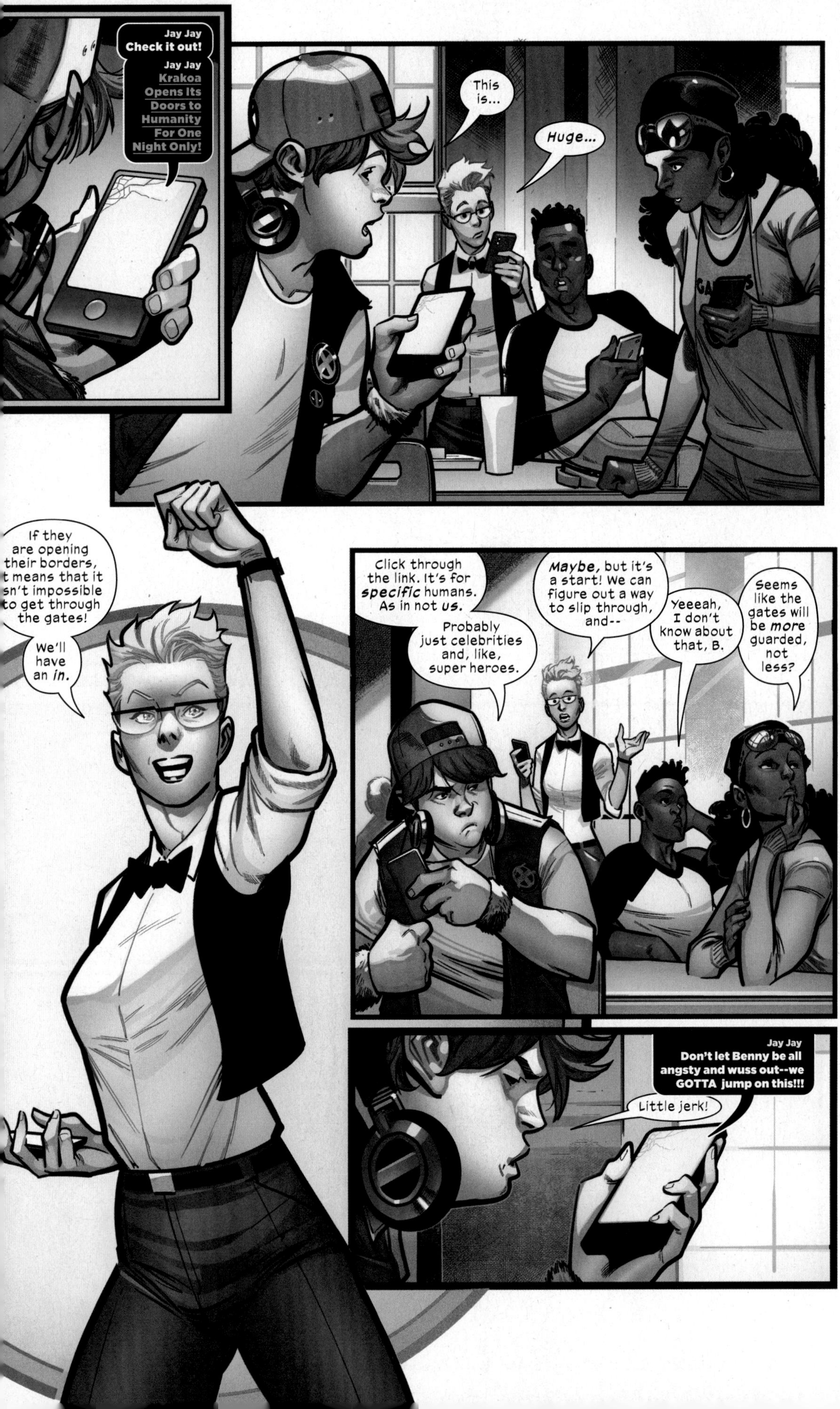
Jay Jay
Check it out!
Jay Jay
Krakoa Opens Its Doors to Humanity For One Night Only!
This is...
Huge...
If they are opening their borders, it means that it isn't impossible to get through the gates!
We'll have an *in.*
Click through the link. It's for *specific* humans. As in not *us.*
Probably just celebrities and, like, super heroes.
Maybe, but it's a start! We can figure out a way to slip through, and--
Yeeeah, I don't know about that, B.
Seems like the gates will be *more* guarded, not less?
Jay Jay
Don't let Benny be all angsty and wuss out--we GOTTA jump on this!!!
Little jerk!

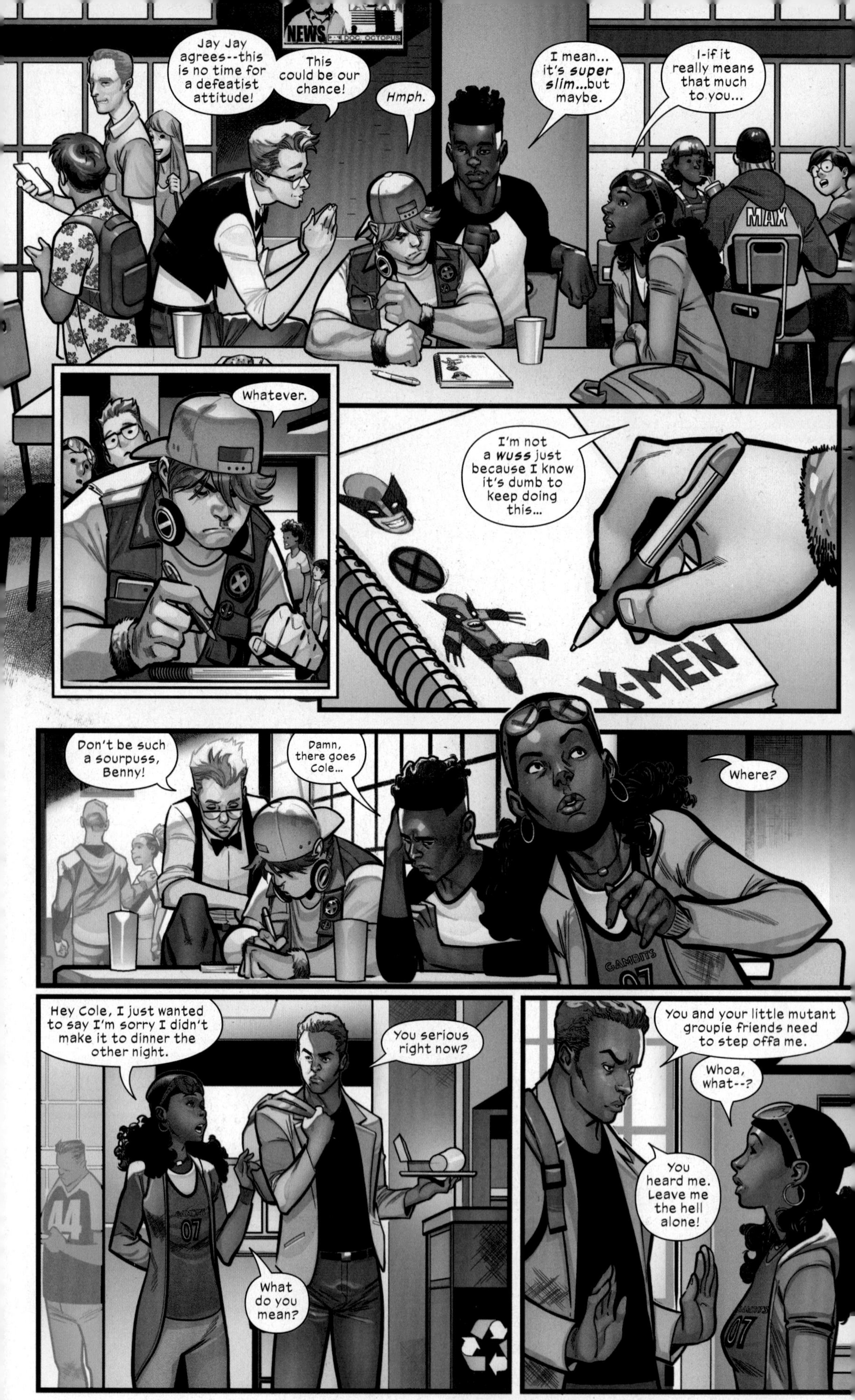
NEWS
DOC OCTOPUS
Jay Jay agrees--this is no time for a defeatist attitude!
This could be our chance!
Hmph.
I mean... it's super slim...but maybe.
I-if it really means that much to you...
MAX
Whatever.
I'm not a wuss just because I know it's dumb to keep doing this...
X-MEN
Don't be such a sourpuss, Benny!
Damn, there goes Cole...
Where?
GAMBITS
Hey Cole, I just wanted to say I'm sorry I didn't make it to dinner the other night.
You serious right now?
What do you mean?
You and your little mutant groupie friends need to step offa me.
Whoa, what--?
You heard me. Leave me the hell alone!

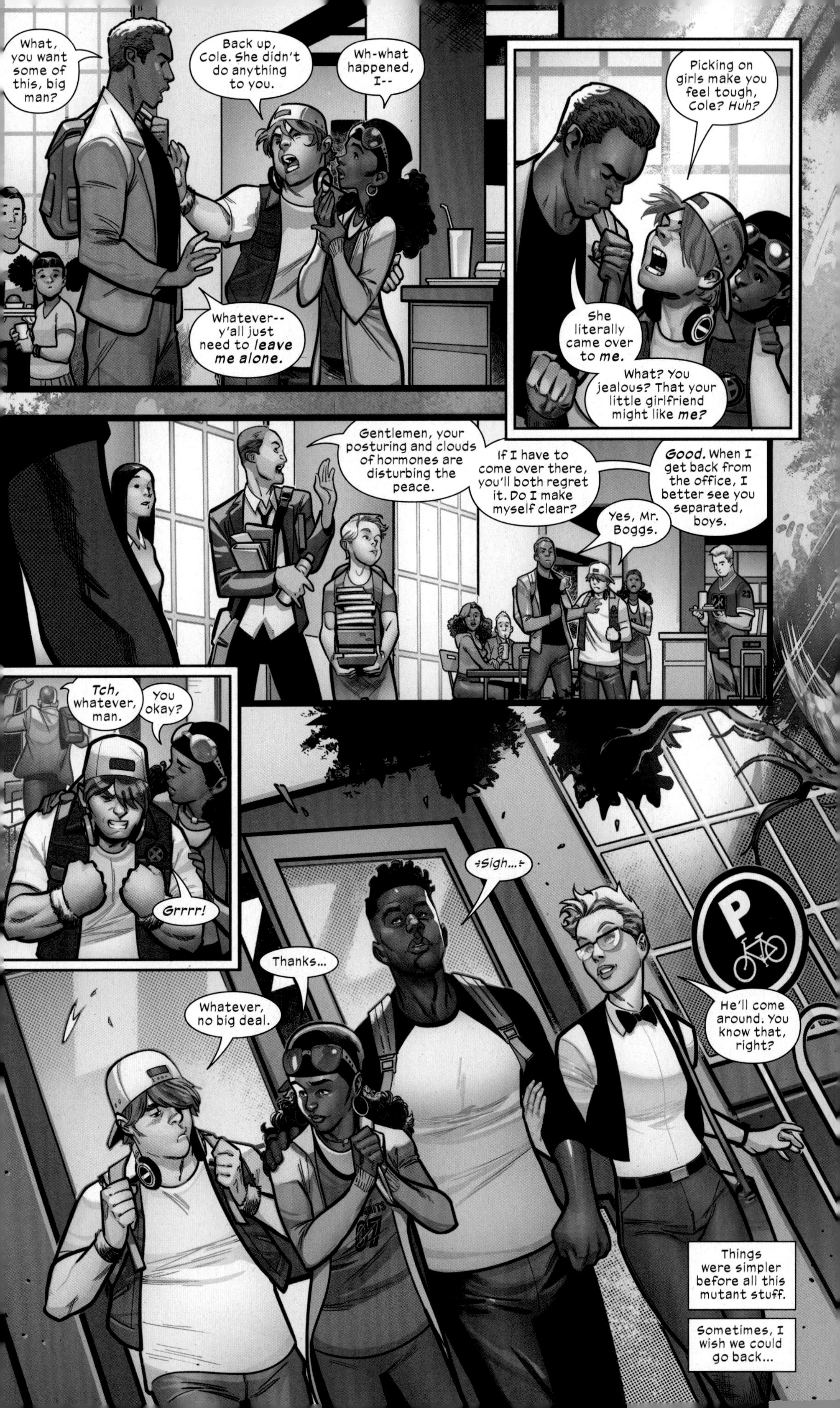

What, you want some of this, big man?
Back up, Cole. She didn't do anything to you.
Wh-what happened, I--
Whatever-- y'all just need to *leave me alone.*
Picking on girls make you feel tough, Cole? *Huh?*
She literally came over to *me.*
What? You jealous? That your little girlfriend might like *me?*
Gentlemen, your posturing and clouds of hormones are disturbing the peace.
If I have to come over there, you'll both regret it. Do I make myself clear?
Yes, Mr. Boggs.
Good. When I get back from the office, I better see you separated, boys.
Tch, whatever, man.
You okay?
Grrrr!
Sigh...
Thanks...
Whatever, no big deal.
He'll come around. You know that, right?
Things were simpler before all this mutant stuff.
Sometimes, I wish we could go back...

FAKE IT TILL YOU MAKE IT

Mutants around the world have flocked to the island-nation of Krakoa for safety, security and to be part of the first mutant society.

Back in New York City, new teen vigilantes CHILDREN OF THE ATOM dream of becoming mutants and joining their heroes, the X-MEN, on Krakoa. The young team has been working tirelessly to find a way through the Krakoan gates, but so far they've had no such luck.

But one among them has secretly started to exhibit traits of a mutant: Carmen, A.K.A. GIMMICK!

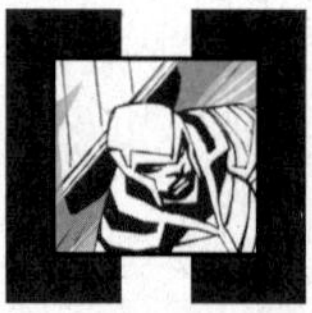

Cherub

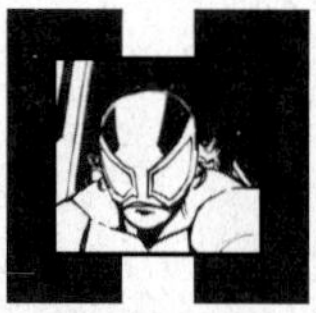

Marvel Guy

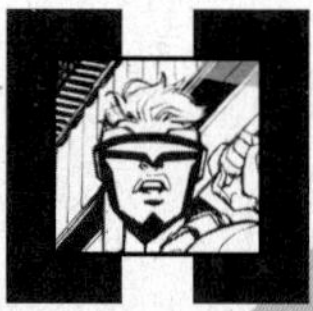

Cyclops-Lass

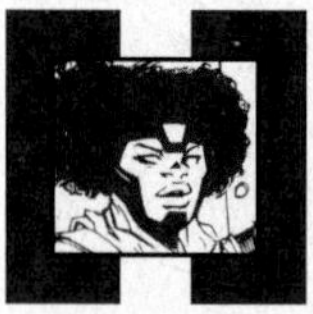

Gimmick

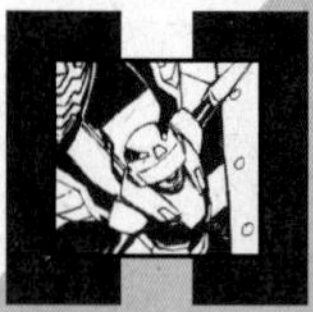

Daycrawler

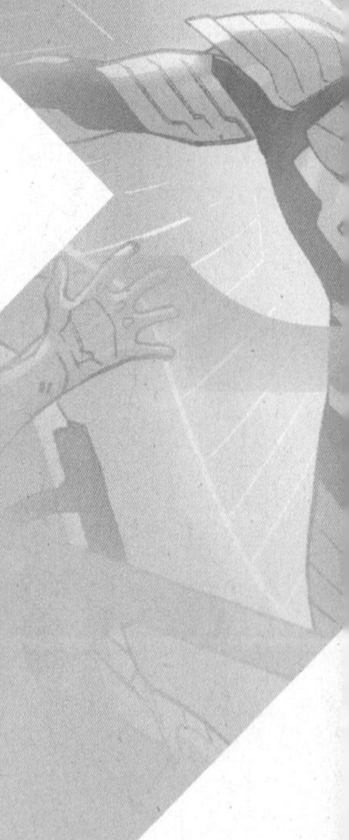

CHILDREN OF THE ATOM

[X_04]

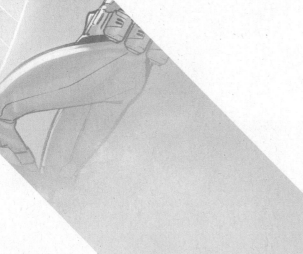

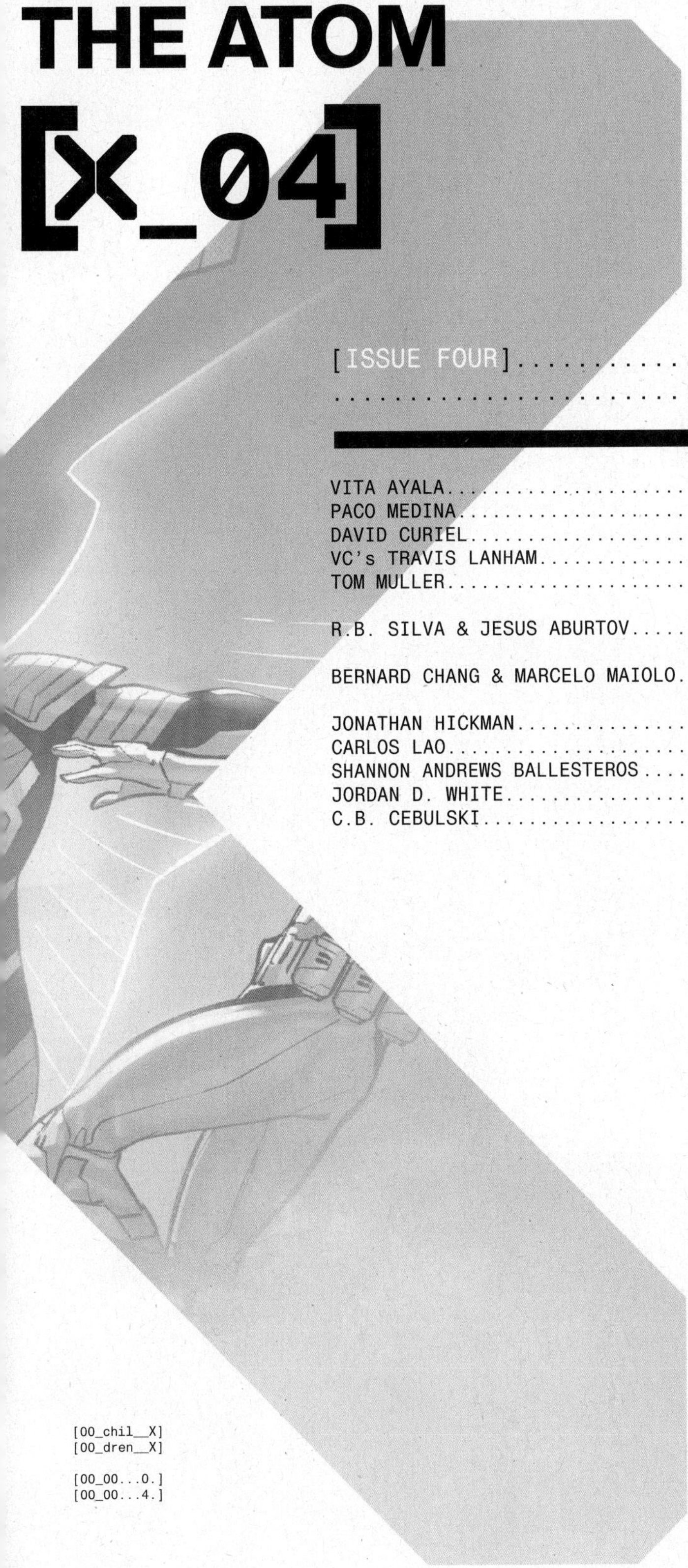

[ISSUE FOUR]...............................
.....................................CAPTURED

VITA AYALA...[WRITER]
PACO MEDINA..[ARTIST]
DAVID CURIEL.................................[COLOR ARTIST]
VC's TRAVIS LANHAM.............................[LETTERER]
TOM MULLER.......................................[DESIGN]

R.B. SILVA & JESUS ABURTOV..................[COVER ARTISTS]

BERNARD CHANG & MARCELO MAIOLO......[VARIANT COVER ARTISTS]

JONATHAN HICKMAN..............................[HEAD OF X]
CARLOS LAO....................................[PRODUCTION]
SHANNON ANDREWS BALLESTEROS.......................[EDITOR]
JORDAN D. WHITE............................[SENIOR EDITOR]
C.B. CEBULSKI............................[EDITOR IN CHIEF]

[00_chil__X]
[00_dren__X]

[00_00...0.]
[00_00...4.]

[00_____]
[00_of___]

[00_the___]

[00__atom__]

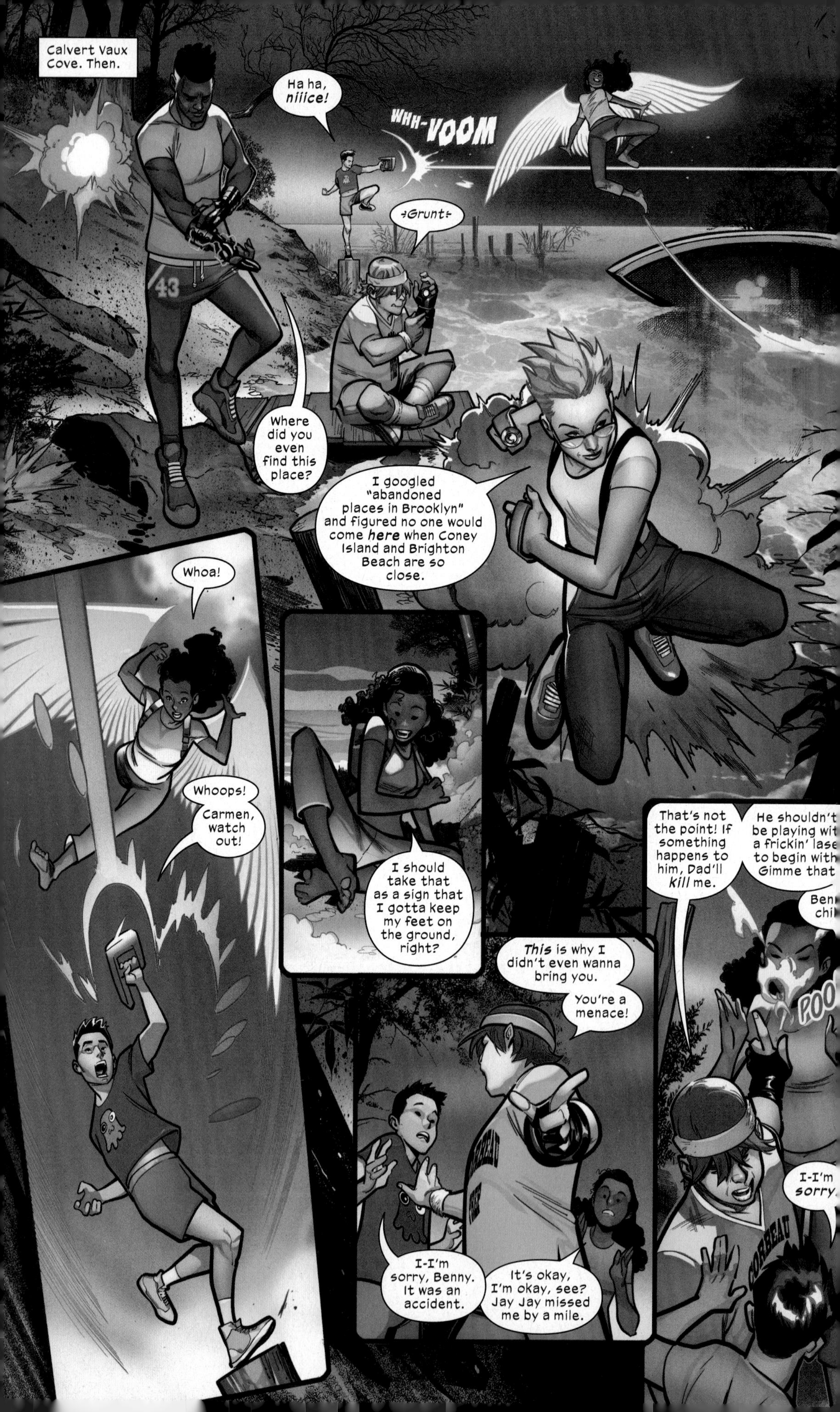
Calvert Vaux Cove. Then.
Ha ha, *niiice!*
WHH-VOOM
-Grunt-
Where did you even find this place?
I googled "abandoned places in Brooklyn" and figured no one would come *here* when Coney Island and Brighton Beach are so close.
Whoa!
Whoops!
Carmen, watch out!
I should take that as a sign that I gotta keep my feet on the ground, right?
This is why I didn't even wanna bring you.
You're a menace!
I-I'm sorry, Benny. It was an accident.
It's okay, I'm okay, see? Jay Jay missed me by a mile.
That's not the point! If something happens to him, Dad'll *kill* me.
I-I'm *sorry.*

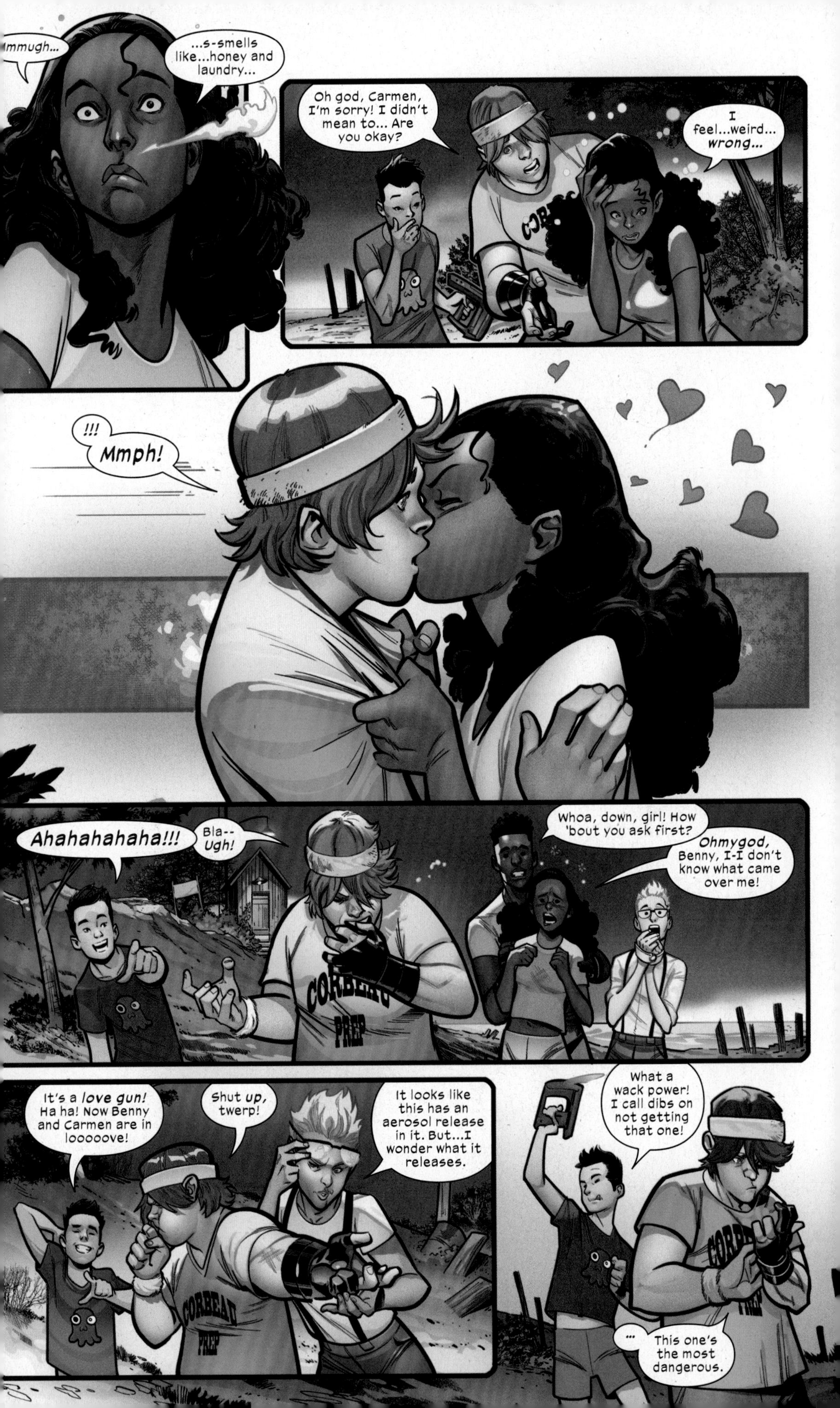

Mmmugh...
...s-smells like...honey and laundry...
Oh god, Carmen, I'm sorry! I didn't mean to... Are you okay?
I feel...weird... *wrong*...
!!!
Mmph!
Ahahahahaha!!!
Bla-- Ugh!
Whoa, down, girl! How 'bout you ask first?
Ohmygod, Benny, I-I don't know what came over me!
It's a *love gun!* Ha ha! Now Benny and Carmen are in looooove!
Shut *up,* twerp!
It looks like this has an aerosol release in it. But...I wonder what it releases.
What a wack power! I call dibs on not getting that one!
...
This one's the most dangerous.

VIBECLOUD/WEAPONXTRA

SNIKT SNAKT FT. DARK COLOSSUS & FEINTLY FROSTED STITCHES

WEAPON XTRA

First single off of the "Grim-Dark Past" EP! Weapon Xtra shreds on guitar and lead vocals, with a verse from Dark Colossus and backups and hook by Feintly Frosted Stitches!

TAGS: {Rock} {Metal} {Punk} {Hip Hop} {Thrash}

WEAPON XTRA
👤 7K
▶ 712
◉ 1

◦ ◉ MUSIC STATION

👤 Follow

••• More

⬜ Share

Comments:

LadyMrSinistyr: This absolutely WHIPS!

XGaveItToYa: wrong wolverine costume, but p cool trak

PapaH: Hope you kids gets signed

DazzlersGlitterLipgloss: yoooo, that DC verse thooooo

LNEx: When am I getting a feature, tho? Lemme know!

ArchivistX: <3

RoboRevolution: Lila Cheney's bettr

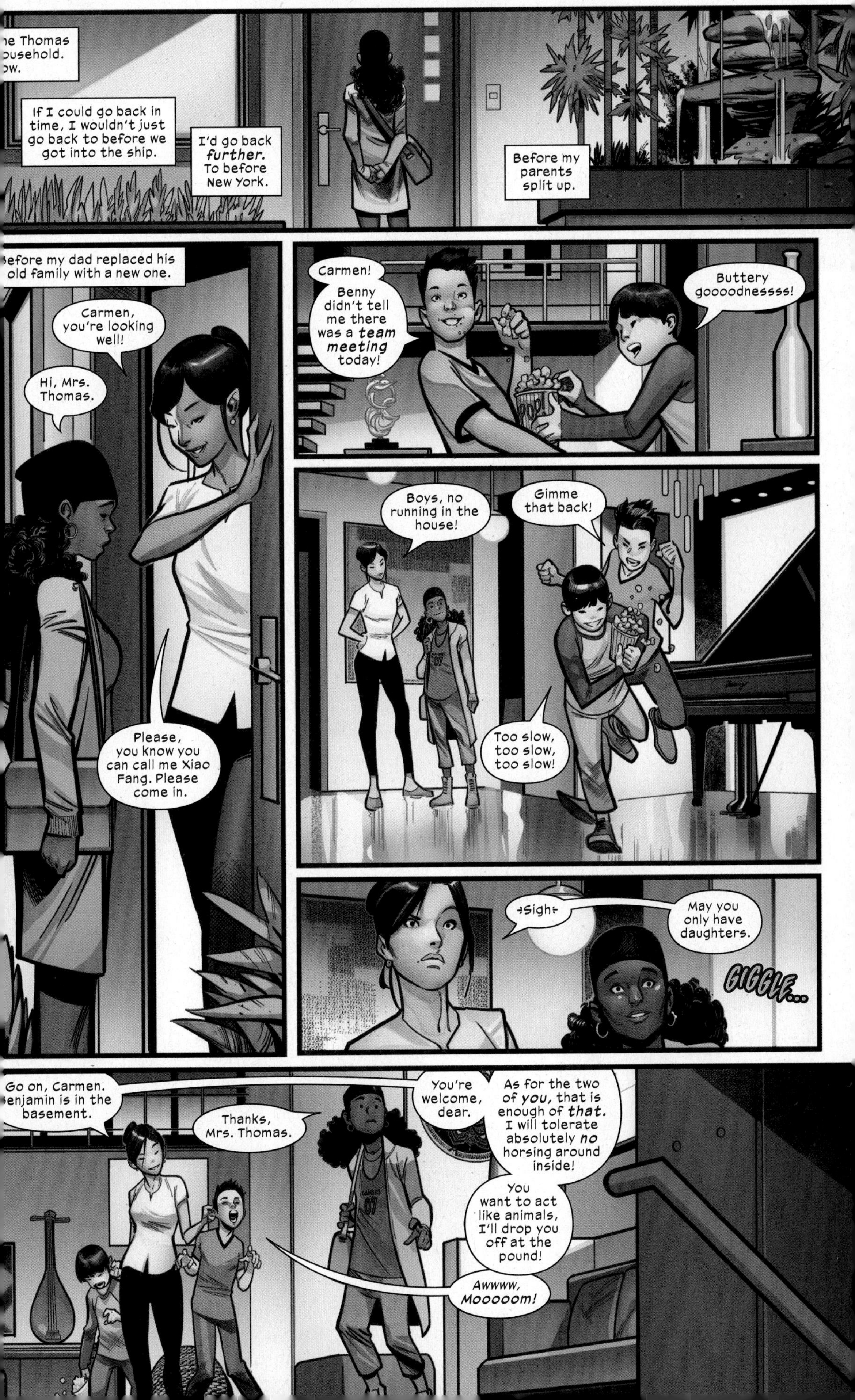

ne Thomas
ousehold.
ow.
If I could go back in time, I wouldn't just go back to before we got into the ship.
I'd go back *further.* To before New York.
Before my parents split up.
Before my dad replaced his old family with a new one.
Carmen, you're looking well!
Hi, Mrs. Thomas.
Please, you know you can call me Xiao Fang. Please come in.
Carmen! Benny didn't tell me there was a *team meeting* today!
Buttery gooodnessss!
Boys, no running in the house!
Gimme that back!
Too slow, too slow, too slow!
Sigh
May you only have daughters.
GIGGLE...
Go on, Carmen. enjamin is in the basement.
Thanks, Mrs. Thomas.
You're welcome, dear.
As for the two of *you,* that is enough of *that.* I will tolerate absolutely *no* horsing around inside!
You want to act like animals, I'll drop you off at the pound!
Awwww, Mooooom!

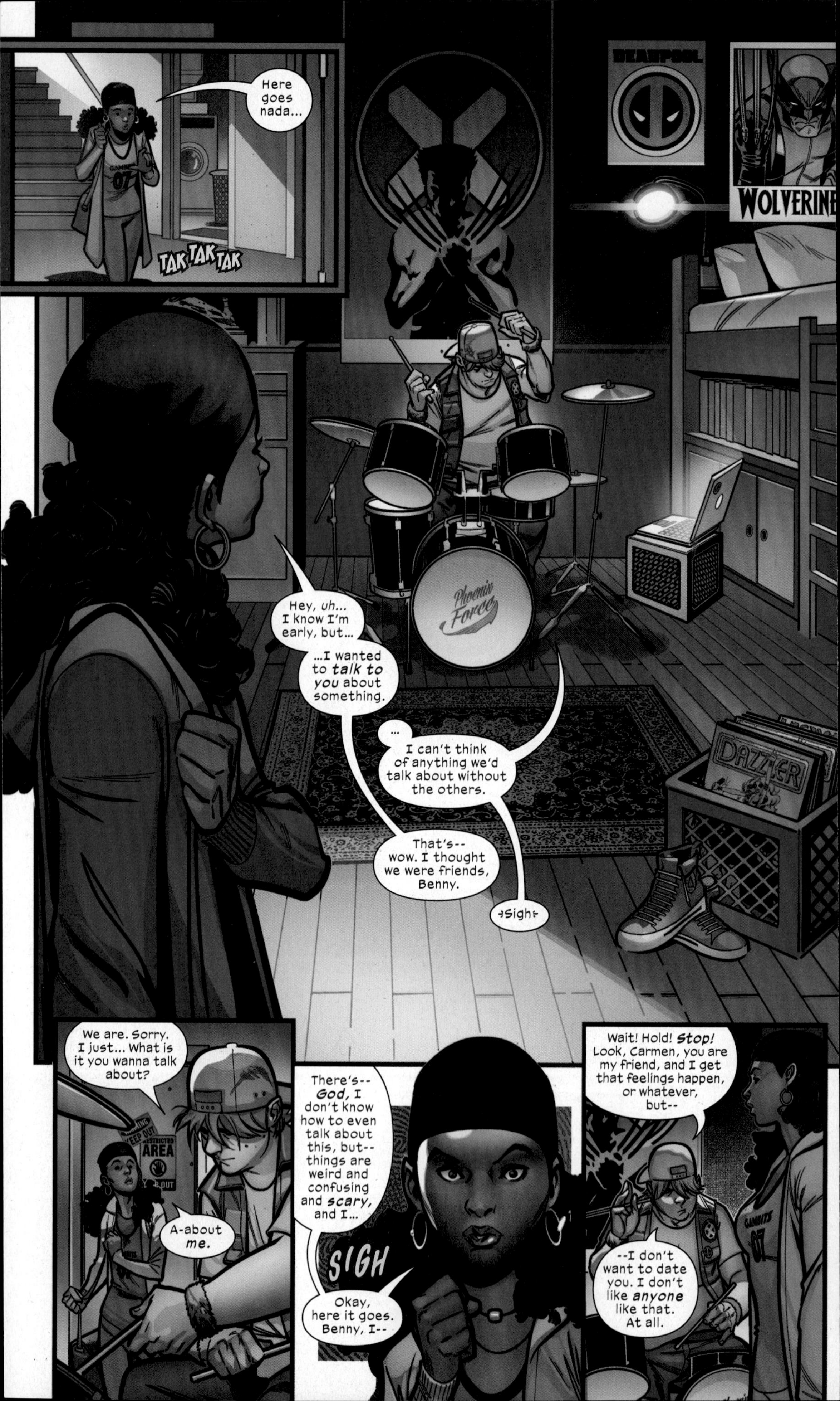

Here goes nada...
TAK TAK TAK
Hey, uh... I know I'm early, but...
...I wanted to talk to you about something.
... I can't think of anything we'd talk about without the others.
That's-- wow. I thought we were friends, Benny.
-Sigh-
DEADPOOL
WOLVERINE
Phoenix Force
DAZZLER
We are. Sorry. I just... What is it you wanna talk about?
A-about me.
KEEP OUT
RESTRICTED AREA
There's-- God, I don't know how to even talk about this, but-- things are weird and confusing and scary, and I...
SIGH
Okay, here it goes. Benny, I--
Wait! Hold! Stop! Look, Carmen, you are my friend, and I get that feelings happen, or whatever, but--
--I don't want to date you. I don't like anyone like that. At all.

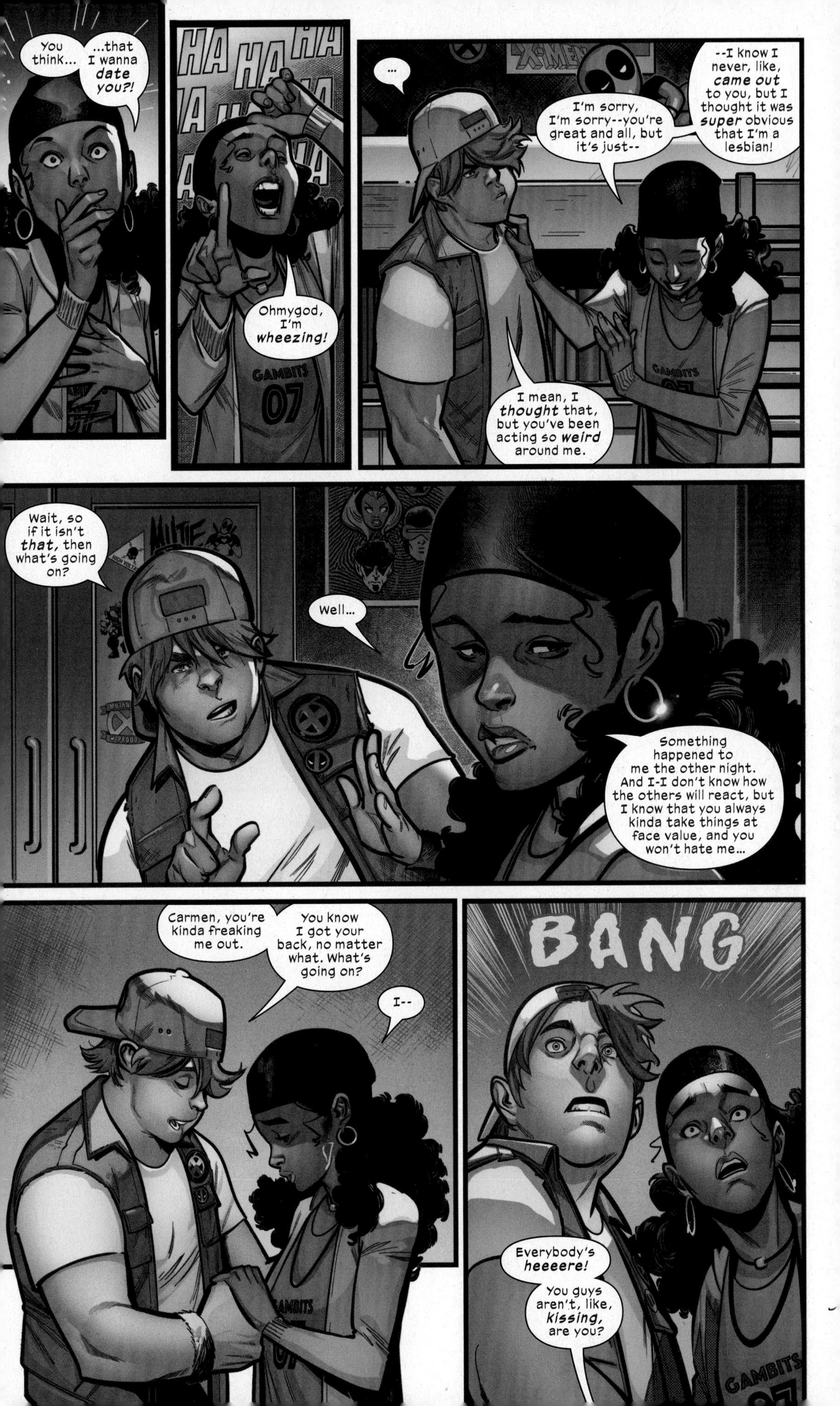
You think...
...that I wanna date you?!
HA HA HA HA HA HA HA HA
Ohmygod, I'm wheezing!
...
I'm sorry, I'm sorry--you're great and all, but it's just--
--I know I never, like, came out to you, but I thought it was super obvious that I'm a lesbian!
I mean, I thought that, but you've been acting so weird around me.
Wait, so if it isn't that, then what's going on?
Well...
Something happened to me the other night. And I-I don't know how the others will react, but I know that you always kinda take things at face value, and you won't hate me...
Carmen, you're kinda freaking me out.
You know I got your back, no matter what. What's going on?
I--
BANG
Everybody's heeeere!
You guys aren't, like, kissing, are you?

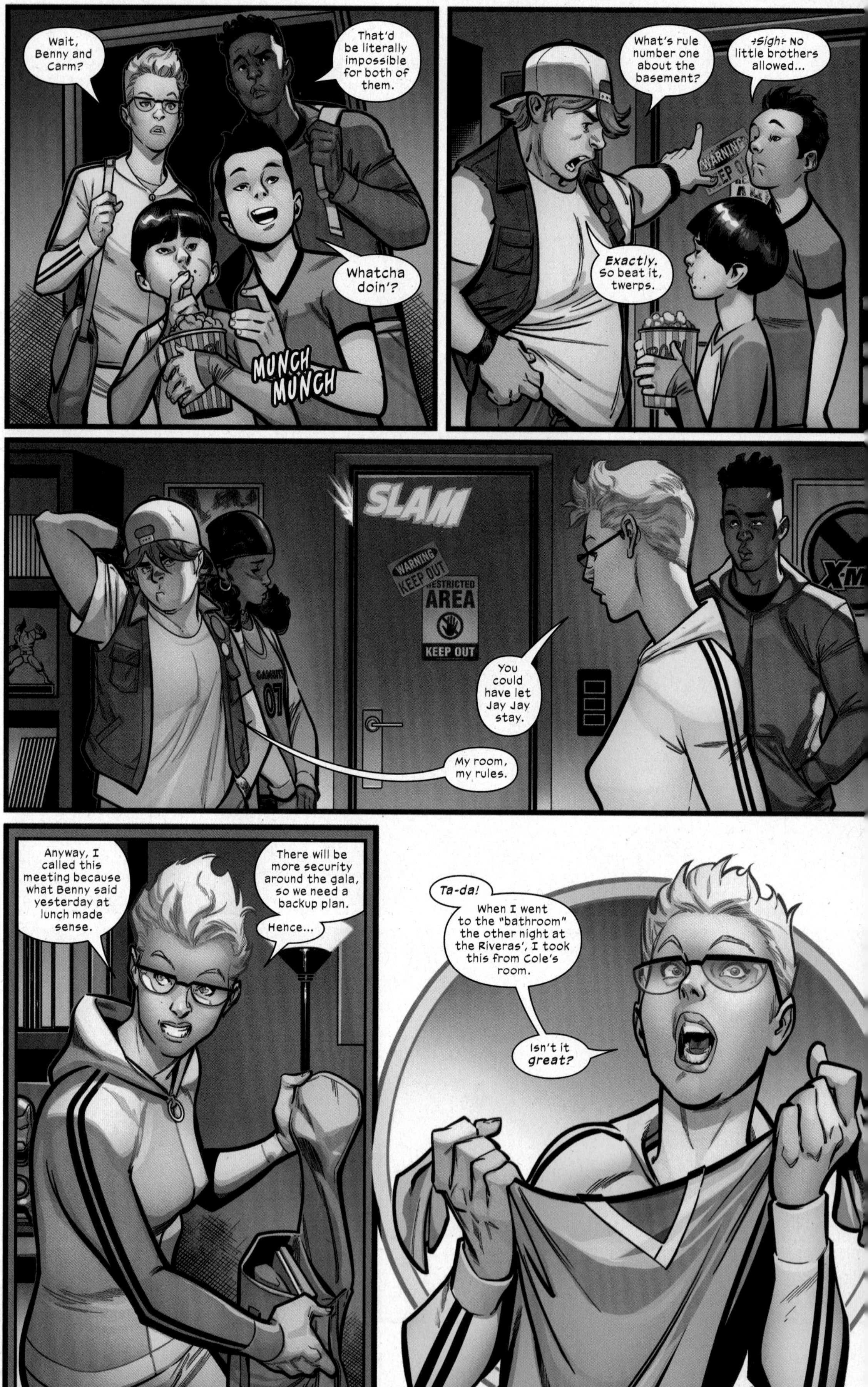
Wait, Benny and Carm?
That'd be literally impossible for both of them.
Whatcha doin'?
MUNCH MUNCH
What's rule number one about the basement?
-Sigh- No little brothers allowed...
Exactly. So beat it, twerps.
SLAM
WARNING KEEP OUT
RESTRICTED AREA
KEEP OUT
You could have let Jay Jay stay.
My room, my rules.
Anyway, I called this meeting because what Benny said yesterday at lunch made sense.
There will be more security around the gala, so we need a backup plan.
Hence...
Ta-da!
When I went to the "bathroom" the other night at the Riveras', I took this from Cole's room.
Isn't it great?

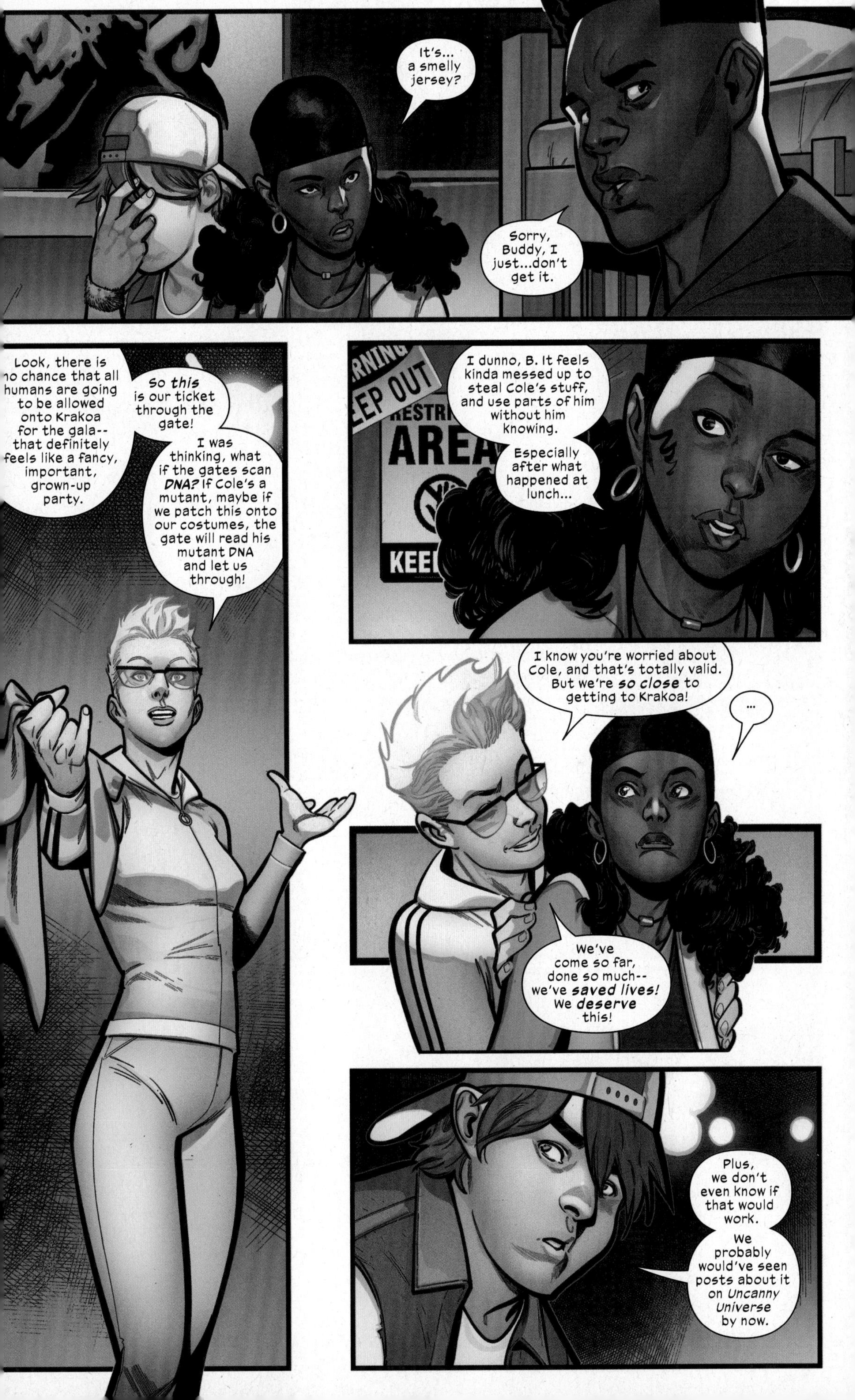

It's... a smelly jersey?
Sorry, Buddy, I just...don't get it.
Look, there is no chance that all humans are going to be allowed onto Krakoa for the gala-- that definitely feels like a fancy, important, grown-up party.
So *this* is our ticket through the gate!
I was thinking, what if the gates scan *DNA?* If Cole's a mutant, maybe if we patch this onto our costumes, the gate will read his mutant DNA and let us through!
WARNING
KEEP OUT
RESTRICTED
AREA
KEEP
I dunno, B. It feels kinda messed up to steal Cole's stuff, and use parts of him without him knowing.
Especially after what happened at lunch...
I know you're worried about Cole, and that's totally valid. But we're *so close* to getting to Krakoa!
...
We've come so far, done so much-- we've *saved lives!* We *deserve* this!
Plus, we don't even know if that would work.
We probably would've seen posts about it on *Uncanny Universe* by now.

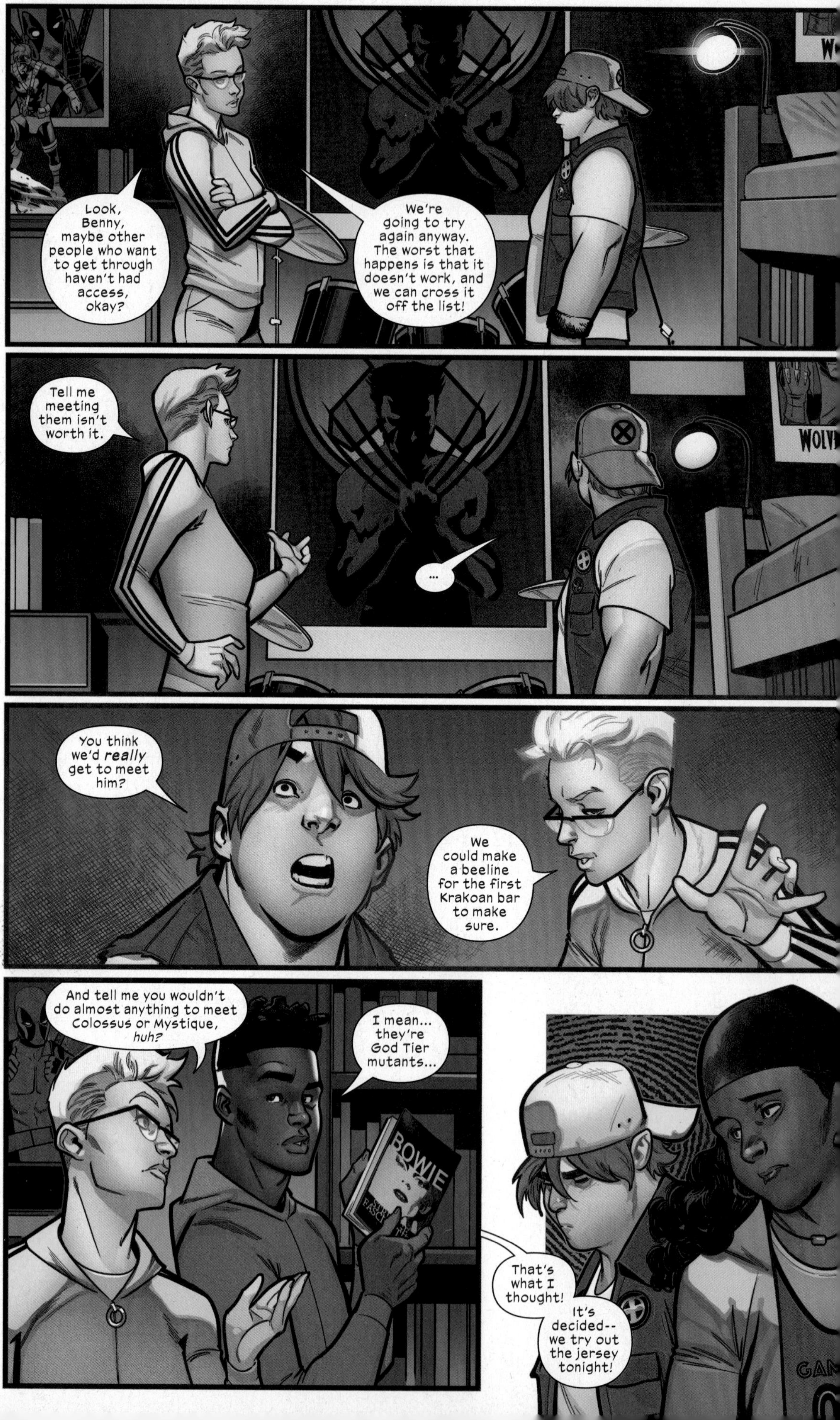
Look, Benny, maybe other people who want to get through haven't had access, okay?
We're going to try again anyway. The worst that happens is that it doesn't work, and we can cross it off the list!
Tell me meeting them isn't worth it.
...
You think we'd *really* get to meet him?
We could make a beeline for the first Krakoan bar to make sure.
And tell me you wouldn't do almost anything to meet Colossus or Mystique, *huh?*
I mean... they're God Tier mutants...
BOWIE
That's what I thought!
It's decided-- we try out the jersey tonight!

......00]
REAM..04]

Login/ Sign up

X-STREAM

Search

Newest Video | Featured Video | News | Forum | Contact Us

UNCANNY UNIVERSE/COLLECTIONS/ SIGHTINGS/THEYOUNGXMEN

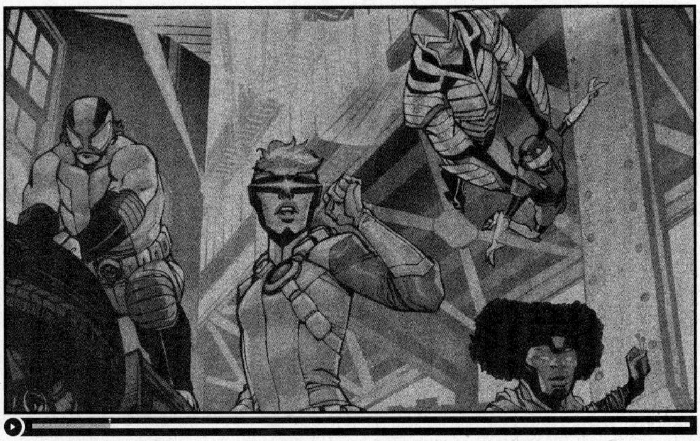

WHO are the Young X-Men?

Description:
The New Kids On The Block Caught Brawling!

A new group of mutants has been seen saving cats from trees and stopping purse-snatchings, but it looks like the wunderkind squad have upgraded to super-powered beefs with D-list villains.

Who are these baby X-Men? Drop any tips in the comments!

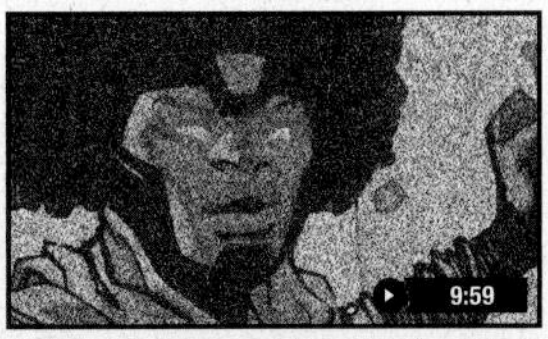
9:59

CURRENTLY PLAYING

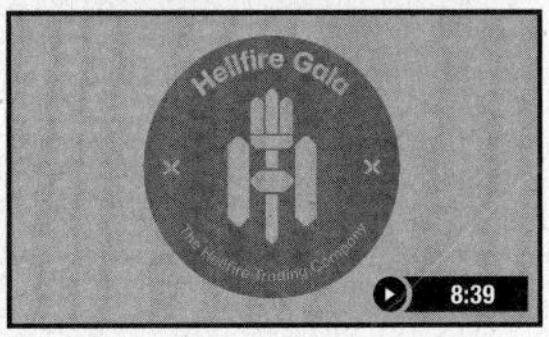
Hellfire Gala
The Hellfire Trading Company
8:39

KRAKOA OPENING ITS DOORS TO HUMANS! MOD REACTION VID

300K VIEWS
X-POSTER

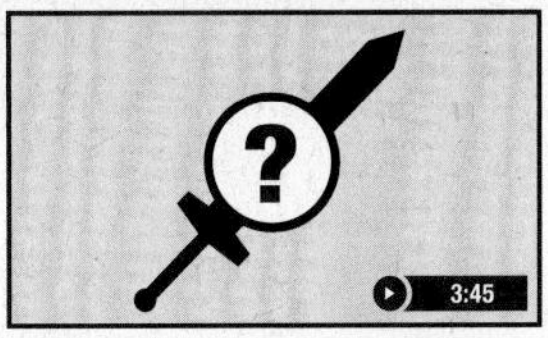
?
3:45

WHAT'S UP WITH THE X-MEN AND SWORDS?

487K VIEWS
MEDIA GAL

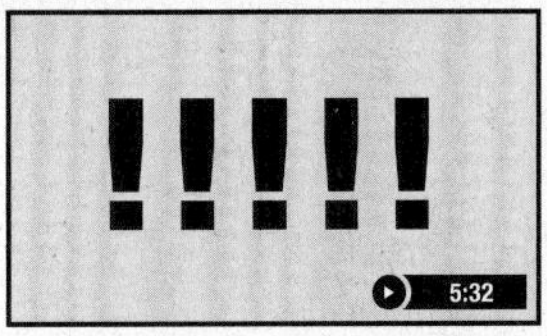
!!!!!
5:32

WHICH HEAVY-HITTING X-MEN HAVE BEEN SEEN CUDDLING IN PUBLIC? THE ANSWER MAY SHOCK YOU!

1.1M VIEWS
KRAKOA VIEWER

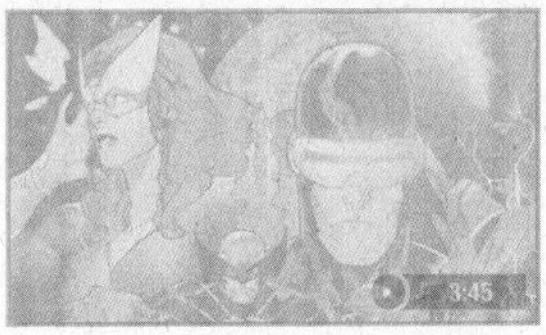
3:45

UP NEXT

1.3M VIEWS
KRAKOA VIEWER

Comments:

ArchivistX: Their code names are - Marvel Guy, Cyclops-Lass, Cherub, Daycrawler, and Gimmick!

NightyNightCrawler: It's actually NightyNightCrawler, not Daycrawler, just fyi.

GeneJunk007: Those are the dumbest names I've ever heard! (Except Cherub, that's pretty legit...)

C.R.A.D.L.E.Official: If anyone has any information as to the whereabouts of these children, please follow this link and let us know. There is a small reward offered. We just want to make sure they are safe.

[reign_of_x]

[kra_]
[koa_]

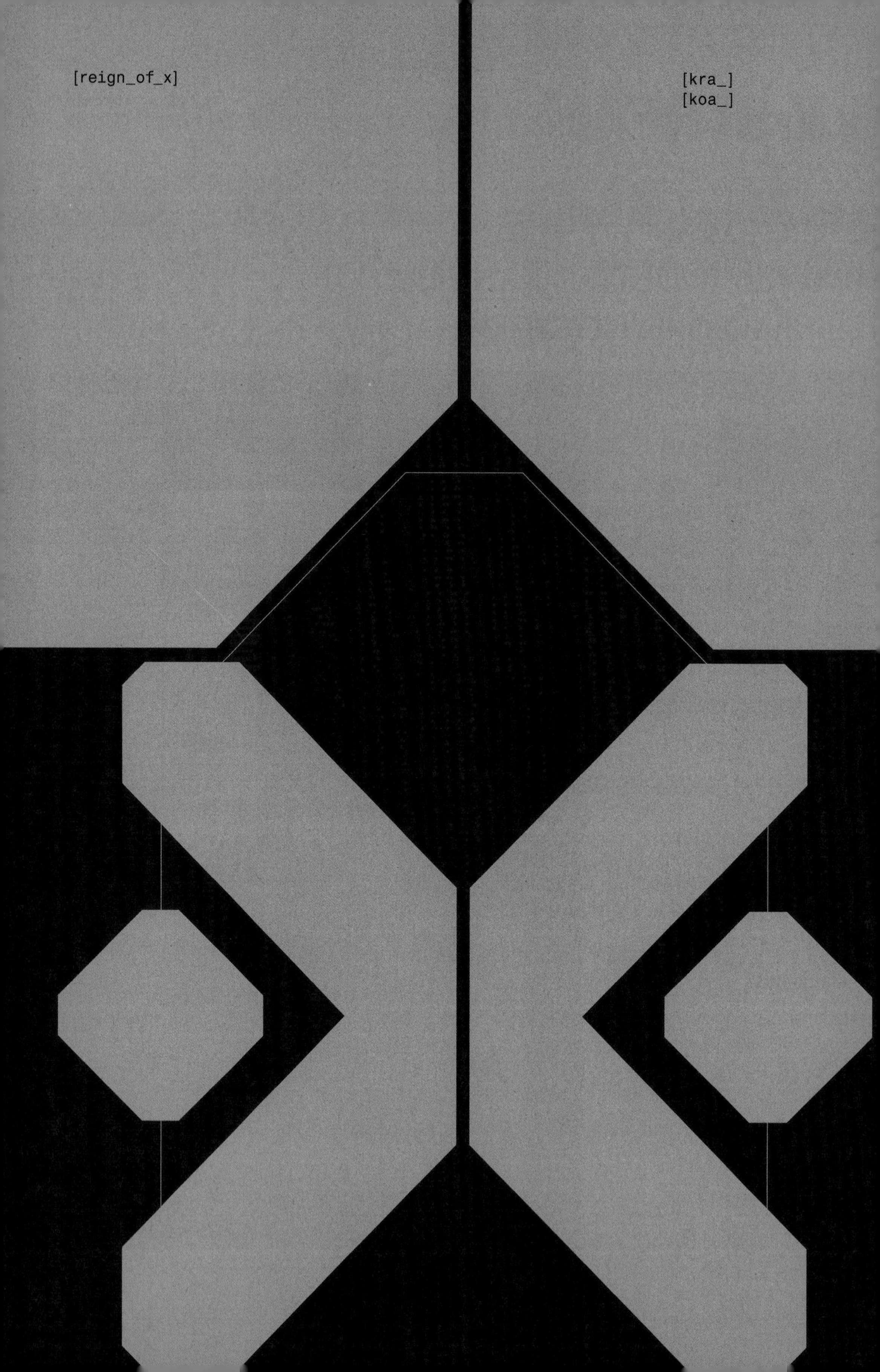

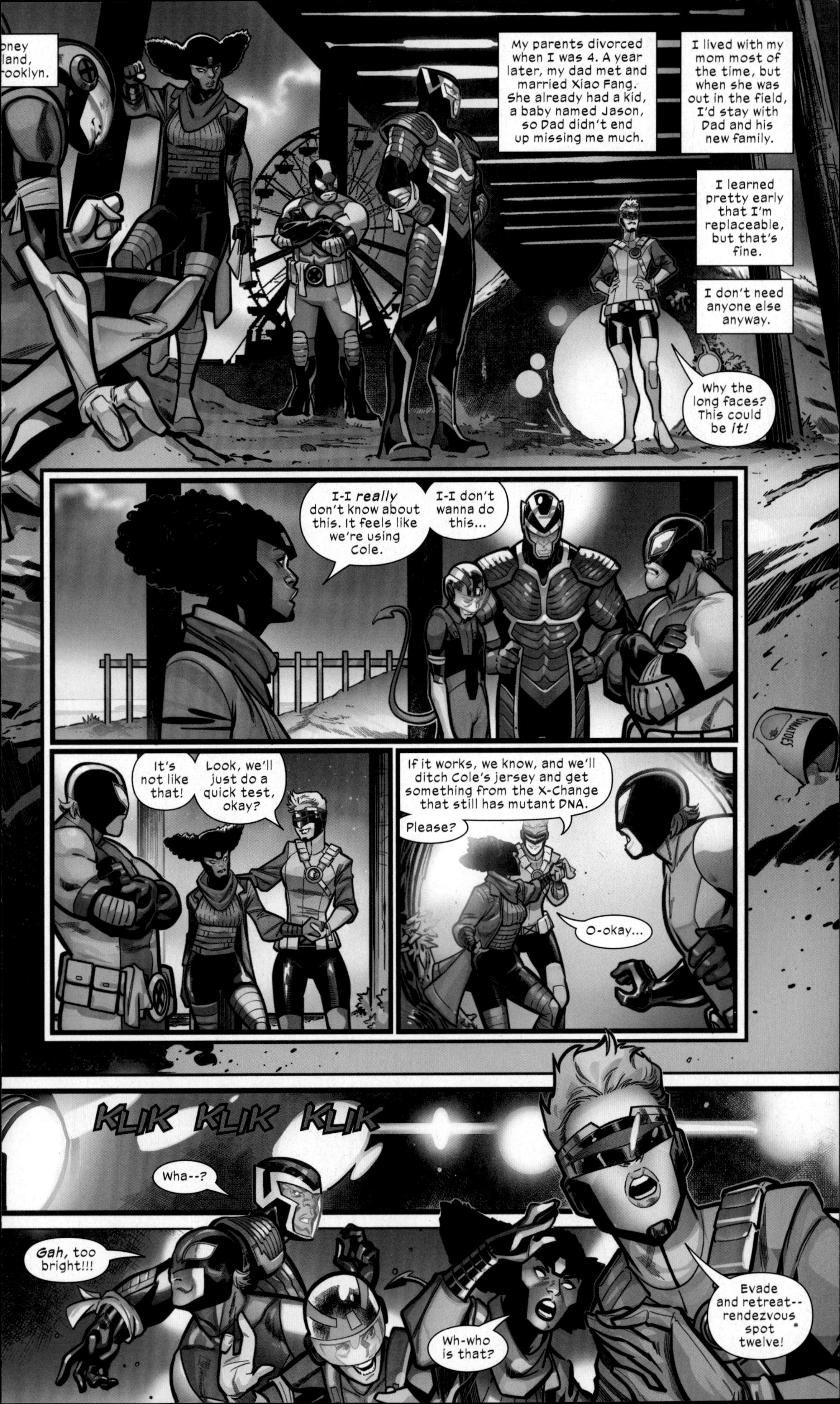

...oney
...land,
...rooklyn.
My parents divorced when I was 4. A year later, my dad met and married Xiao Fang. She already had a kid, a baby named Jason, so Dad didn't end up missing me much.
I lived with my mom most of the time, but when she was out in the field, I'd stay with Dad and his new family.
I learned pretty early that I'm replaceable, but that's fine.
I don't need anyone else anyway.
Why the long faces? This could be *it!*
I-I *really* don't know about this. It feels like we're using Cole.
I-I don't wanna do this...
It's not like that!
Look, we'll just do a quick test, okay?
If it works, we know, and we'll ditch Cole's jersey and get something from the X-Change that still has mutant DNA.
Please?
O-okay...
KLIK KLIK KLIK
Wha--?
Gah, too bright!!!
Wh-who is that?
Evade and retreat-- rendezvous spot twelve!

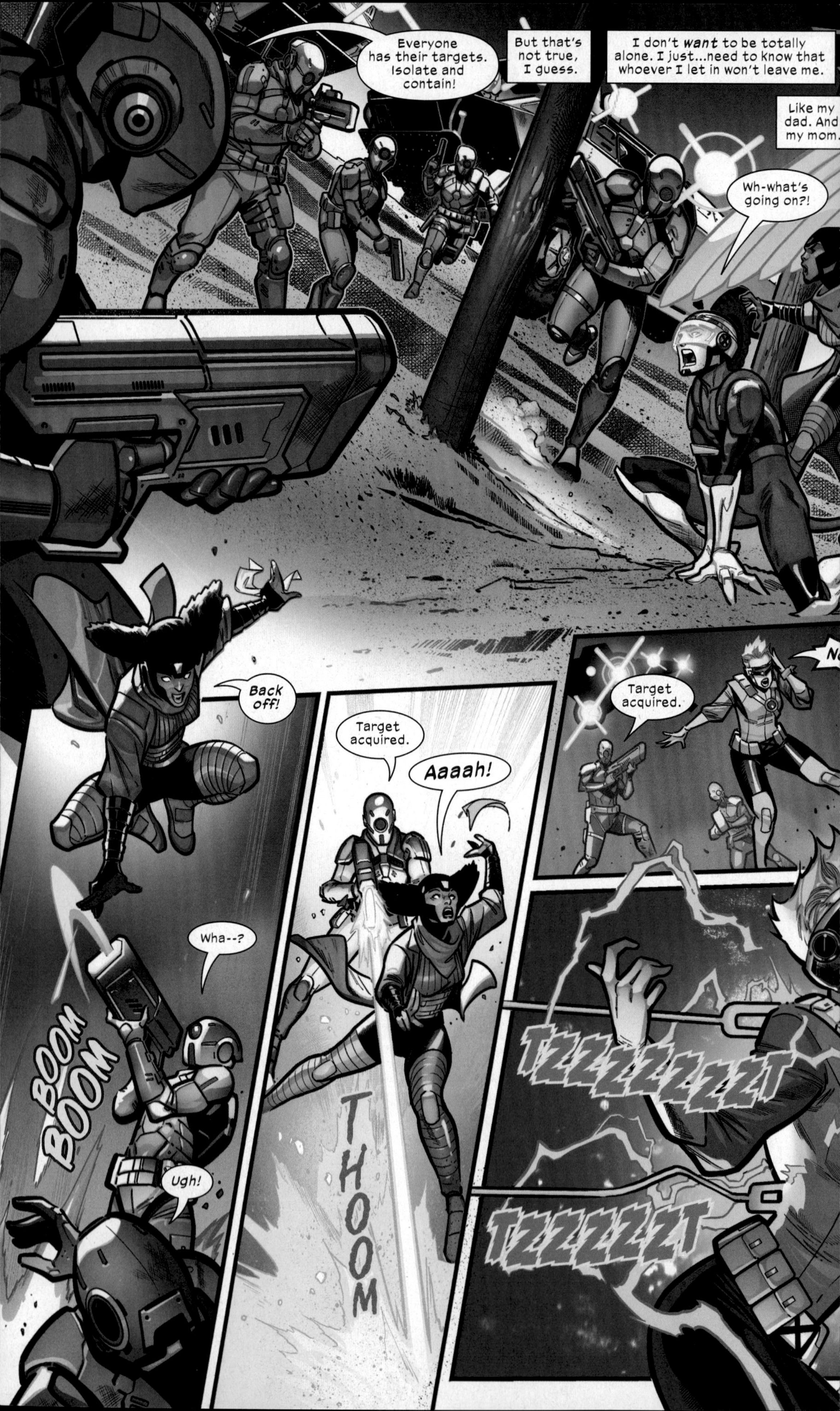
Everyone has their targets. Isolate and contain!
But that's not true, I guess.
I don't *want* to be totally alone. I just...need to know that whoever I let in won't leave me.
Like my dad. And my mom.
Wh-what's going on?!
Back off!
Target acquired.
Aaaah!
Target acquired.
Wha--?
BOOM BOOM
Ugh!
THOOM
TZZZZZZZZT
TZZZZZT

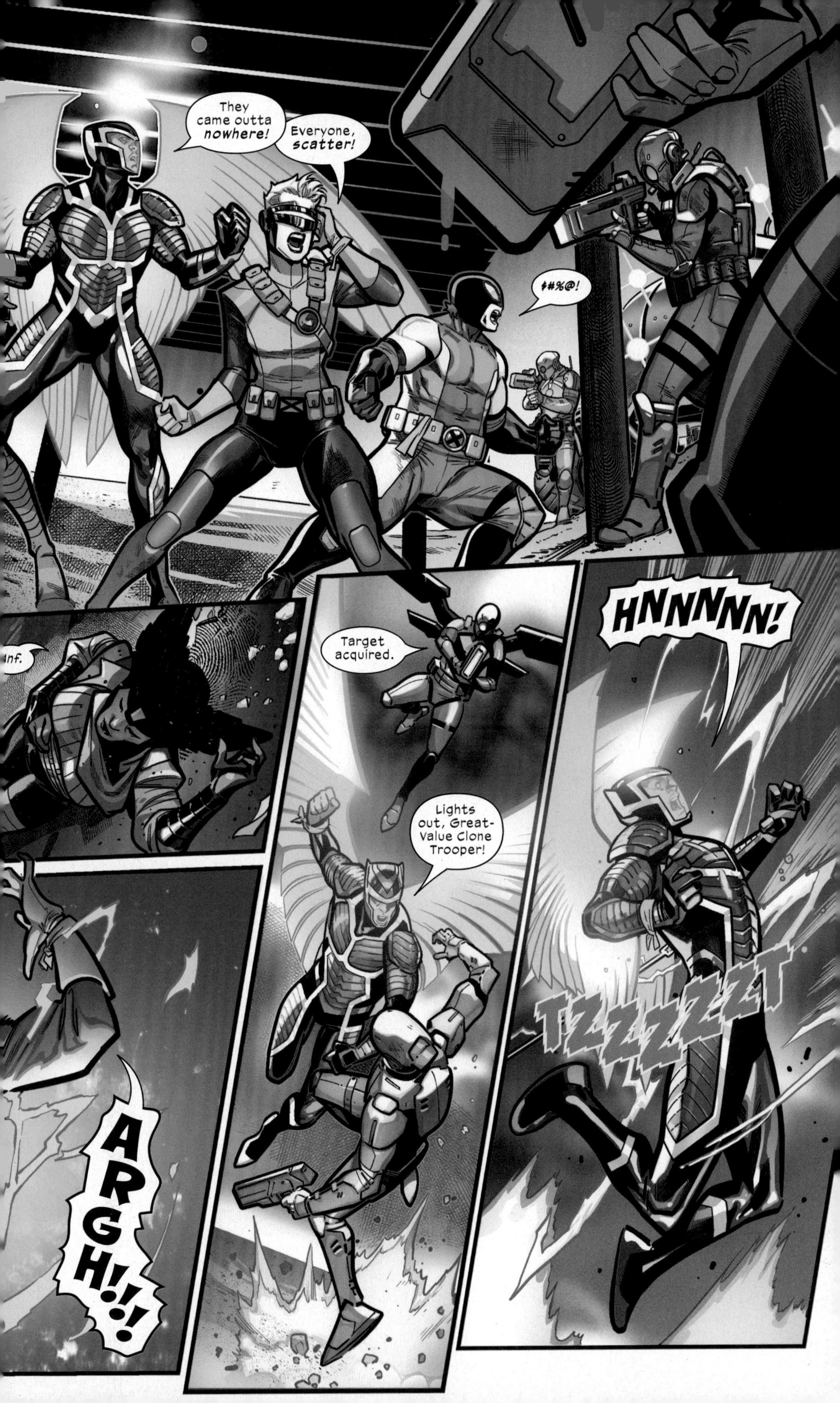
They came outta *nowhere!*
Everyone, *scatter!*
$#%@!
Target acquired.
Lights out, Great-Value Clone Trooper!
HNNNNN!
ARGH!!!
TZZZZZT

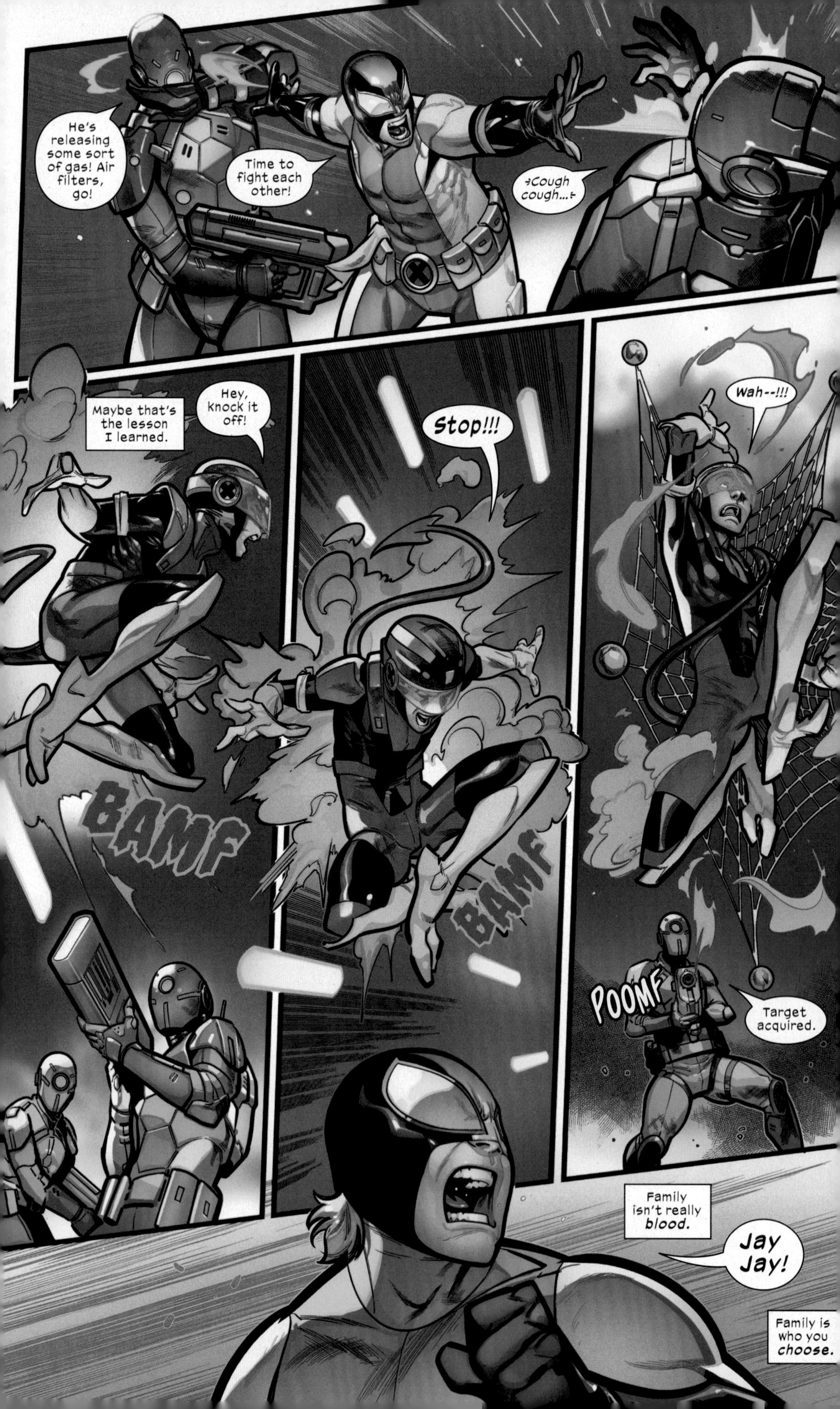
He's releasing some sort of gas! Air filters, go!
Time to fight each other!
≠Cough cough...≠
Maybe that's the lesson I learned.
Hey, knock it off!
Stop!!!
Wah--!!!
BAMF
BAMF
POOMF
Target acquired.
Family isn't really *blood*.
Jay Jay!
Family is who you *choose*.

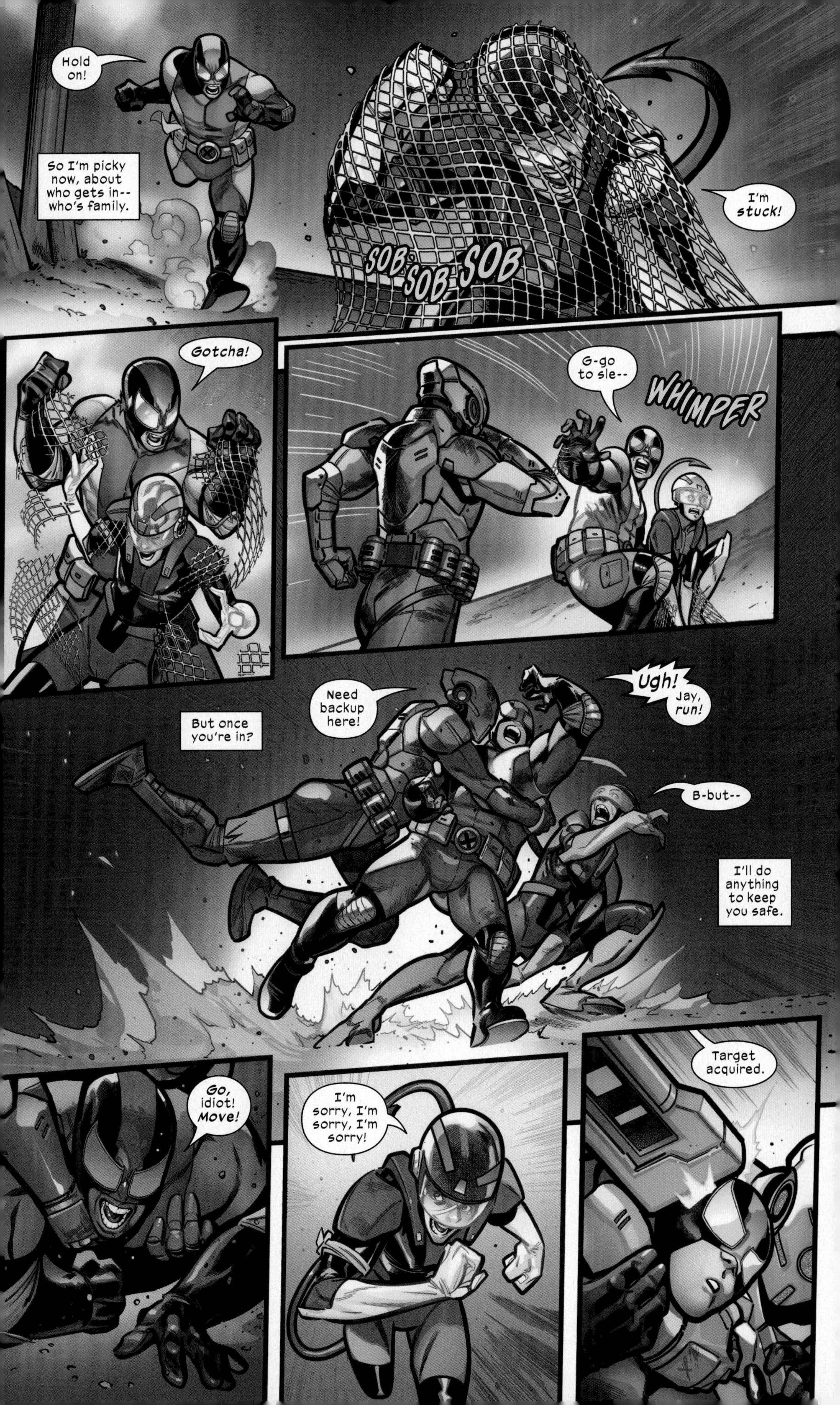
Hold on!
So I'm picky now, about who gets in-- who's family.
I'm stuck!
SOB SOB SOB
Gotcha!
G-go to sle--
WHIMPER
But once you're in?
Need backup here!
Ugh! Jay, run!
B-but--
I'll do anything to keep you safe.
Go, idiot! Move!
I'm sorry, I'm sorry, I'm sorry!
Target acquired.

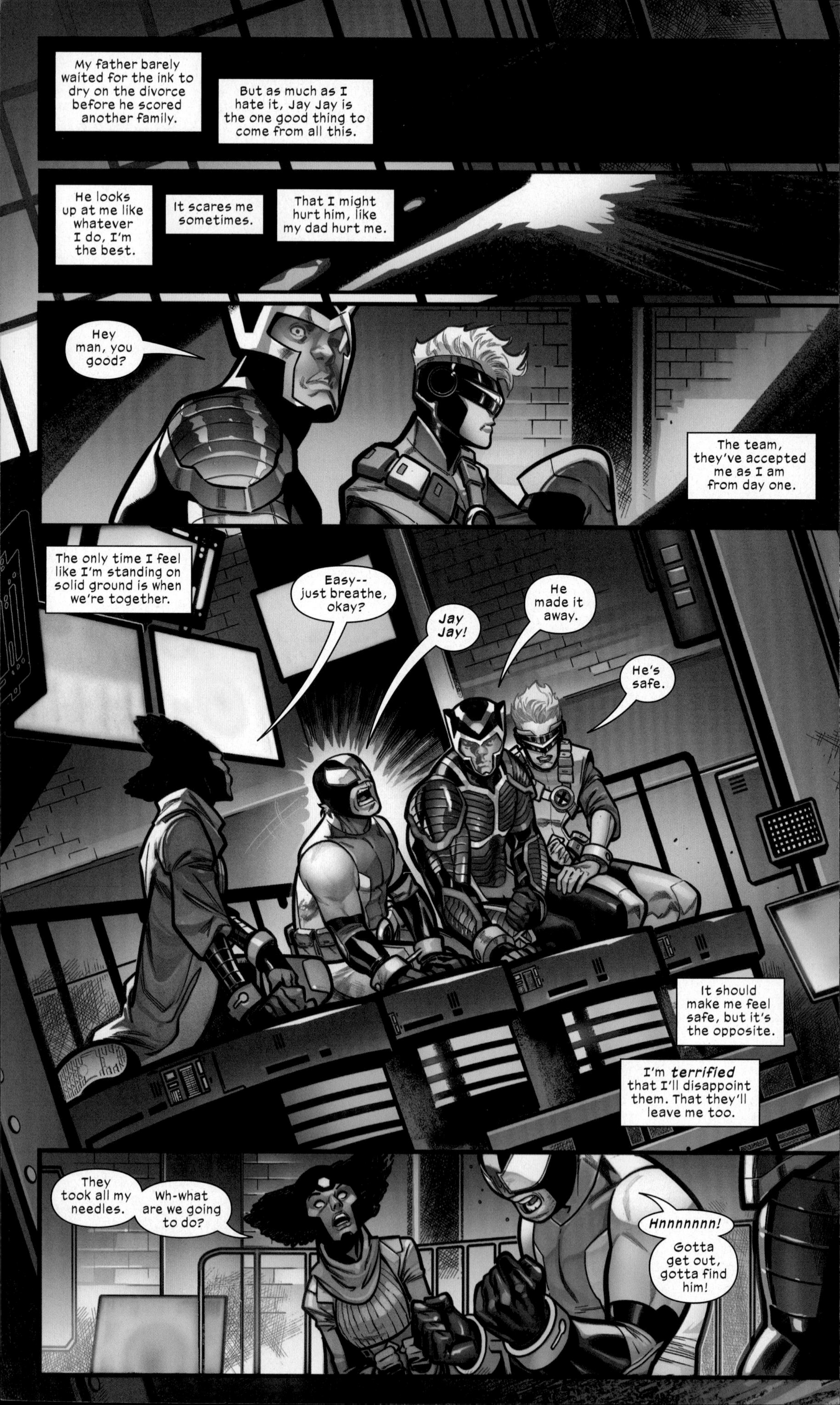

My father barely waited for the ink to dry on the divorce before he scored another family.
But as much as I hate it, Jay Jay is the one good thing to come from all this.
He looks up at me like whatever I do, I'm the best.
It scares me sometimes.
That I might hurt him, like my dad hurt me.
Hey man, you good?
The team, they've accepted me as I am from day one.
The only time I feel like I'm standing on solid ground is when we're together.
Easy-- just breathe, okay?
Jay Jay!
He made it away.
He's safe.
It should make me feel safe, but it's the opposite.
I'm *terrified* that I'll disappoint them. That they'll leave me too.
They took all my needles.
Wh-what are we going to do?
Hnnnnnnn!
Gotta get out, gotta find him!

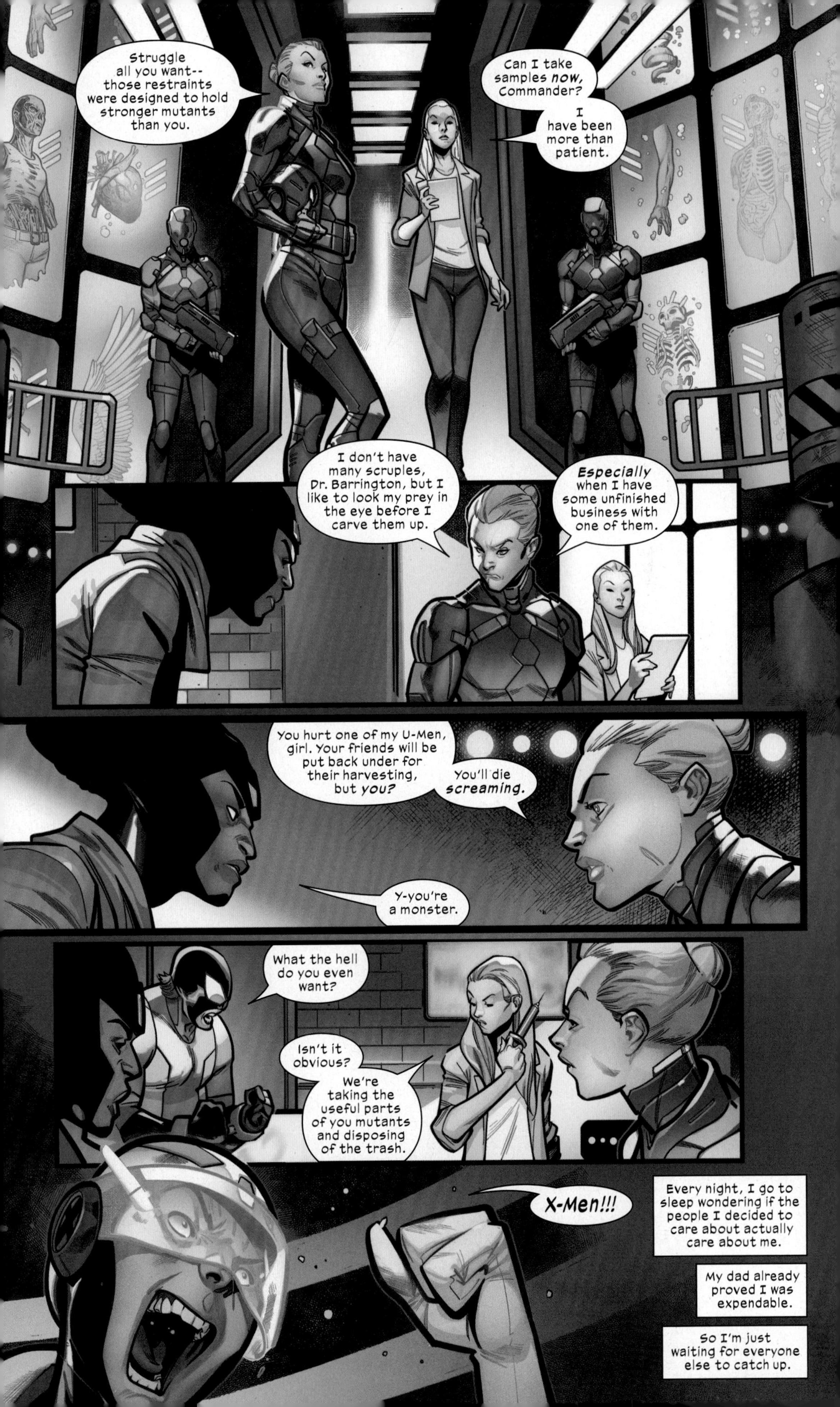

Struggle all you want-- those restraints were designed to hold stronger mutants than you.
Can I take samples *now,* Commander?
I have been more than patient.
I don't have many scruples, Dr. Barrington, but I like to look my prey in the eye before I carve them up.
Especially when I have some unfinished business with one of them.
You hurt one of my U-Men, girl. Your friends will be put back under for their harvesting, but *you?*
You'll die *screaming.*
Y-you're a monster.
What the hell do you even want?
Isn't it obvious?
We're taking the useful parts of you mutants and disposing of the trash.
X-Men!!!
Every night, I go to sleep wondering if the people I decided to care about actually care about me.
My dad already proved I was expendable.
So I'm just waiting for everyone else to catch up.

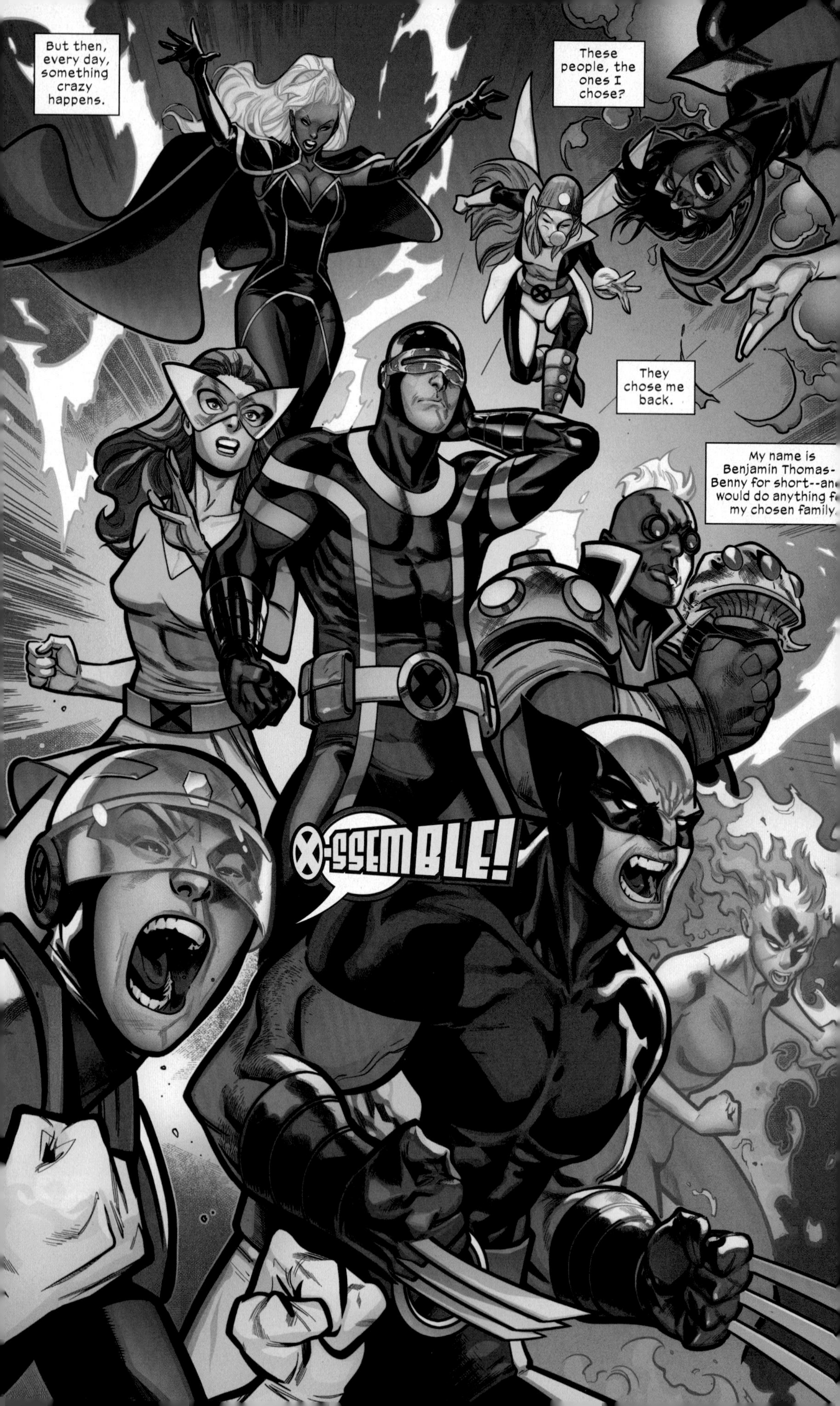
But then, every day, something crazy happens.
These people, the ones I chose?
They chose me back.
My name is Benjamin Thomas-Benny for short--and would do anything for my chosen family.
X-SSEMBLE!

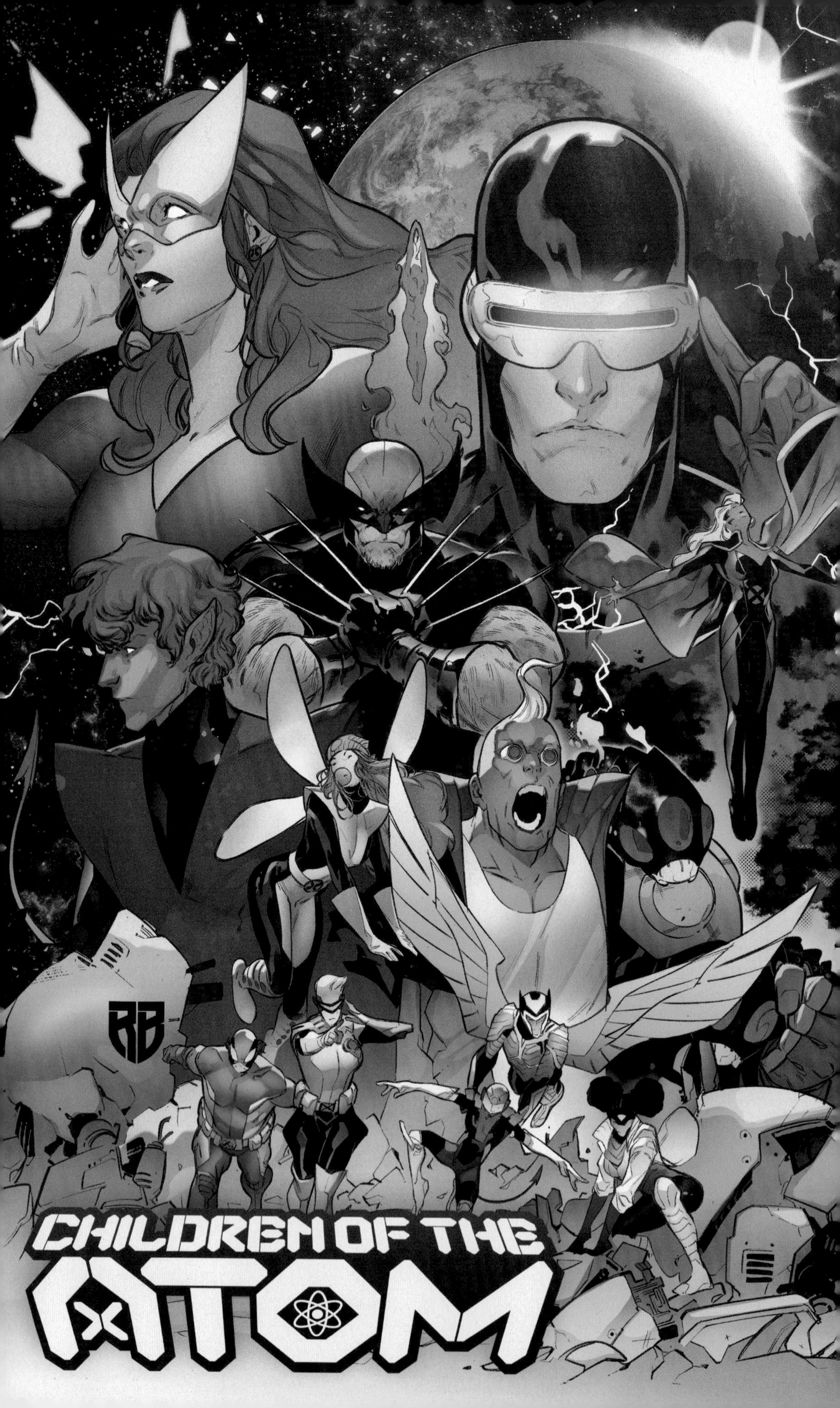
RB
CHILDREN OF THE
ATOM

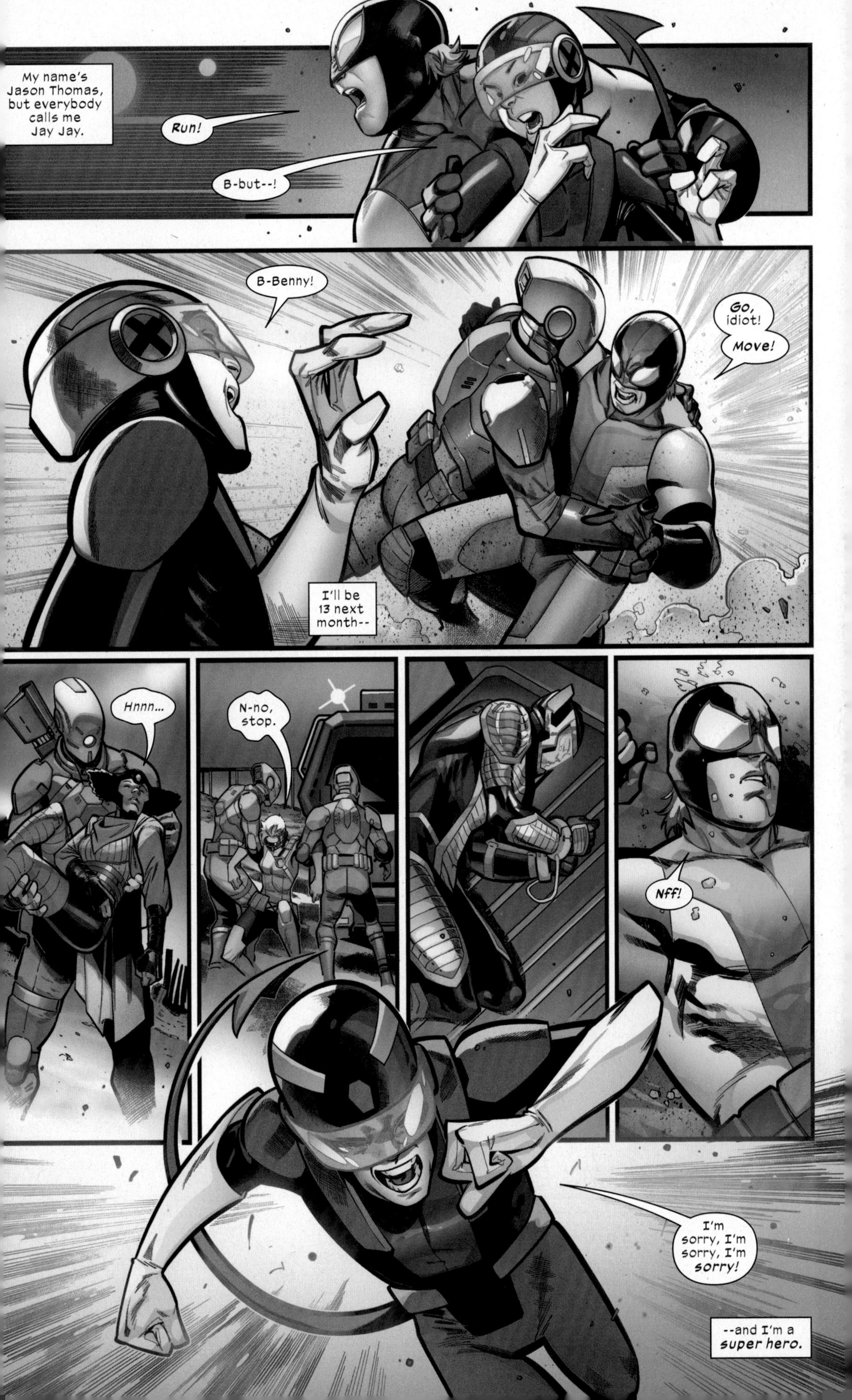
My name's Jason Thomas, but everybody calls me Jay Jay.
Run!
B-but--!
B-Benny!
Go, idiot!
Move!
I'll be 13 next month--
Hnnn...
N-no, stop.
Nff!
I'm sorry, I'm sorry, I'm sorry!
--and I'm a super hero.

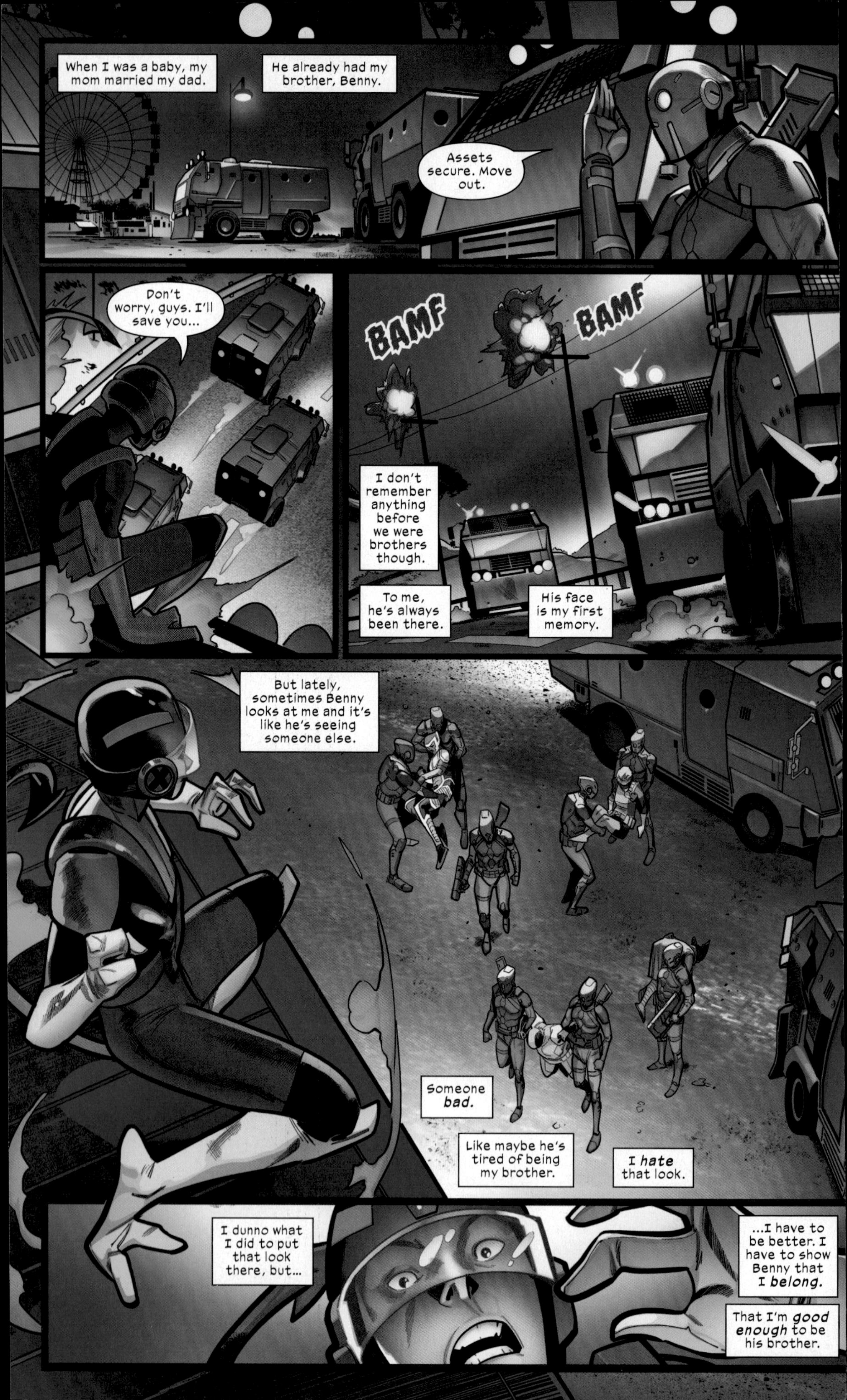

When I was a baby, my mom married my dad.
He already had my brother, Benny.
Assets secure. Move out.
Don't worry, guys. I'll save you...
BAMF
BAMF
I don't remember anything before we were brothers though.
To me, he's always been there.
His face is my first memory.
But lately, sometimes Benny looks at me and it's like he's seeing someone else.
Someone *bad.*
Like maybe he's tired of being my brother.
I *hate* that look.
I dunno what I did to put that look there, but...
...I have to be better. I have to show Benny that I *belong.*
That I'm *good enough* to be his brother.

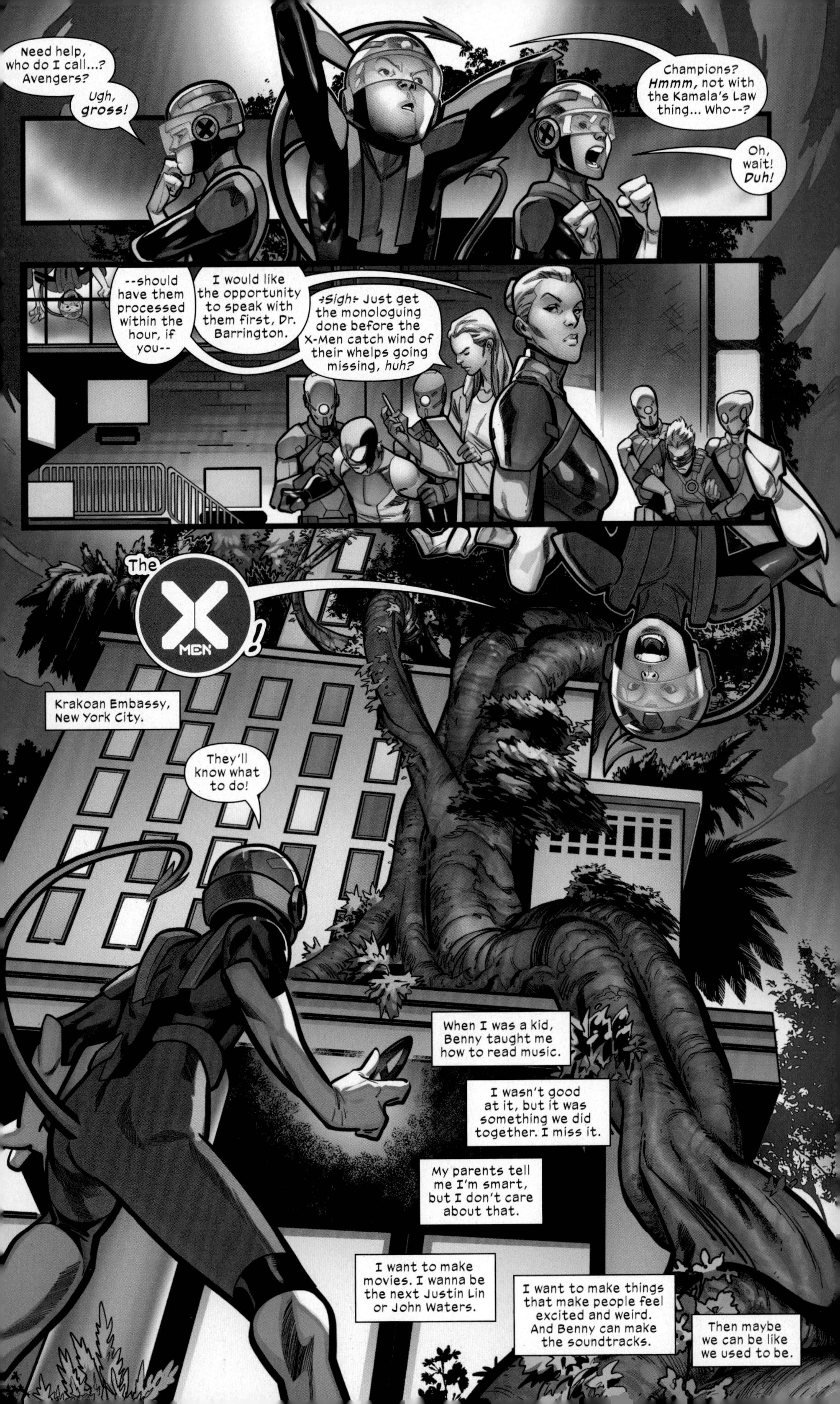
Need help, who do I call...? Avengers?
Ugh, gross!
Champions? Hmmm, not with the Kamala's Law thing... Who--?
Oh, wait! Duh!
--should have them processed within the hour, if you--
I would like the opportunity to speak with them first, Dr. Barrington.
Sigh Just get the monologuing done before the X-Men catch wind of their whelps going missing, huh?
The X-MEN!
Krakoan Embassy, New York City.
They'll know what to do!
When I was a kid, Benny taught me how to read music.
I wasn't good at it, but it was something we did together. I miss it.
My parents tell me I'm smart, but I don't care about that.
I want to make movies. I wanna be the next Justin Lin or John Waters.
I want to make things that make people feel excited and weird. And Benny can make the soundtracks.
Then maybe we can be like we used to be.

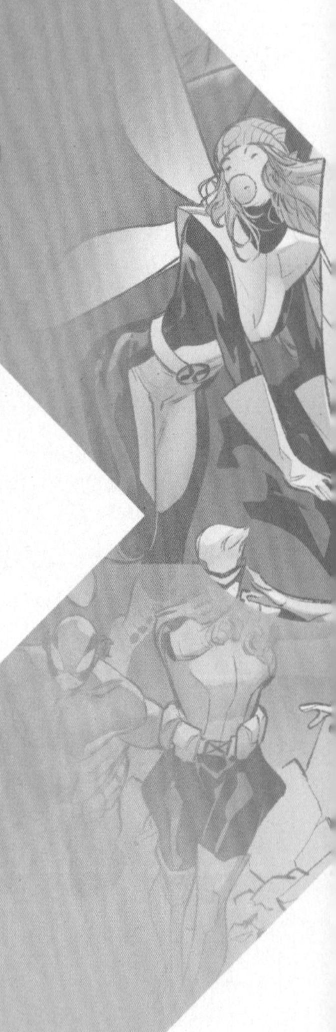

SECRETS REVEALED

Mutants around the world have flocked to the island-nation of Krakoa for safety, security and to be part of the first mutant society.

Back in New York City, new teen vigilantes CHILDREN OF THE ATOM dream of becoming mutants and joining their heroes, the X-MEN, on Krakoa. One among them has secretly started to exhibit traits of a mutant: Carmen, A.K.A. GIMMICK!

During the COTA kids' latest attempt to sneak through the Krakoan gates, Dr. Barrington and her army of U-Men seized the young heroes, mistaking them all for mutants! Only Jay Jay escaped and came back with a whole team of real deal mutants to rescue them!

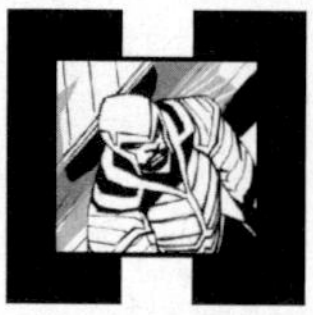

Cherub

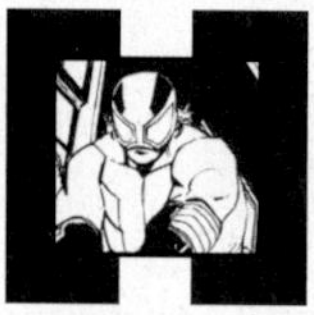

Marvel Guy

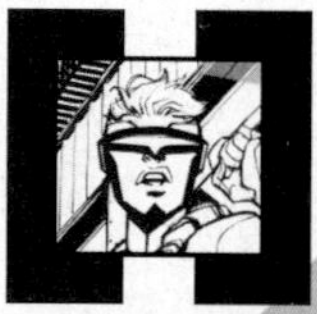

Cyclops-Lass

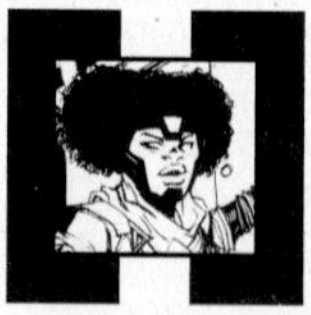

Gimmick

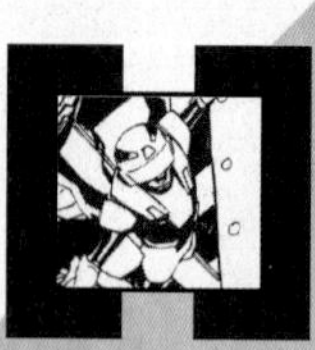

Daycrawler

CHILDREN OF THE ATOM

[X_05]

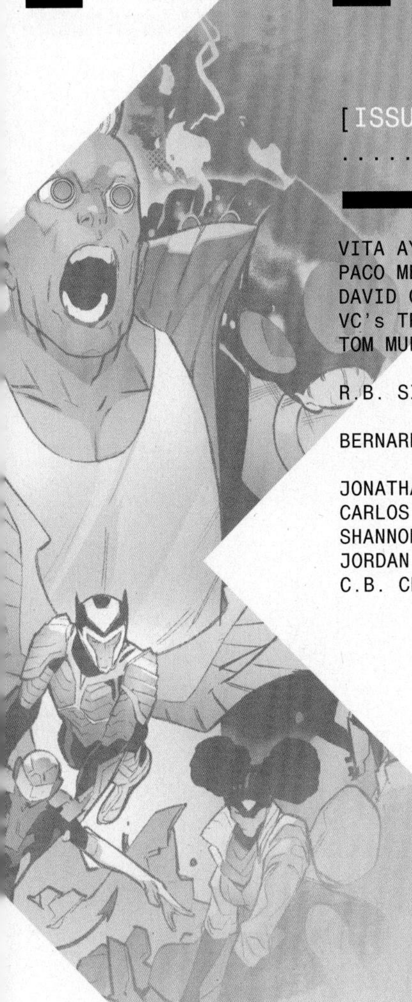

[ISSUE FIVE]..REINFORCEMENTS

VITA AYALA....................[WRITER]
PACO MEDINA....................[ARTIST]
DAVID CURIEL....................[COLOR ARTIST]
VC's TRAVIS LANHAM....................[LETTERER]
TOM MULLER....................[DESIGN]

R.B. SILVA & ERICK ARCINIEGA....................[COVER ARTISTS]

BERNARD CHANG & MARCELO MAIOLO......[VARIANT COVER ARTISTS]

JONATHAN HICKMAN....................[HEAD OF X]
CARLOS LAO....................[PRODUCTION]
SHANNON ANDREWS BALLESTEROS....................[EDITOR]
JORDAN D. WHITE....................[SENIOR EDITOR]
C.B. CEBULSKI....................[EDITOR IN CHIEF]

[00_chil__X]
[00_dren__X]

[00_00...0.]
[00_00...5.]

[00______]
[00_of____]

[00_the___]

[00__atom__]

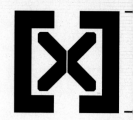

A STUDY OF THE POWERFUL GEAR
USED BY THE CHILDREN OF THE ATOM

Source: Alien technology of unknown origin

Beatrice "Buddy" Bartholomew, A.K.A. Cyclops-Lass

Heat beam/laser-cutting tech inside her visor. The kids theorize that this is welding technology.

Gabriel "Gabe" Brathwaite, A.K.A. Cherub

Flight via thrusters that look like wings, and a sonic/acoustic blast from a tool that is disguised as a hand harp. The kids theorize that this is mobility and demolition tech.

Carmen Maria Cruz, A.K.A. Gimmick

Absorption and manipulation of kinetic energy and the ability to charge objects with that energy through gauntlets/gloves -- charged objects discharge energy through controlled explosions. The kids theorize that this is some sort of excavation technology.

Benjamin "Benny" Thomas, A.K.A. Marvel Guy

Can affect living beings through pheromones via a small handheld tool incorporated into his gloves -- it appears as if it is psychic suggestion, but is closer to a chemically induced empathic suggestion. The kids theorize this tech was primarily used to clear areas of animals or maybe as a perimeter control, as it doesn't cause any lasting changes/harm.

Jason "Jay Jay" Thomas, A.K.A. Daycrawler, A.K.A. Nighty-Nightcrawler

Short-range teleportation of self and/or of other objects via a small teleportation-field generator on his belt controlled by tech in his gloves, which operates a little like folding space or creating a small wormhole. The kids theorize this tech is to aid in sample gathering. (Note: The smoke comes from a small smoke machine that Carmen rigged to go off whenever Jay Jay teleports.)

The Children of the Atom also have headgear that blocks telepathy -- they got them off the mutant paraphernalia black market. Some are pieces of old Magneto helmets that were modified and sold, others are from unknown origins. Carmen modified them and incorporated them into the costumes.

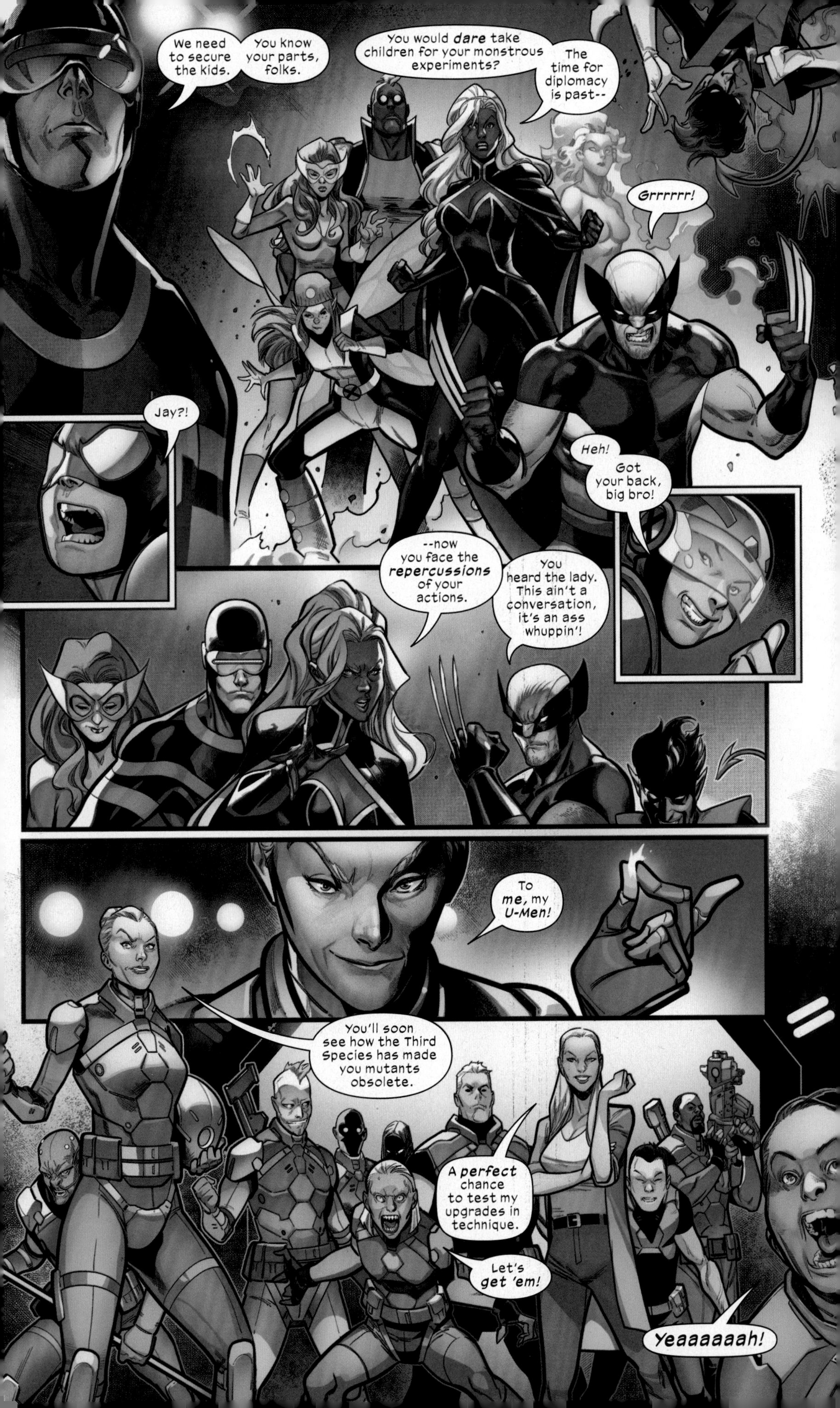
We need to secure the kids.
You know your parts, folks.
You would *dare* take children for your monstrous experiments?
The time for diplomacy is past--
Grrrrrr!
Jay?!
Heh!
Got your back, big bro!
--now you face the *repercussions* of your actions.
You heard the lady. This ain't a conversation, it's an ass whuppin'!
To *me,* my *U-Men!*
You'll soon see how the Third Species has made you mutants obsolete.
A *perfect* chance to test my upgrades in technique.
Let's *get 'em!*
Yeaaaaaah!

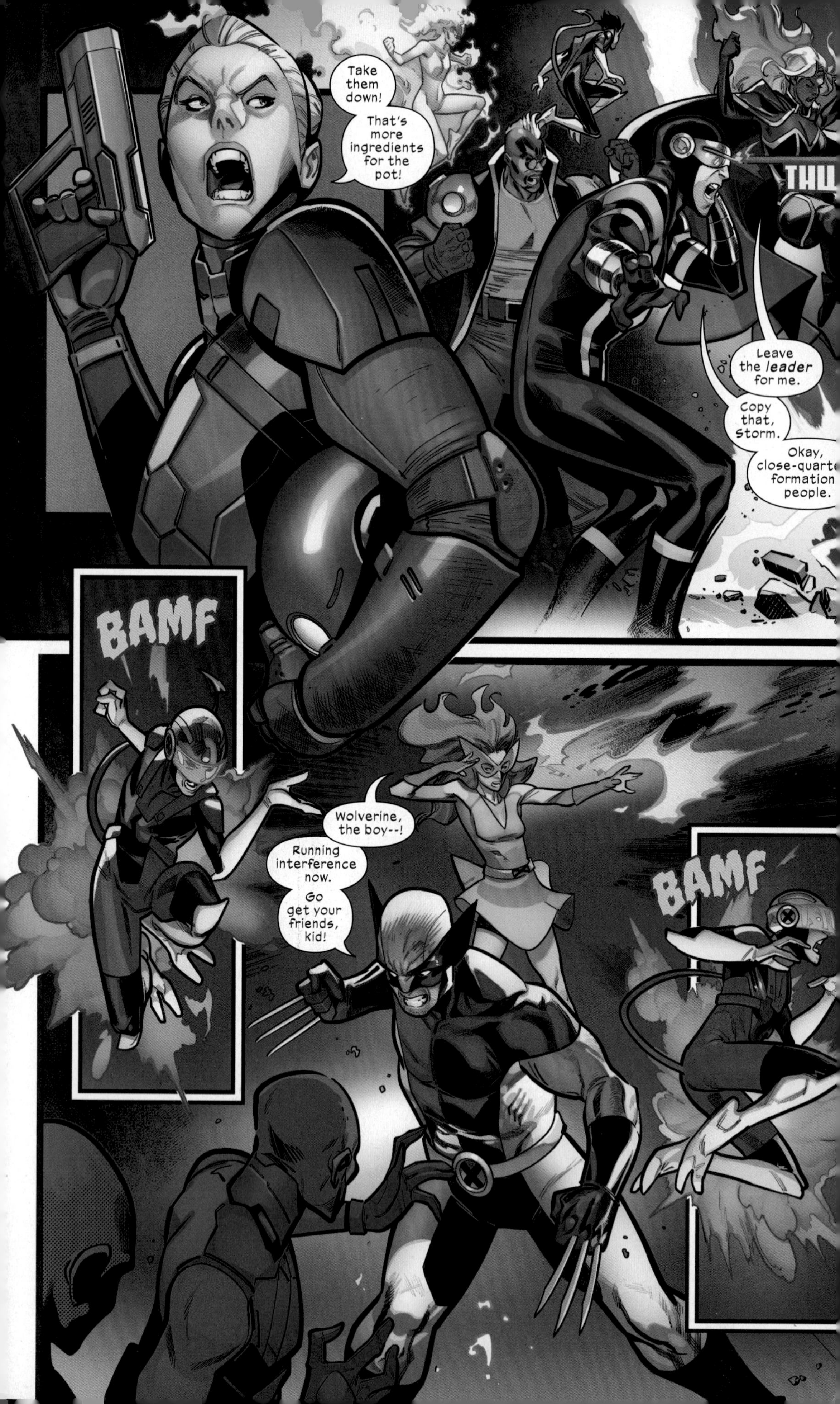

Take them down!
That's more ingredients for the pot!
THU
Leave the *leader* for me.
Copy that, Storm.
Okay, close-quarte formation people.
BAMF
Wolverine, the boy--!
Running interference now.
Go get your friends, kid!
BAMF

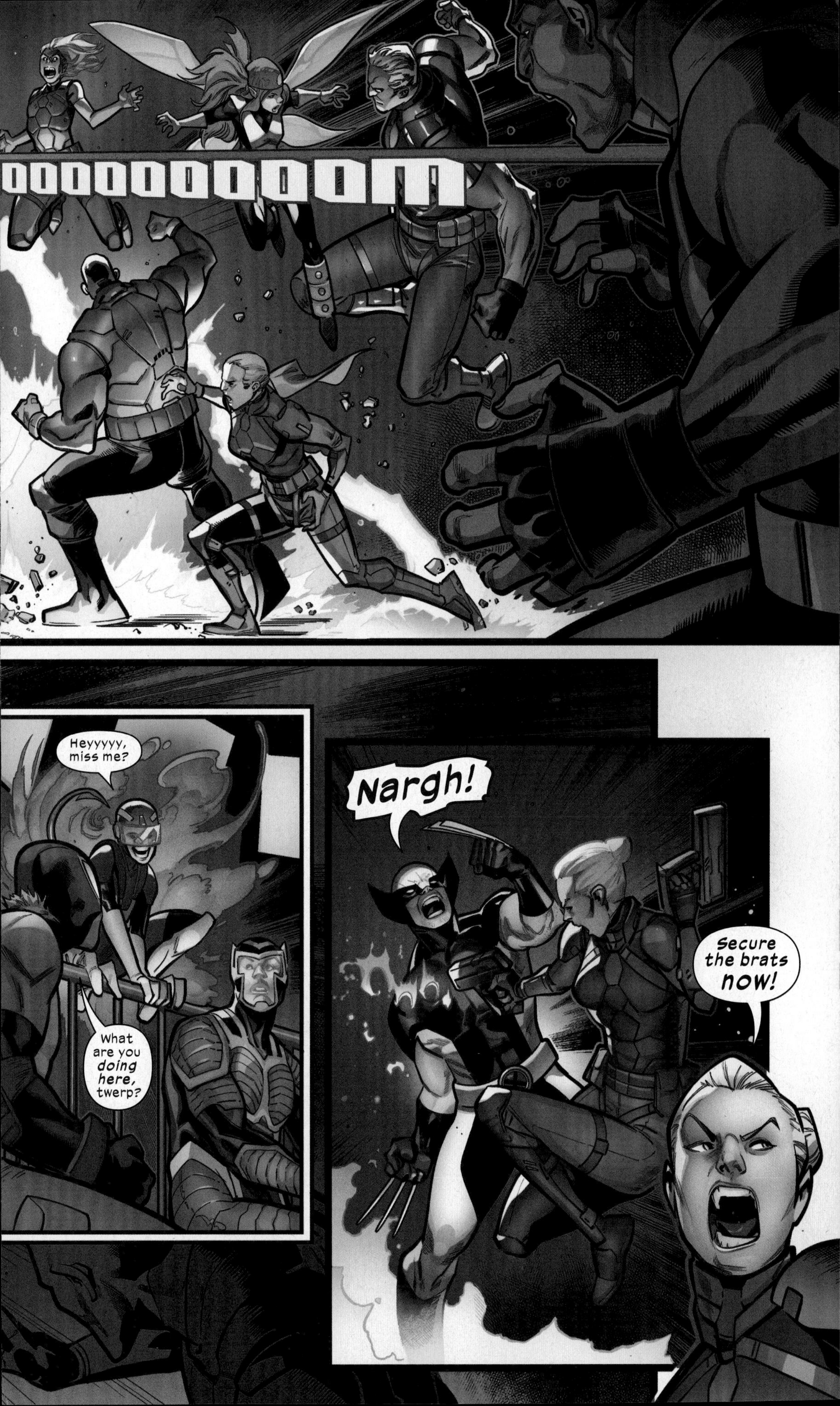
OOOOOOOOOOM
Heyyyyy, miss me?
What are you doing here, twerp?
Nargh!
Secure the brats now!

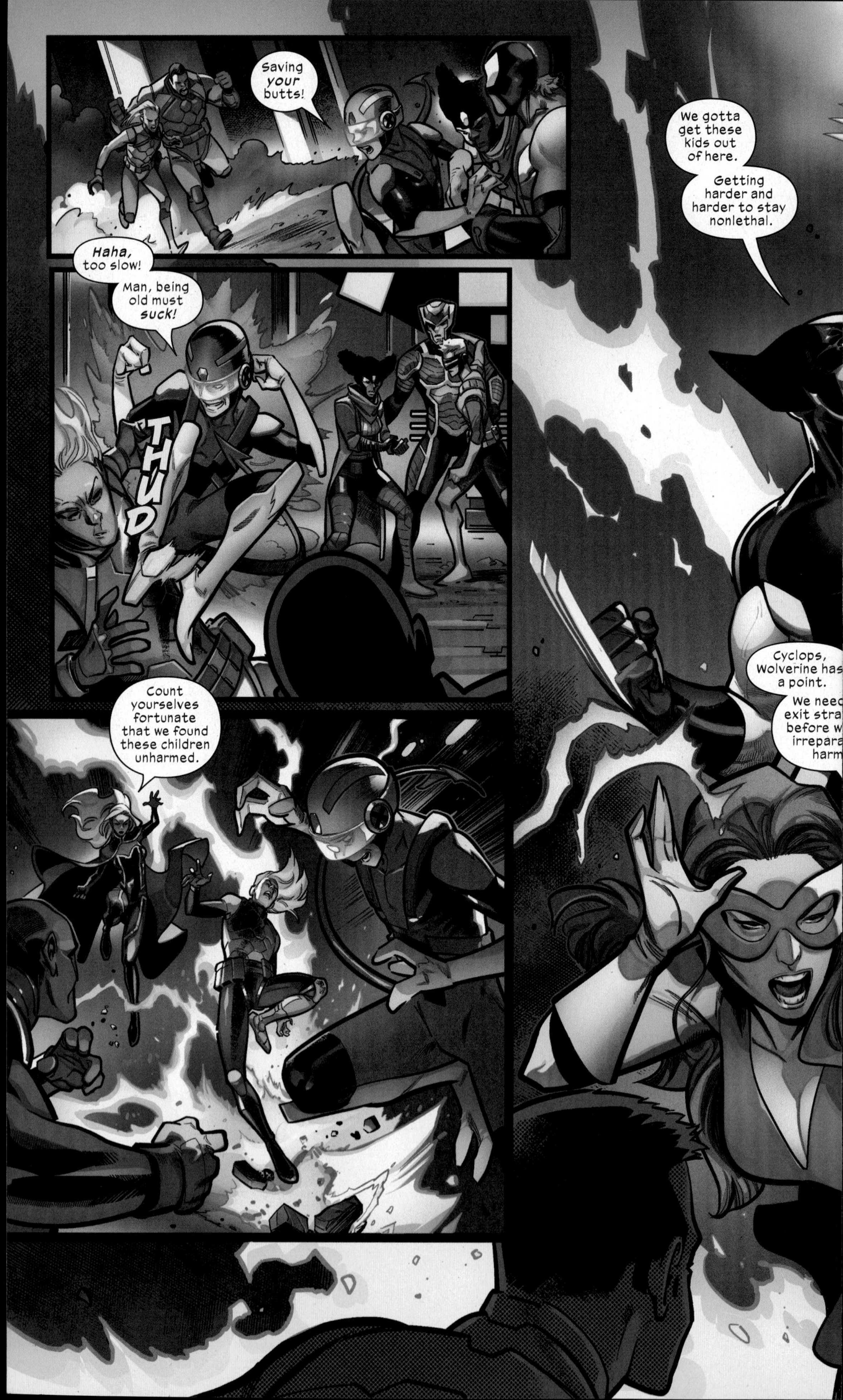

Saving *your* butts!
We gotta get these kids out of here.
Getting harder and harder to stay nonlethal.
Haha, too slow!
Man, being old must *suck!*
THUD
Count yourselves fortunate that we found these children unharmed.
Cyclops, Wolverine has a point.

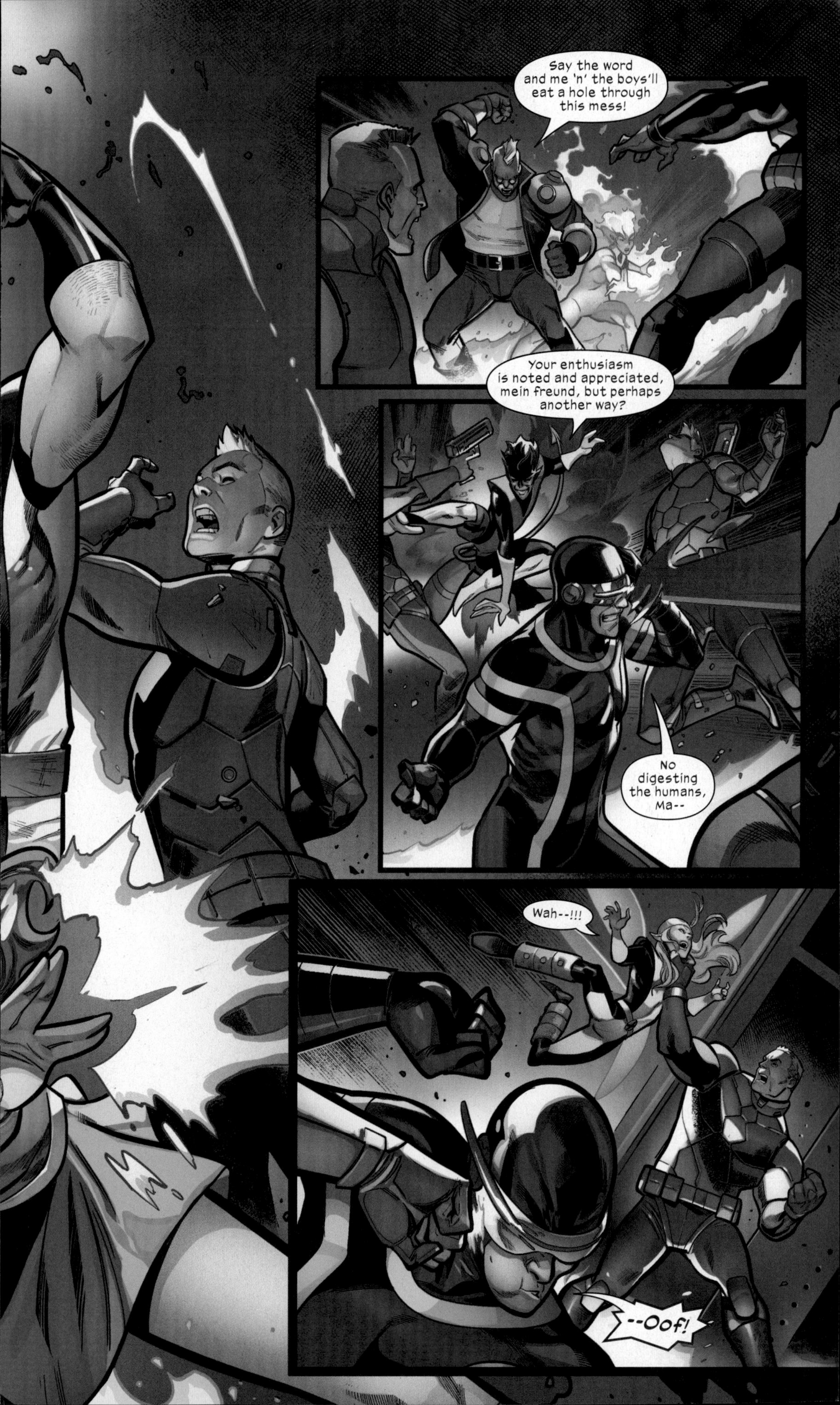
Say the word and me 'n' the boys'll eat a hole through this mess!
Your enthusiasm is noted and appreciated, mein freund, but perhaps another way?
No digesting the humans, Ma--
Wah--!!!
--Oof!

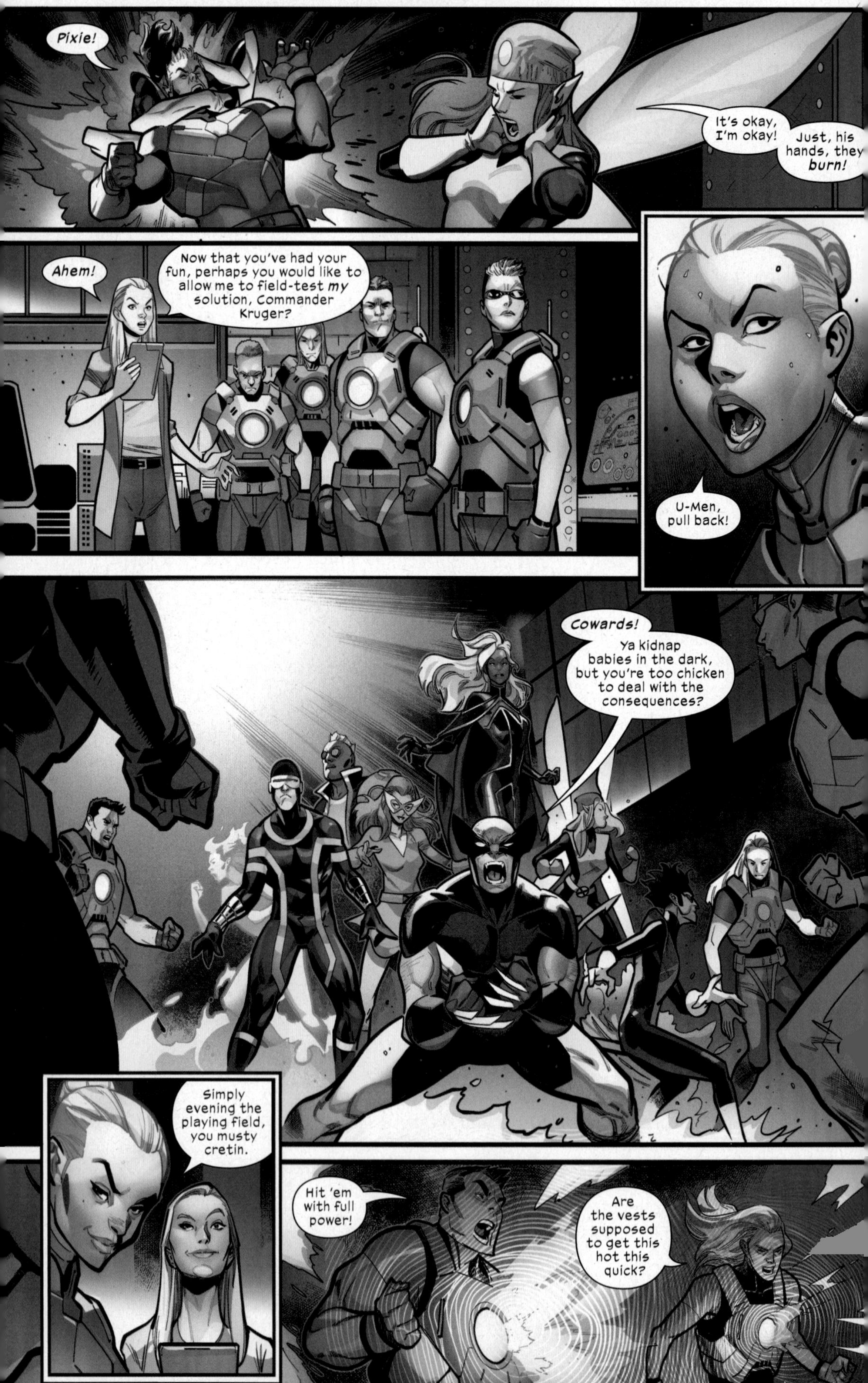

Pixie!
It's okay, I'm okay!
Just, his hands, they *burn!*
Ahem!
Now that you've had your fun, perhaps you would like to allow me to field-test *my* solution, Commander Kruger?
U-Men, pull back!
Cowards!
Ya kidnap babies in the dark, but you're too chicken to deal with the consequences?
Simply evening the playing field, you musty cretin.
Hit 'em with full power!
Are the vests supposed to get this hot this quick?

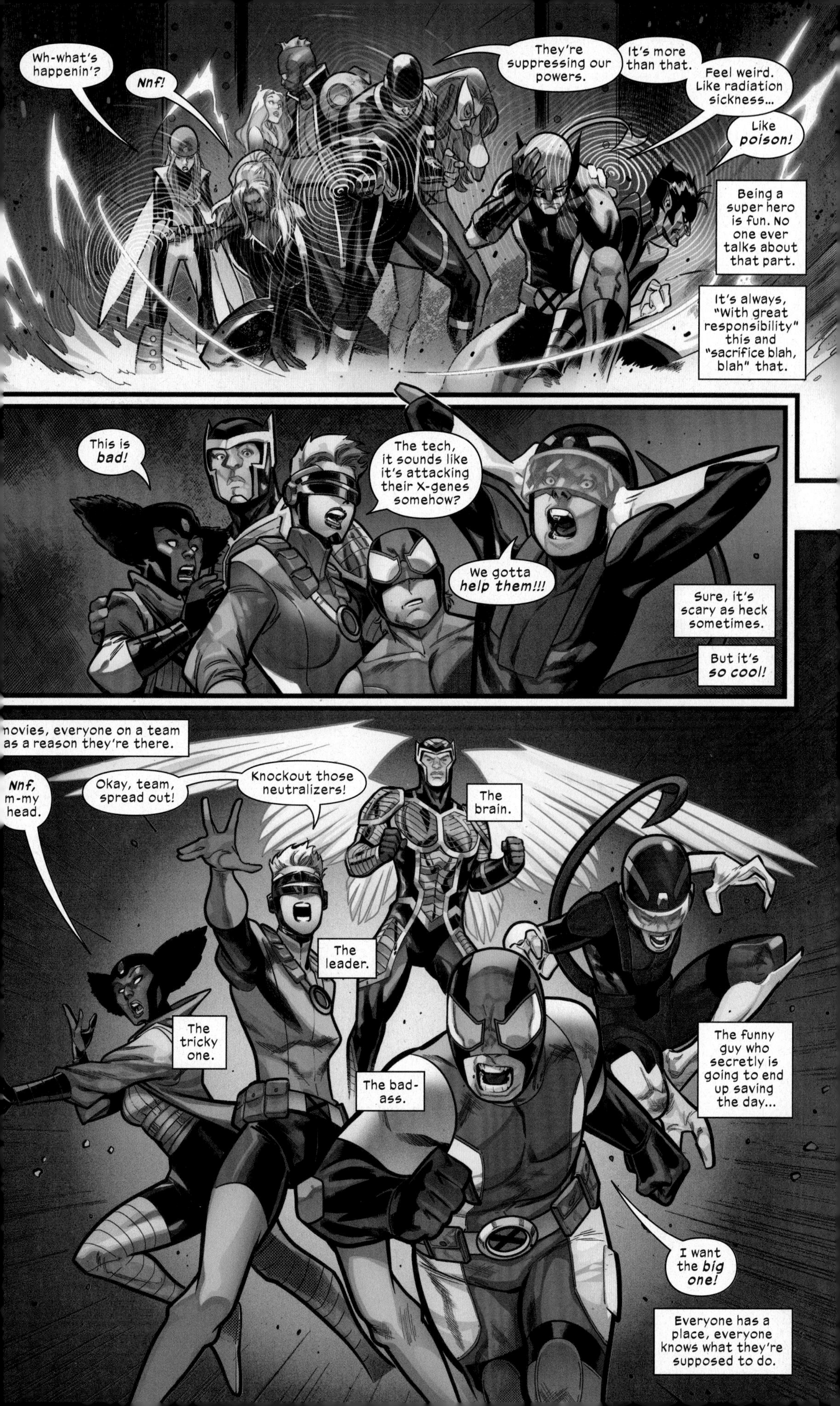

Wh-what's happenin'?
Nnf!
They're suppressing our powers.
It's more than that.
Feel weird. Like radiation sickness...
Like poison!
Being a super hero is fun. No one ever talks about that part.
It's always, "With great responsibility" this and "sacrifice blah, blah" that.
This is bad!
The tech, it sounds like it's attacking their X-genes somehow?
We gotta help them!!!
Sure, it's scary as heck sometimes.
But it's so cool!
movies, everyone on a team as a reason they're there.
Nnf, m-my head.
Okay, team, spread out!
Knockout those neutralizers!
The brain.
The leader.
The tricky one.
The bad-ass.
The funny guy who secretly is going to end up saving the day...
I want the big one!
Everyone has a place, everyone knows what they're supposed to do.

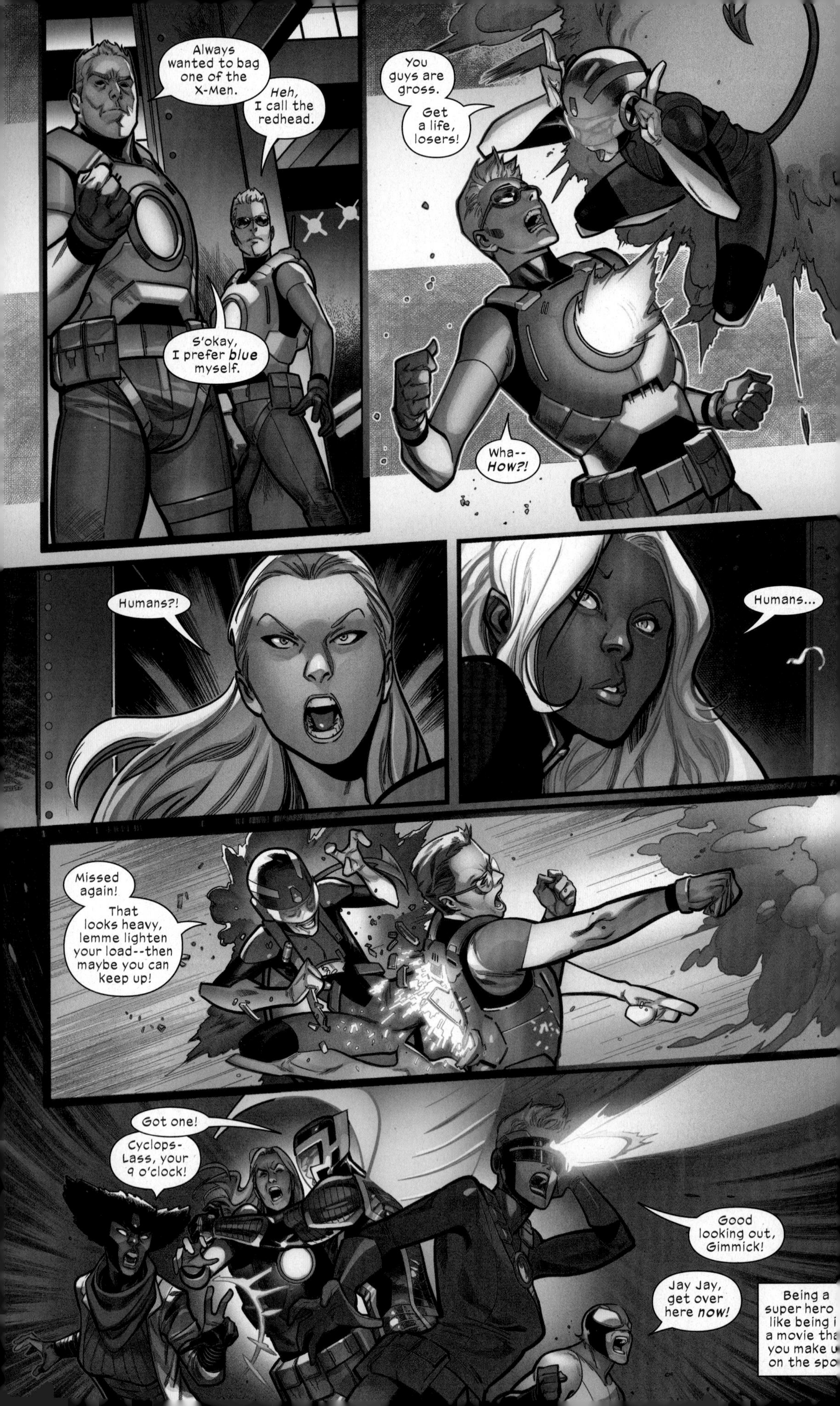
Always wanted to bag one of the X-Men.
Heh, I call the redhead.
S'okay, I prefer *blue* myself.
You guys are gross.
Get a life, losers!
Wha-- *How?!*
Humans?!
Humans...
Missed again!
That looks heavy, lemme lighten your load--then maybe you can keep up!
Got one!
Cyclops-Lass, your 9 o'clock!
Good looking out, Gimmick!
Jay Jay, get over here *now!*

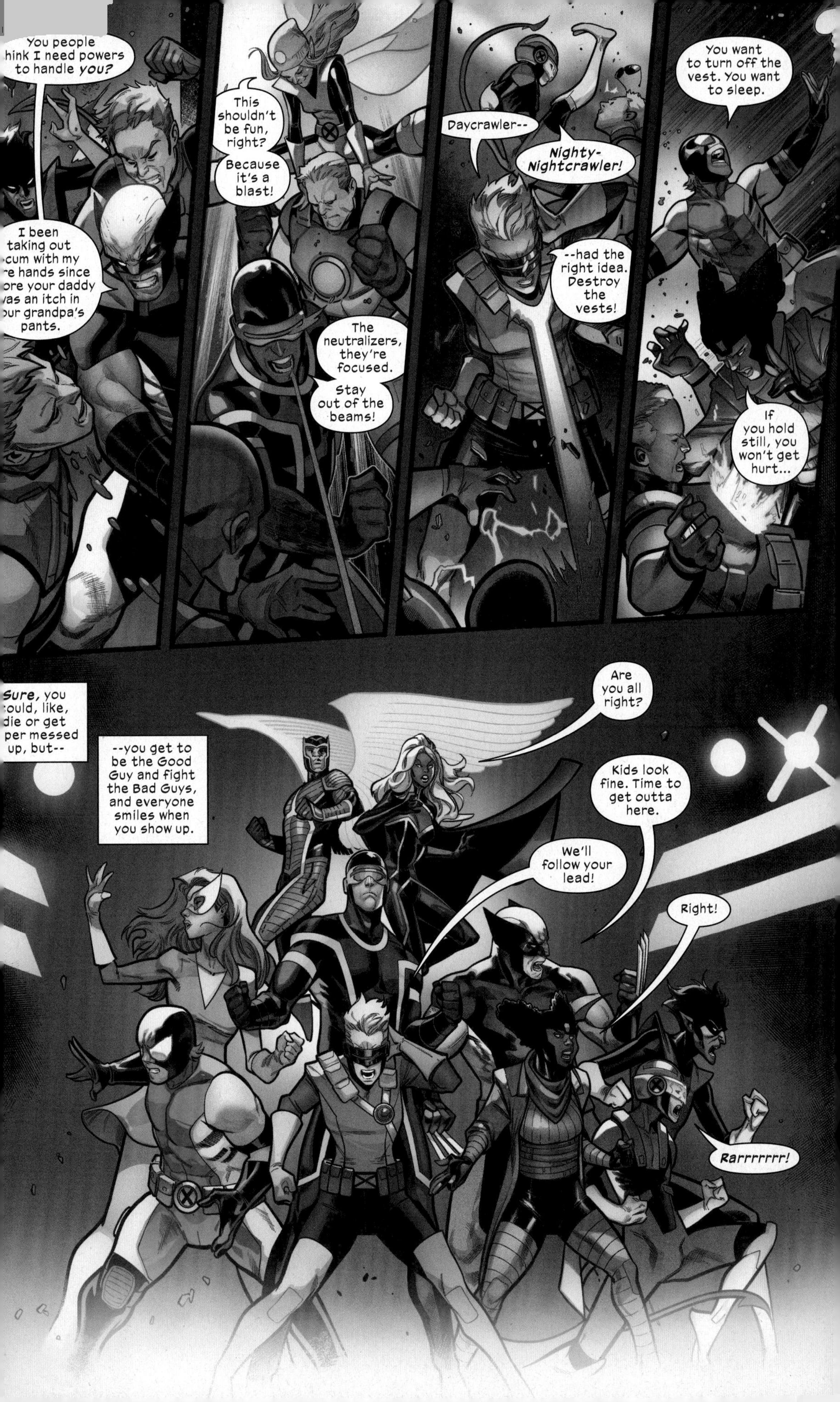

You people
hink I need powers to handle *you?*
I been taking out
cum with my
e hands since
ore your daddy
as an itch in
ur grandpa's pants.
This shouldn't be fun, right?
Because it's a blast!
The neutralizers, they're focused.
Stay out of the beams!
Daycrawler--
Nighty-Nightcrawler!
--had the right idea. Destroy the vests!
You want to turn off the vest. You want to sleep.
If you hold still, you won't get hurt...
Sure, you
ould, like,
die or get
per messed
up, but--
--you get to be the Good Guy and fight the Bad Guys, and everyone smiles when you show up.
Are you all right?
Kids look fine. Time to get outta here.
We'll follow your lead!
Right!
Rarrrrrrr!

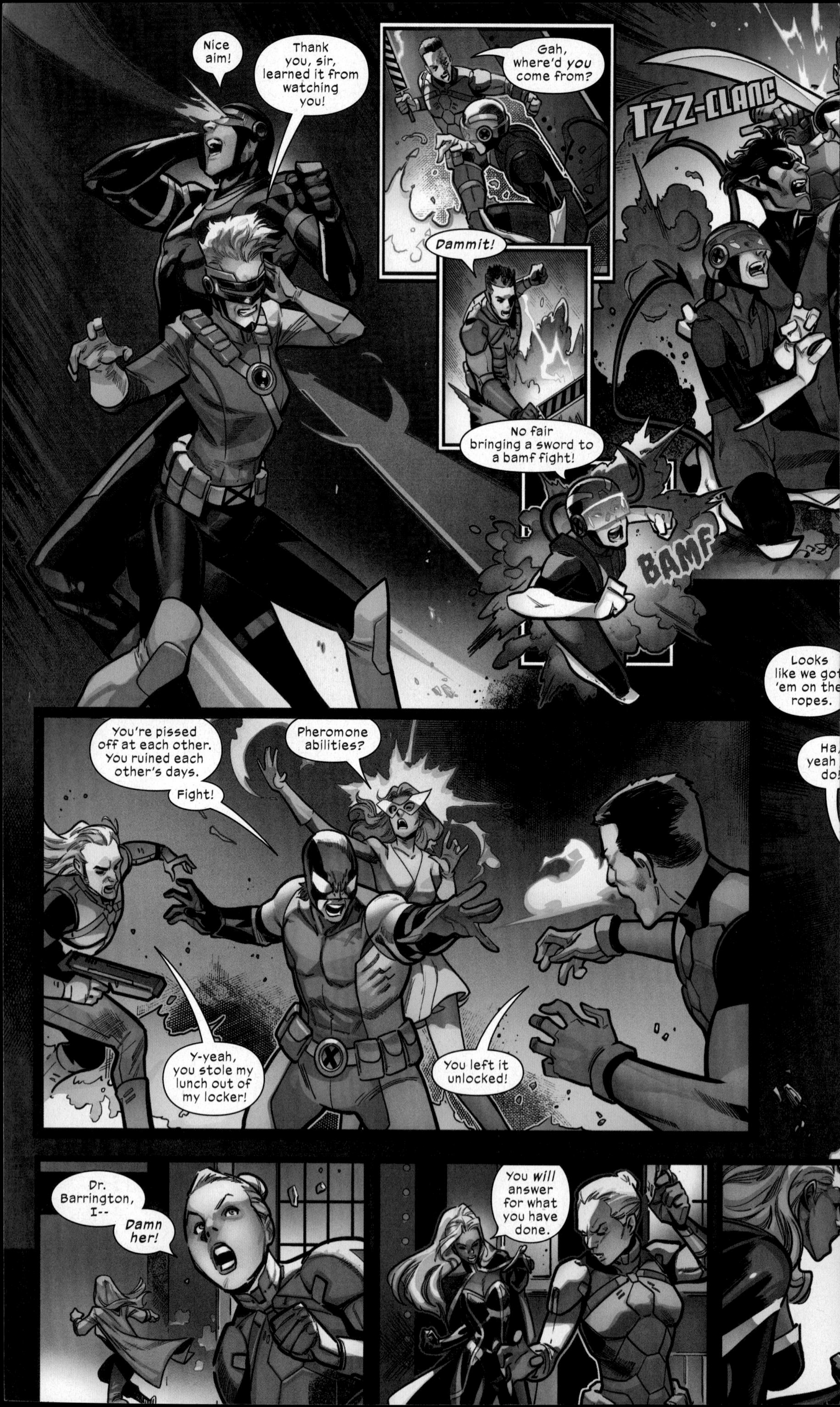
Nice aim!
Thank you, sir, learned it from watching you!
Gah, where'd you come from?
TZZ-CLANC
Dammit!
No fair bringing a sword to a bamf fight!
BAMF
Looks like we got 'em on the ropes.
Ha, yeah do!
You're pissed off at each other. You ruined each other's days.
Fight!
Pheromone abilities?
Y-yeah, you stole my lunch out of my locker!
You left it unlocked!
Dr. Barrington, I--
Damn her!
You will answer for what you have done.

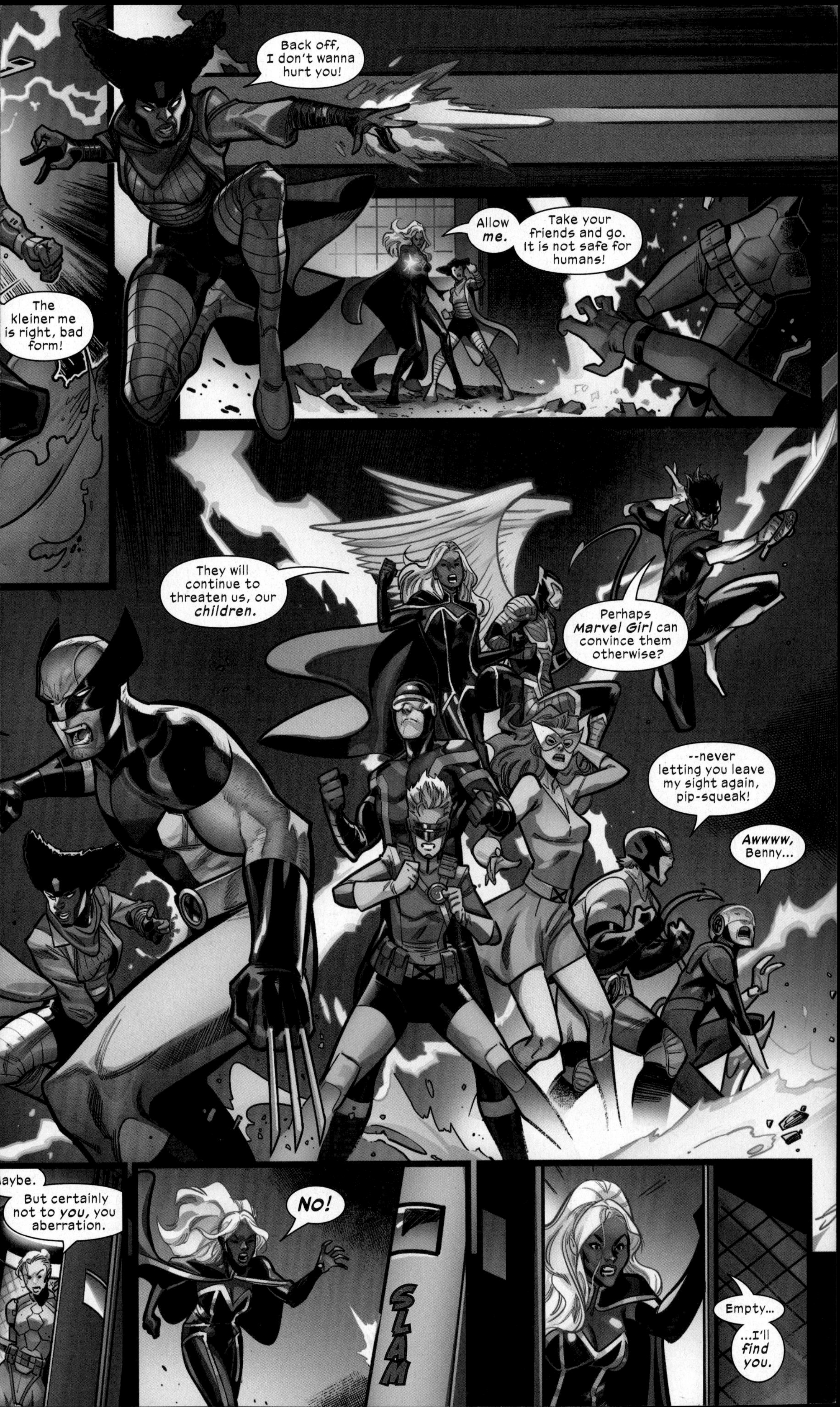
Back off, I don't wanna hurt you!
The kleiner me is right, bad form!
Allow me.
Take your friends and go. It is not safe for humans!
They will continue to threaten us, our children.
Perhaps Marvel Girl can convince them otherwise?
--never letting you leave my sight again, pip-squeak!
Awwww, Benny...
aybe.
But certainly not to you, you aberration.
NO!
SLAM
Empty...
...I'll find you.

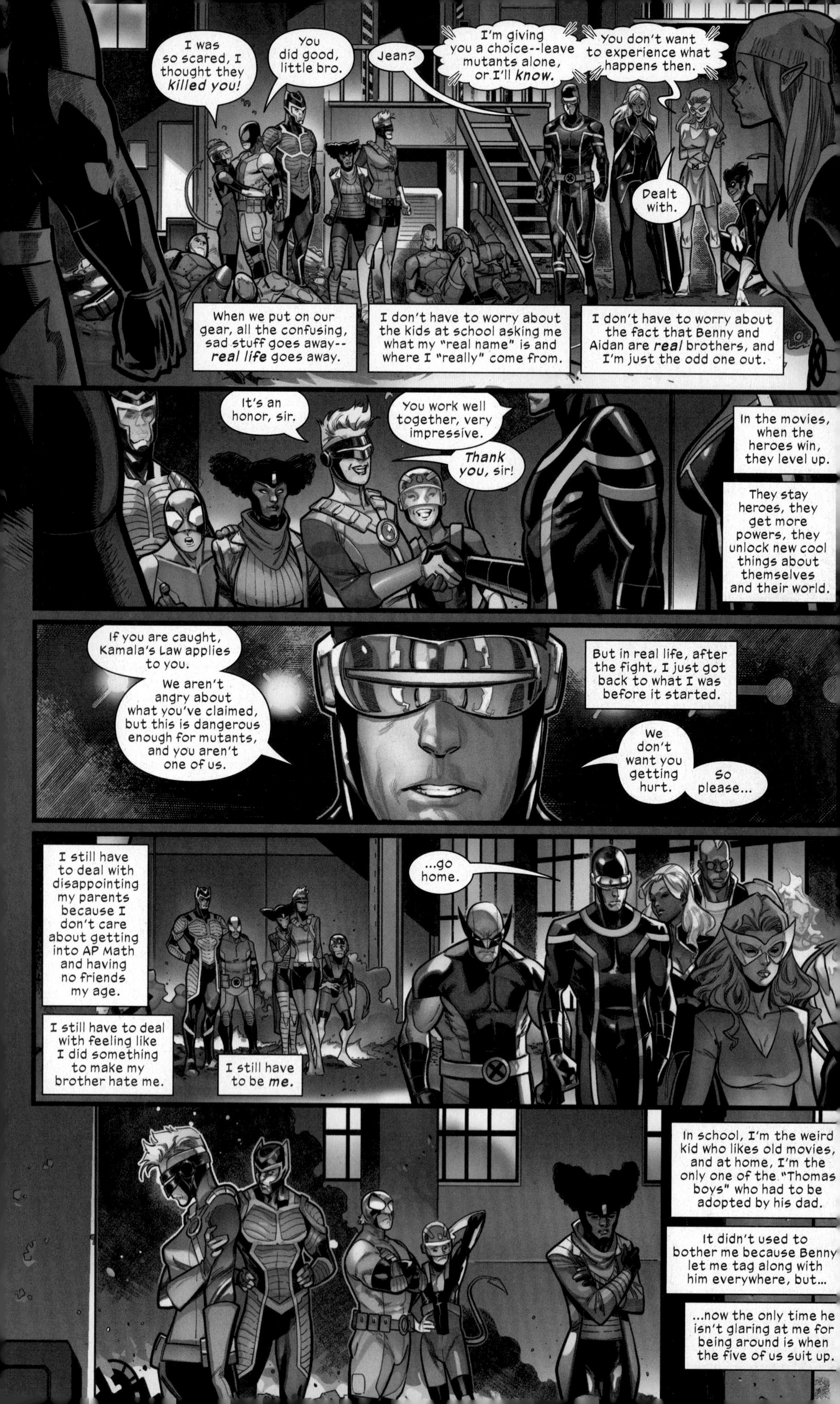

I was so scared, I thought they *killed you!*
You did good, little bro.
Jean?
I'm giving you a choice--leave mutants alone, or I'll *know.*
You don't want to experience what happens then.
Dealt with.
When we put on our gear, all the confusing, sad stuff goes away-- *real life* goes away.
I don't have to worry about the kids at school asking me what my "real name" is and where I "really" come from.
I don't have to worry about the fact that Benny and Aidan are *real* brothers, and I'm just the odd one out.
It's an honor, sir.
You work well together, very impressive.
Thank you, sir!
In the movies, when the heroes win, they level up.
They stay heroes, they get more powers, they unlock new cool things about themselves and their world.
If you are caught, Kamala's Law applies to you.
We aren't angry about what you've claimed, but this is dangerous enough for mutants, and you aren't one of us.
But in real life, after the fight, I just got back to what I was before it started.
We don't want you getting hurt.
So please...
I still have to deal with disappointing my parents because I don't care about getting into AP Math and having no friends my age.
I still have to deal with feeling like I did something to make my brother hate me.
I still have to be *me.*
...go home.
In school, I'm the weird kid who likes old movies, and at home, I'm the only one of the "Thomas boys" who had to be adopted by his dad.
It didn't used to bother me because Benny let me tag along with him everywhere, but...
...now the only time he isn't glaring at me for being around is when the five of us suit up.

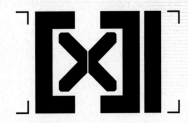

 DAYCRAWLER'S CHATTER FEED

 C.R.A.D.L.E._OFFICIAL 1h

The purpose of the UNDERAGE SUPERHUMAN WELFARE ACT, also known as Kamala's Law, is to protect both minors with extra-human abilities and their non-powered peers. In making un-mentored "super hero activity" illegal, we hope to encourage all minors who want to pursue such a noble calling to seek adult guidance and to dissuade those who are not serious about helping others to seek their thrills elsewhere.

Such guidance is available through C.R.A.D.L.E., the Child Hero Reconnaissance and Disruption Law Enforcement organization, as well as many other approved sources.

It has come to the attention of this organization that a group of teenage mutants calling themselves the Children of the Atom have been operating in New York as vigilantes without proper approvals and mentors. They are putting themselves and the city at risk.

If anyone has information about these children, click through the link:
HELP C.R.A.D.L.E.

📧 1,726

Trending: *#YoungXMen, #ChildrenOfTheAtom, #KamalasLaw*

 KRAKOA_OFFICIAL 3h

Through their actions, the group known as the Children of the Atom have helped Krakoa find and welcome back three lost citizens, as well as locate and disband a violent anti-mutant hate group.

Though they are not in any way a state-sanctioned group, the Children of the Atom, being involved with mutant affairs in New York City, have prevented the incarceration, dismemberment and death of countless mutants, and Krakoa thanks them for their service.

 13,189 6,511

Trending: *#YoungXMen, #ChildrenOfTheAtom, #KamalasLaw*

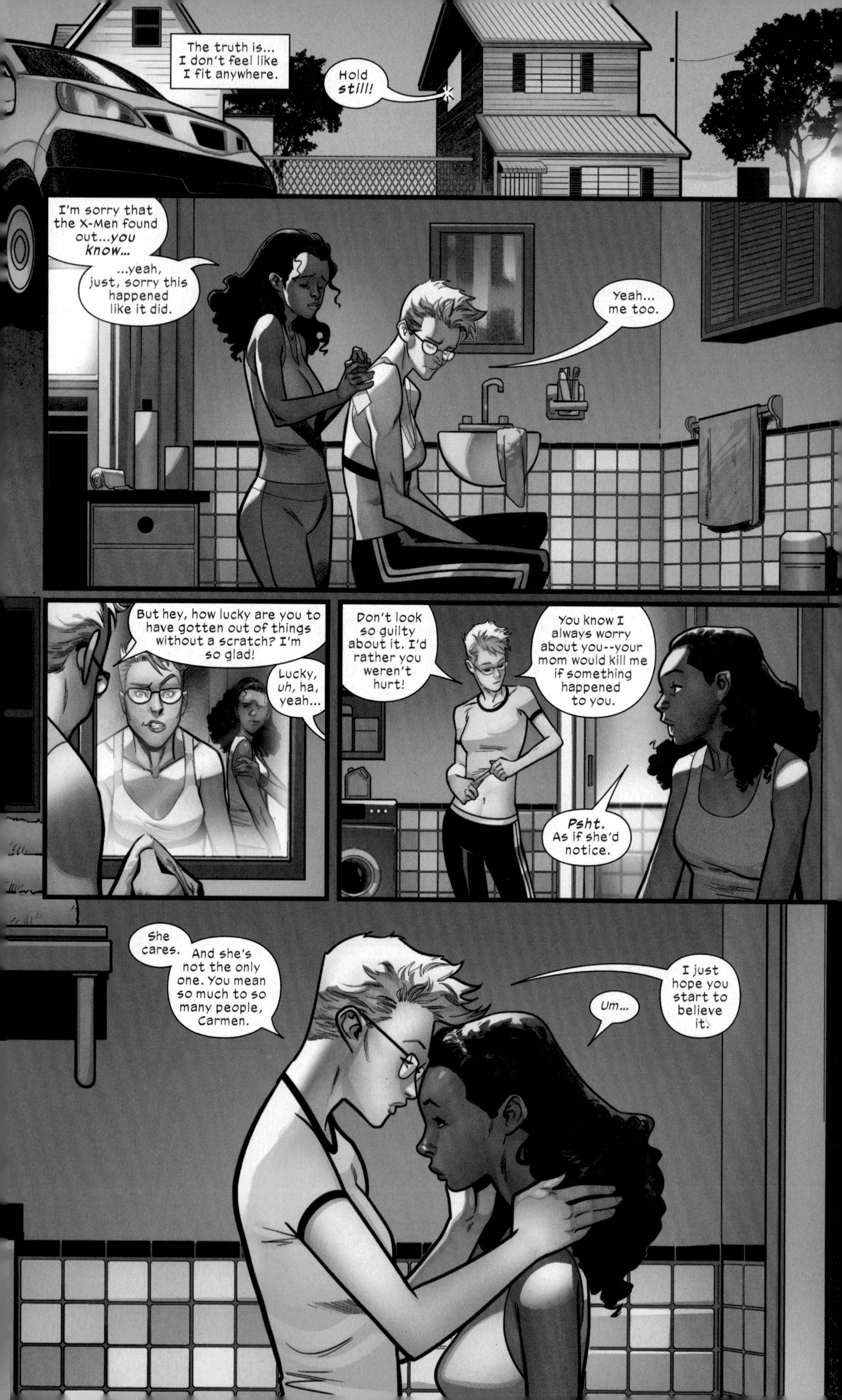

The truth is... I don't feel like I fit anywhere.
Hold *still!*
I'm sorry that the X-Men found out...*you know...*
...yeah, just, sorry this happened like it did.
Yeah... me too.
But hey, how lucky are you to have gotten out of things without a scratch? I'm so glad!
Lucky, *uh,* ha, yeah...
Don't look so guilty about it. I'd rather you weren't hurt!
You know I always worry about you--your mom would kill me if something happened to you.
Psht. As if she'd notice.
She cares.
And she's not the only one. You mean so much to so many people, Carmen.
Um...
I just hope you start to believe it.

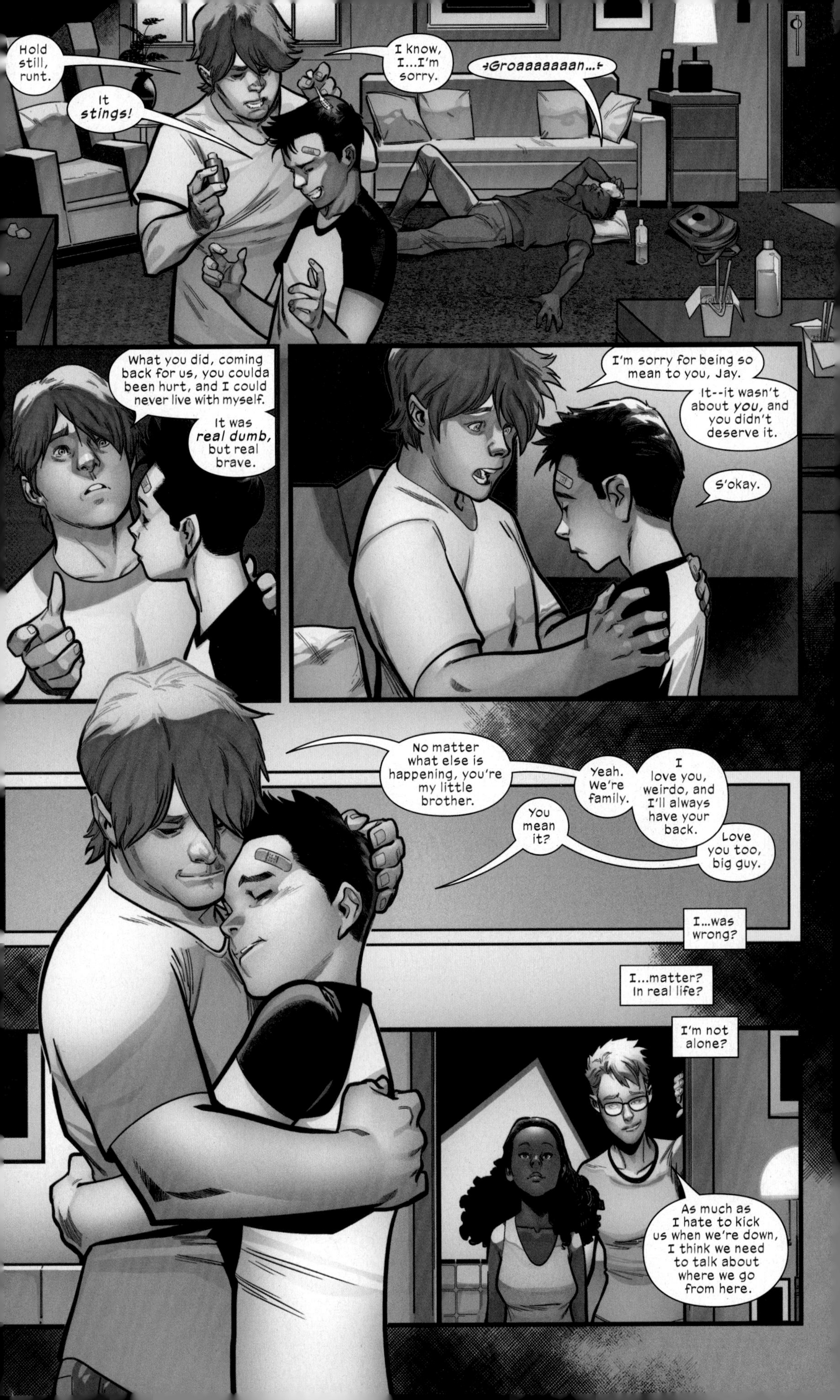
Hold still, runt.
It *stings!*
I know, I...I'm sorry.
Groaaaaaaan...
What you did, coming back for us, you coulda been hurt, and I could never live with myself.
It was *real dumb,* but real brave.
I'm sorry for being so mean to you, Jay.
It--it wasn't about *you,* and you didn't deserve it.
S'okay.
No matter what else is happening, you're my little brother.
You mean it?
Yeah. We're family.
I love you, weirdo, and I'll always have your back.
Love you too, big guy.
I...was wrong?
I...matter? In real life?
I'm not alone?
As much as I hate to kick us when we're down, I think we need to talk about where we go from here.

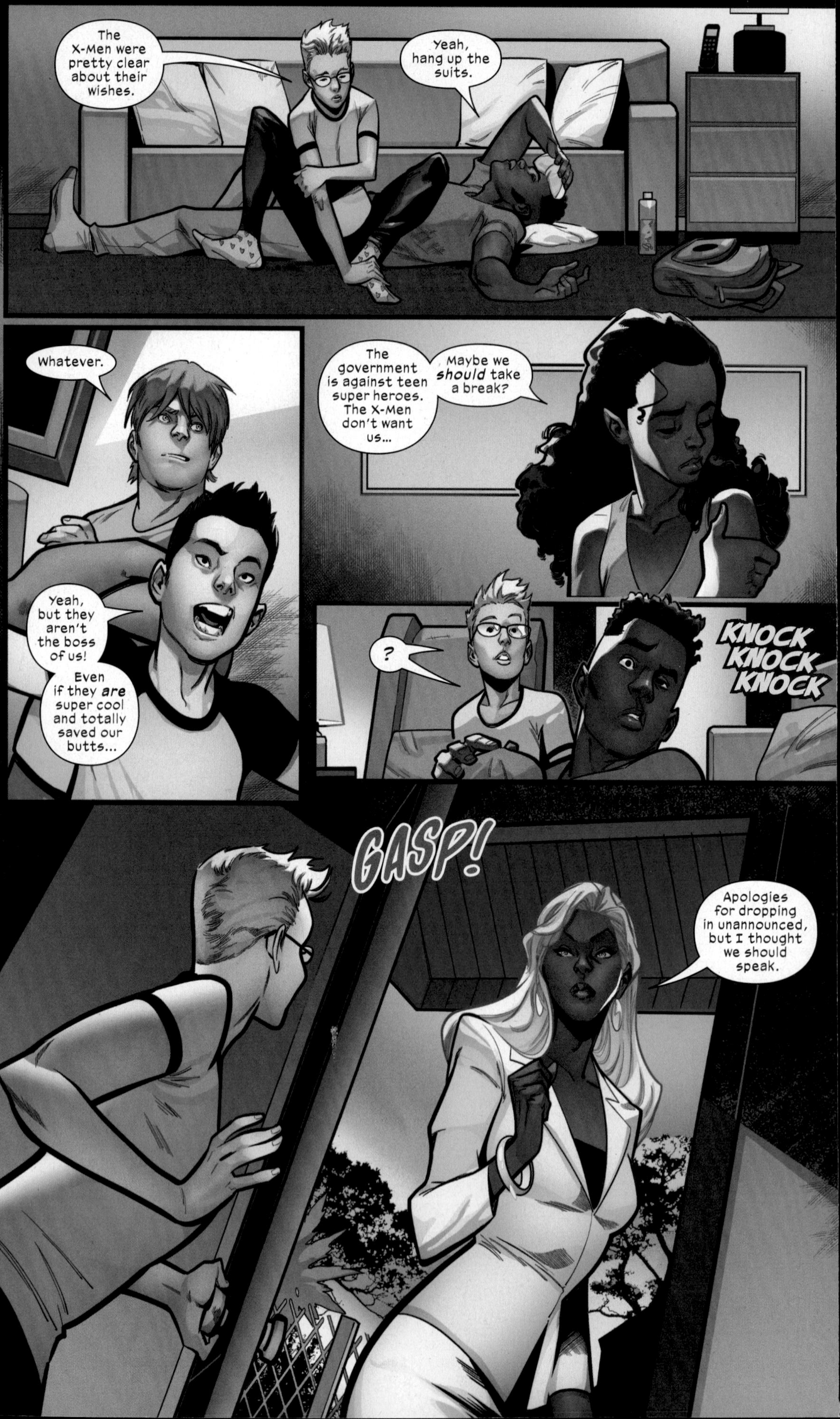
The X-Men were pretty clear about their wishes.
Yeah, hang up the suits.
Whatever.
Yeah, but they aren't the boss of us!
Even if they *are* super cool and totally saved our butts...
The government is against teen super heroes. The X-Men don't want us...
Maybe we *should* take a break?
?
KNOCK KNOCK KNOCK
GASP!
Apologies for dropping in unannounced, but I thought we should speak.

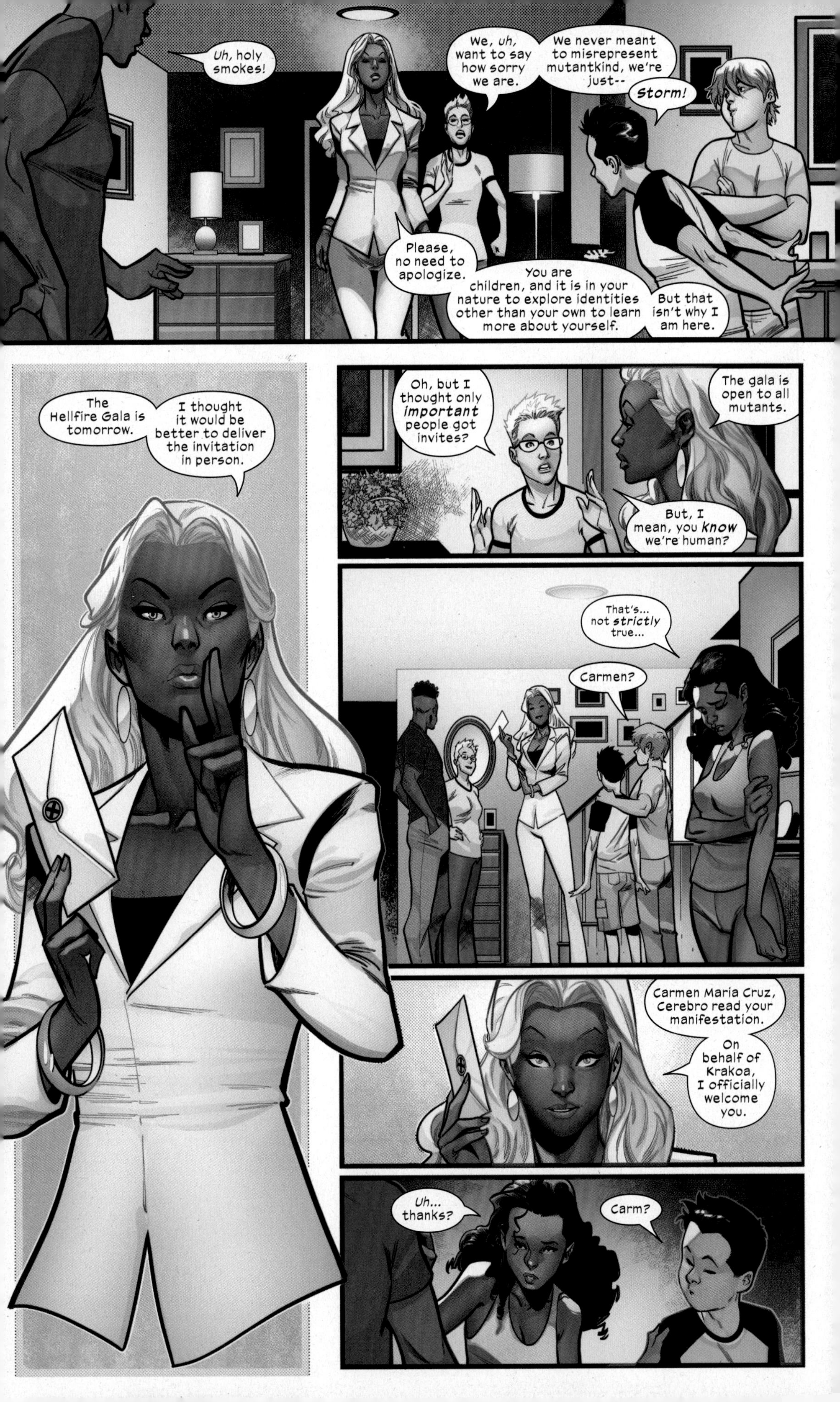

Uh, holy smokes!
We, uh, want to say how sorry we are.
We never meant to misrepresent mutantkind, we're just--
Storm!
Please, no need to apologize.
You are children, and it is in your nature to explore identities other than your own to learn more about yourself.
But that isn't why I am here.
The Hellfire Gala is tomorrow.
I thought it would be better to deliver the invitation in person.
Oh, but I thought only important people got invites?
The gala is open to all mutants.
But, I mean, you know we're human?
That's... not strictly true...
Carmen?
Carmen Maria Cruz, Cerebro read your manifestation.
On behalf of Krakoa, I officially welcome you.
Uh... thanks?
Carm?

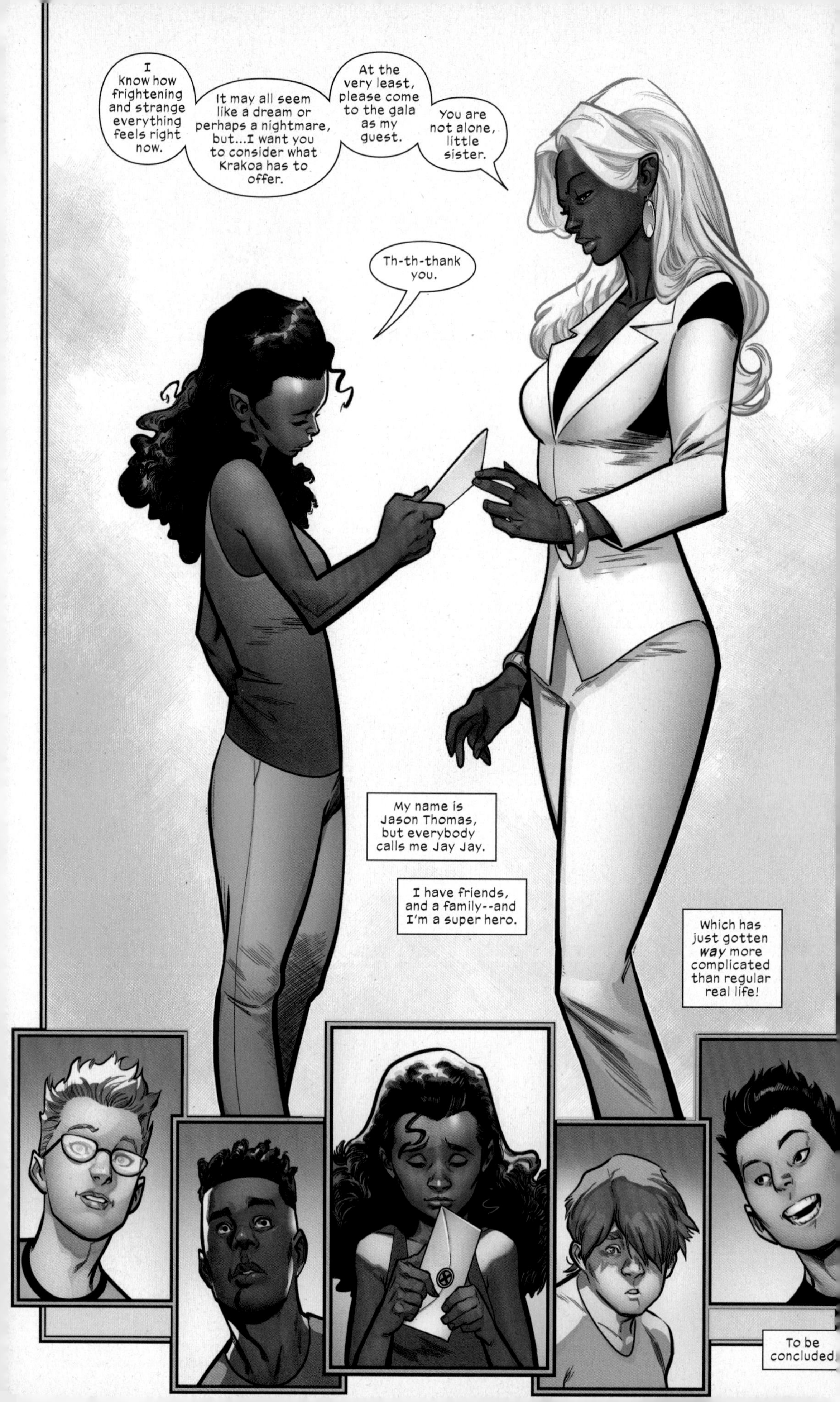
I know how frightening and strange everything feels right now.
It may all seem like a dream or perhaps a nightmare, but...I want you to consider what Krakoa has to offer.
At the very least, please come to the gala as my guest.
You are not alone, little sister.
Th-th-thank you.
My name is Jason Thomas, but everybody calls me Jay Jay.
I have friends, and a family--and I'm a super hero.
Which has just gotten way more complicated than regular real life!
To be concluded.

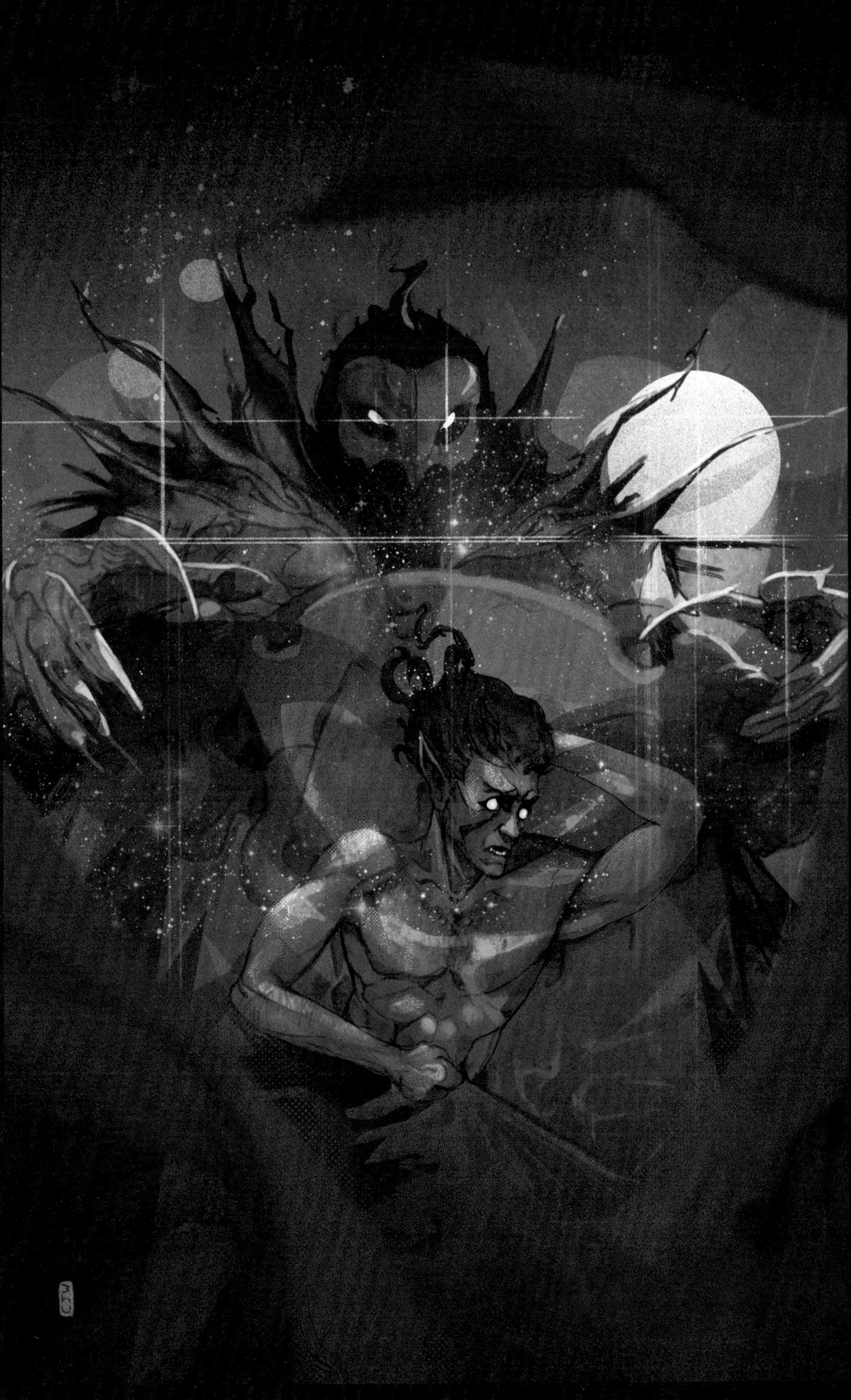

Way of X #2 Variant Cover by Christian Ward

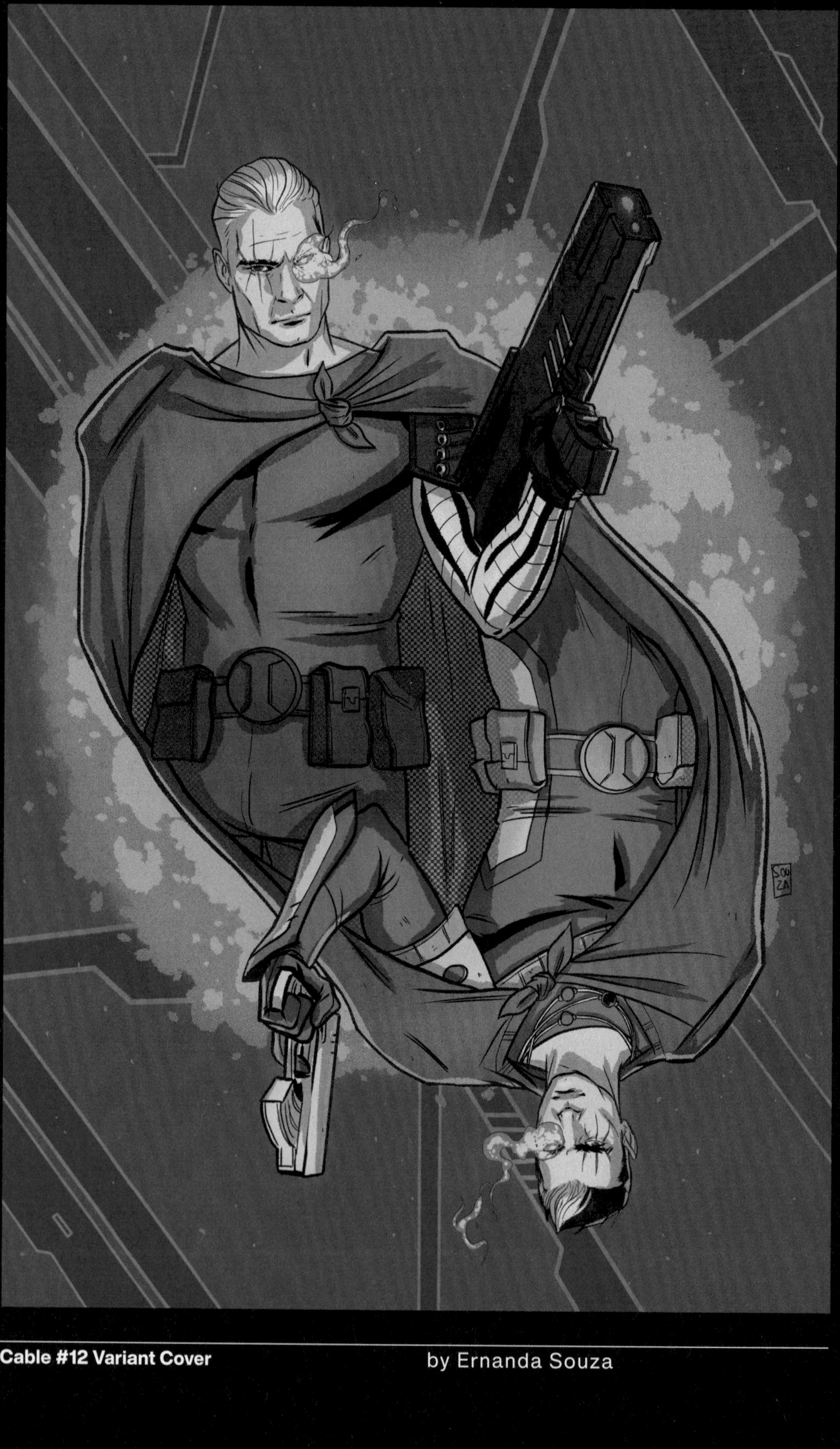
SOU
ZA

Cable #12 Variant Cover by Ernanda Souza

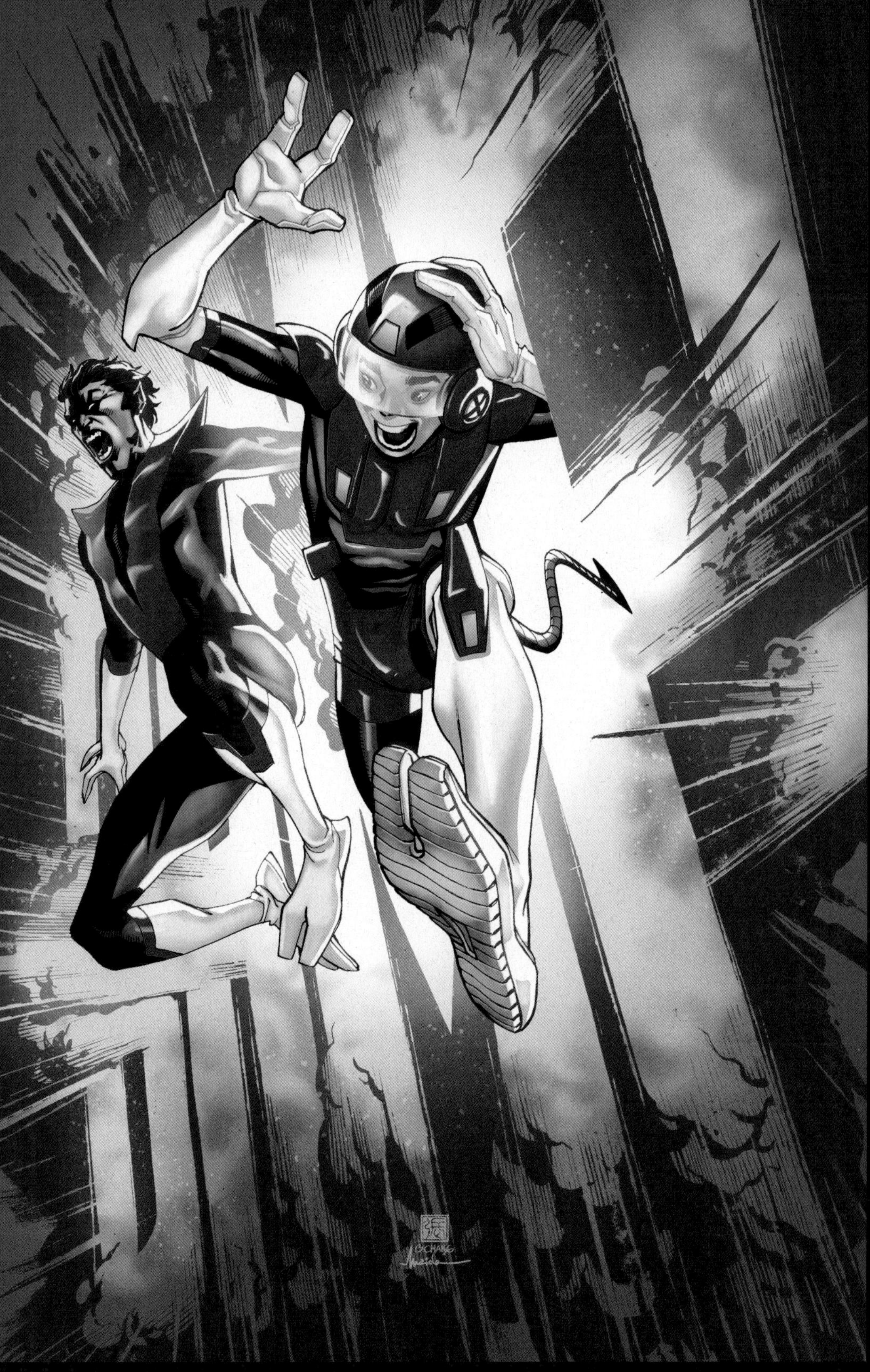

Children of the Atom #4 Variant Cover by Bernard Chang & Marcelo Maiolo

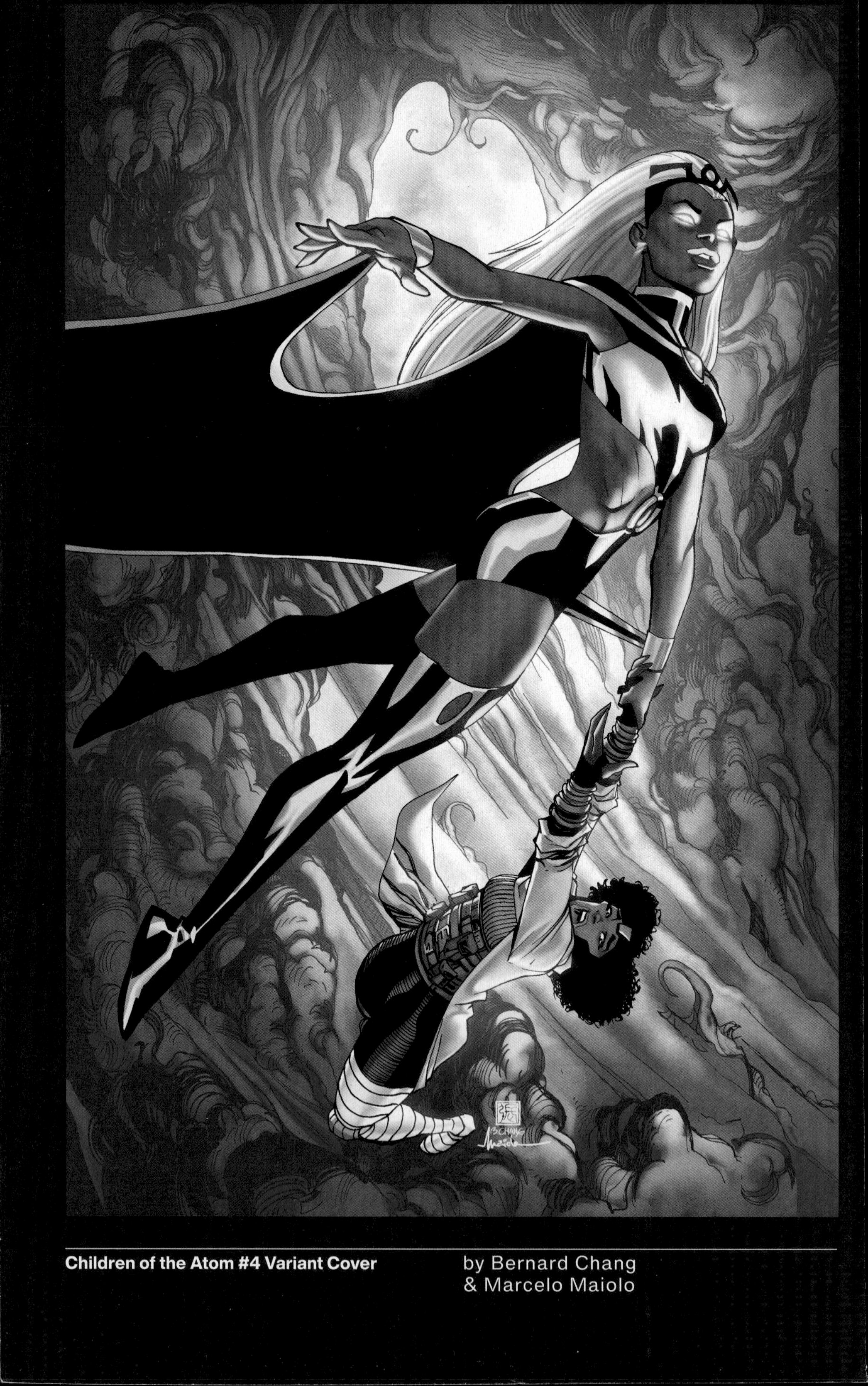
B.CHANG

Children of the Atom #4 Variant Cover

by Bernard Chang
& Marcelo Maiolo